Frontal LISP
Lateral LISP

Frontal Lisp, Lateral Lisp
© 2007 by Pam Marshalla. All rights reserved

ISBN 978-0-9791749-0-2

Marshalla Speech and Language
914 - 164th Street SE #128
Mill Creek, WA 98012-6339

The contents of this book may not be reproduced or transmitted in any form or by any means, electronic or mechanical, including photocopying and recording, or by any information storage and retrieval system, without written permission from the author.

Illustrations
All illustrations were created in Microsoft PowerPoint by Pam Marshalla.

Disclaimer
This text describes invasive oral-motor stimulation techniques intended for use by the professional speech and language pathologist. The book has been written with the knowledge that some readers are new to the area of oral-motor therapy while others are well-versed in it. Professionals who utilize these techniques must have thorough knowledge of the oral mechanism, including its structure, sensitivities, reflexes and movements. Professional judgment and common sense must rule the application of these techniques with specific clients. As such, the reader is solely responsible for discretionary use of the oral-motor techniques contained herein.

Dedication

This book is dedicated to Dr. Charles Van Riper, a pioneer in the field of speech-language treatment and an original thinker who set forth the basics of traditional articulation therapy.

Dr. Van Riper was interested in the process and the procedures of speech-language therapy. In the early 1980's he worried that we were beginning to lose sight of these practical things as our research began to focus increasingly on the minutia of speech and language. I never met Dr. Van Riper in person, but he wrote to me about his concern. "It is as if we are spending all our time counting the number of angels dancing on the head of a pin." He said that we needed people who could keep us focused on the big picture and the nuts and bolts of therapy. He liked the speech and language therapy newsletter I was writing at the time, and strongly urged me to continue writing therapy-based material.

I was a very young speech-language pathologist at the time I received Dr. Van Riper's letter. The idea for this book was just an idea back then. But thirty years of clinical experience later I think I finally have enough insight and experience to write it. My hope is that it will serve Dr. Van Riper's honorable goal of keeping us focused on the process of speech and language treatment no matter how many angels we count on the head of that pin.

Please Note

- Male pronouns (*he, him, his*) are used to represent clients. Female pronouns (*she, her, hers*) are used to denote speech-language pathologists and other adults. This method has been adopted for simplicity.

- The official title of "speech-language pathologist" is understood as the title of those professionals for whom this book is written. However, other terms such as "speech teacher," "speech therapist," "communication specialist," "trainer" and "facilitator" are employed to add color to the text. The shorthand version, SLP, also is used.

- It is understood that "speech-language therapy" is the proper phrase for describing the work of the speech-language pathologist. Nevertheless, other terms such as "speech therapy," "speech correction," "therapy," "speech exercises," "work," "facilitation" and "treatment" have been used to add color to the text.

- The term "normal" is used in the classic sense, that is, as a description of speech which exists without impairment. For example, "A midline air stream is employed in *normal* production of all the sibilants."

- Terms used to designate the parts of the tongue are based on the "Zones of the Tongue" system proposed in *Oral-Motor Techniques in Articulation and Phonological Therapy* by Pam Marshalla.

- It is understood that the terms *prevocalic* and *postvocalic* are the correct terms used to describe a consonant's position within a syllable. However, the terms *initial*, *medial* and *final* have been adopted for use in this text. These older terms adequately describe the position of a consonant within a whole word for our purposes here. The choice to use these out-of-favor terms has been the author's.

- Definitions for phonetic terms have been taken from two sources: (1) Carrell, James and William Tiffany, (1960). *Phonetics: Theory and Application to Speech Improvement*. McGraw-Hill Book Company: New York, New York, and (2) Nicolosi, Lucille, Elizabeth Harryman and Janet Kresheck, (1983). *Terminology of Communication Disorders*. Williams and Wilkins: Baltimore, Maryland.

Contents

Introduction		9
1	The Phonemes	11
2	Oral Position for Sibilant Production	15
3	Deep Analysis of the Frontal Lisp	25
4	Deep Analysis of the Lateral Lisp	51
5	Developmental Considerations in Sibilant Acquisition	67
6	The Long T Method	75
7	The Cornerstone Approach	83
8	Remediation Specific to the Frontal Lisp	97
9	Remediation Specific to the Lateral Lisp	127
10	Auditory Training Through the Program	143
11	Onward to the Other Sibilants	155
12	Oral Habits, Oral Structure, Oral Rest and Swallowing	167
13	Achieving Carryover	175
14	Real Clients in Real Therapy	193
Appendices		203
Glossary		223
References		227

Introduction

The frontal lisp and the lateral lisp are two common articulation errors that receive very little attention today. Speech-language pathology students who emerge from university training programs overwhelmingly report that they have spent little if any time discussing these error patterns in classes, and literally no time practicing diagnostic and therapeutic approaches to these problems in their internal and external practice therapy assignments. This has not always been the case. Historically, speech-language pathologists were known by the titles of "elocutionists," "speech correctionists" and "speech teachers." Remediation of the lisps used to be one of the primary concerns of our professional pioneers.

Today however it seems that everything else we learn – from literacy in the classroom to swallowing evaluations – takes precedence over the simple process of articulation therapy. Correcting speech sound error has been put on the back burner. Yet the frontal and lateral lisps are two of the most common error patterns we see in all types of speech and language disordered people. The remediation of articulation errors in general, and the lisps in particular, is one area the professional speech-language pathologist is uniquely suited to address. If we do not help clients correct these errors, nobody will.

Our lack of focus on so-called "mild" articulation errors has reared its ugly head in the public forum. Broad observation of speakers of all dialects of North American English reveals that both the frontal and lateral lisp have slowly crept back into the discourse of the educated class. We find these errors – especially the lateral lisp – in doctors, lawyers, teachers, preachers, scientists and writers. We even find lisps in politicians, radio talk show hosts, television journalists, actors and news broadcasters. These are people for whom public speaking is a way of life! I find it troublesome to discover lisps in professionals. Their errors usually are controlled, but they are not corrected. In other words, they have learned to speak as clearly as possible with the error they have. In my view this is a symptom of a society that is losing focus on the details of proper pronunciation.

In school, children with frontal or lateral lisps often suffer silently with these problems, and their parents worry that their kids will be held back socially or educationally. The elementary student with a lisp often is viewed as baby-like, and the middle school student as different, stupid or weird. High school students sometimes receive low grades on oral reports because their spoken language is hard to understand when they have either of these lisps.

It is this author's opinion that we have let go of correct pronunciation as a sign of intelligence and of education. It is also my opinion that this is largely the fault of my own profession. Some may feel that the presence of a lisp is no big deal. But I can tell you that our clients and their parents think it IS a big deal. They want help to eliminate this error.

These children are our future leaders. They deserve, no, they NEED to have excellent communication skills.

I have spent the better part of thirty years diagnosing, treating and thinking about frontal and lateral lisps. Although generally viewed as "mild" articulation errors, the lisps can be difficult to correct. While most clients fix up these problems in no time, some spend years in therapy and are dismissed with limited or no success. Children who fail in this therapy often quit speech sessions sometime during the middle school years when it becomes less embarrassing to retain the misarticulation than it is to be pulled out of class for therapy. Even clients who receive private speech and language therapy can have a very difficult time getting rid of these errors, especially the lateral lisp.

The information presented in this book is based on the author's clinical experiences and information obtained from other speech-language pathologists who have participated in continuing education workshops throughout the United States and Canada. My own therapy has been shaped through trial and error by combining strategies from articulation, phonological, oral-motor and feeding therapy. I have not tried to prove my insights and techniques in this volume: I have only tried to explain them. This book is not a textbook or a lab research summary. This book only contains the insights, advice and experiences of one therapist gained through thirty years of direct clinical experience.

My immediate goal in writing this book is to aid speech-language pathologists in their own work with clients who lisp. My bigger goal is that millions of English-speaking clients will be able to move on to better speech by using the methods contained herein. And my ultimate goal is that eventually every new class of speech-language pathology students will receive instruction on these techniques before they face these clients on the job.

Chapter 1

The Phonemes

The frontal lisp and the lateral lisp represent two different problems imposed on the same set of phonemes. The phonemes that are affected are these six sounds: /s/, /z/, /ʃ/, /ʒ/, /tʃ/ and /dʒ/. The phonemes of concern to us comprise six distinct sounds, however each is represented by several spelling patterns. Table 1 presents a list of each phoneme and their spelling options.

Sibilants, Stridents, Fricatives and Affricates

The individual phonemes in our set have been called *sibilants, stridents, fricatives* and *affricates*. The following definitions contain quoted elements from Nicolosi, Harryman and Kresheck.

1. *Sibilant:* A sibilant is a phoneme "whose production is accompanied by a hissing noise." This set includes /s/, /z/, /ʃ/, /ʒ/, /tʃ/ and /dʒ/. The term comes from the phonetics literature.
2. *Strident:* A strident phoneme is one that is "characterized by noisiness resulting from a fast rate of air flow directed against the hard surfaces of the teeth." This set includes /f/, /v/, /s/, /z/, /ʃ/, /ʒ/, /tʃ/ and /dʒ/. The term comes from the phonology literature.
3. *Fricative:* A fricative phoneme is one that is formed "by directing the breath stream with adequate pressure against one or more surfaces, principally the hard palate,

Table 1

Phoneme	Spelling	Sample Word
/s/	s	soup
	c	city
	sc	scene
	ss	boss
/z/	z	zoo
	zz	buzz
	s	his
/ʃ/	sh	shoe
	ss	passion
	t	nation
	sch	schilling
	c	appreciate
	ch	Chicago
	s	sugar
/ʒ/	s	television
	g	beige
	z	azure
/tʃ/	ch	chew
	tch	watch
	t	question
	c	cello
/dʒ/	j	jump
	g	gem
	dg	edge
	dj	adjust
	gg	exaggerate
	ld	soldier

alveolar ridge behind the upper teeth, and lips." This set includes /f/, /v/, /s/, /z/, /ʃ/, /ʒ/, /θ/ and /ð/. The term comes from the phonetics literature.

4. *Affricate:* An affricate phoneme is one that begins as a stop and ends as a fricative. This set includes /tʃ/ and /dʒ/. The term comes from the phonetics literature.

The term "sibilant" is the only one of these descriptors that encompasses all six of our target phonemes and no other, therefore it is the term we shall use the most often throughout this text. All four of these terms refer to the "hissing" quality of air turbulence that occurs when the sounds are made correctly. Learning Exercise 1 is designed to help the reader become aware of this hissing element in our target phonemes. It is one of the most critical factors in understanding the frontal and lateral lisp misarticulations.

LEARNING EXERCISE 1*
Discover the Hissing Element

In a quiet location, produce each of the six phonemes individually: /s/, /z/, /ʃ/, /ʒ/, /tʃ/, /dʒ/. Prolong each so you have time to attend to its features. Listen to the hissing quality or sharp edge of each. Also notice how each phoneme sounds distinct from the rest.

* The exercises contained throughout this text assume that the reader can and does produce the sibilant phonemes within the acceptable range.

The Cognate Pairs

Our six subject phonemes occur in three pairs. Each pair contains one voiceless and one voiced phoneme. These are known as *cognate pairs*. The voiceless and voiced cognate pairs are:

1. /s/ and /z/
2. /ʃ/ and /ʒ/
3. /tʃ/ and /dʒ/

The two phonemes within each pair are nearly identical in terms of oral position but different in terms of voicing and tension. Thus, /s/ and /z/ are made with essentially identical oral positions, however /z/ is made with voice while /s/ is not. Likewise, /ʃ/ and /ʒ/ are made with identical oral position but different voicing. And, /tʃ/ and /dʒ/ are made with nearly identical oral position but different voicing. Thus while diagnosis and therapy must address all six individual phonemes, our therapeutic efforts can be toward only three individual oral movement patterns: one for /s/ and /z/, one for /ʃ/ and /ʒ/ and one for /tʃ/ and /dʒ/. Learning Exercise 2 will help readers attune themselves to the cognate pairs.

Application to Therapy

The reader will have noticed through the exercises in this first chapter that all six of our subject phonemes are quite similar. That is why they are classified together. They are very

> **LEARNING EXERCISE 2**
> **Attune to the Cognate Pairs**
>
> Prolong /s/ and then add voice to produce /z/. Make these two sounds back-and-forth in a continuous sequence. Notice that /s/ is produced without voice whereas /z/ is produced with voice. Also notice that oral position is virtually the same for both. Repeat for the pairs /ʃ/ and /ʒ/, and then again with /tʃ/ and /dʒ/.

similar in the way they *sound* and the way they are *made*. A client who is to achieve correct articulation of these phonemes must possess excellent skills in these two areas. He must be able to hear the differences between the phonemes, and he must have the ability to perceive his own oral movements well enough to position his mouth differentially in these ways. These skills are known respectively as *auditory discrimination* and *kinesthetic awareness*. A client must have excellent auditory discrimination skill as well as a well-developed sense of kinesthetic awareness to produce these six phonemes differentially and correctly. Therapy to facilitate these sounds includes techniques to enhance these underlying processes. Therapy encourages clients to listen carefully and to control oral movement.

Chapter 1 Summary
The Phonemes

- The frontal lisp and the lateral lisp represent two different problems imposed on the same set of phonemes: /s/, /z/, /ʃ/, /ʒ/, /tʃ/ and /dʒ/.

- These phonemes are classified together phonetically and phonologically because of their "hissing" quality.

- Diagnosis and therapy must address all six individual phonemes, however, therapeutic efforts can be directed toward only three individual oral movement patterns.

- Clients must have excellent auditory discrimination skill and a well-developed sense of oral kinesthetic awareness to produce these six phonemes differentially and correctly.

- Therapy encourages clients to listen carefully and to control oral movement.

Chapter 2

Oral Position for Sibilant Production

The oral mechanism must be positioned in precise ways in order to achieve the hissing element necessary for correct production of each of our six target phonemes. We shall discuss this idea generally for all six of the phonemes, and then specifically for the characteristics that differentiate one pair from another.

Midline Stridency

Midline stridency is the most important element of sibilant production. Stridency is created upon exhalation through the mouth. As we exhale, we direct our voiced or voiceless air stream through the oral cavity along a mid line channel from back to front. The basic groove shape is created by elevating the sides of the tongue and by keeping its midline low (figures 01 and 02). This fundamental grooved tongue pattern is essential for correct production of all six phonemes because it ensures that the exhaled air stream will strike against the lingual surfaces of the incisors in such as way as to create air turbulence right at midline. Turbulence is created as the air stream (1) tumbles around between the tongue and the incisors, (2) cuts between the upper and lower teeth, and (3) exits the mouth between the lips.

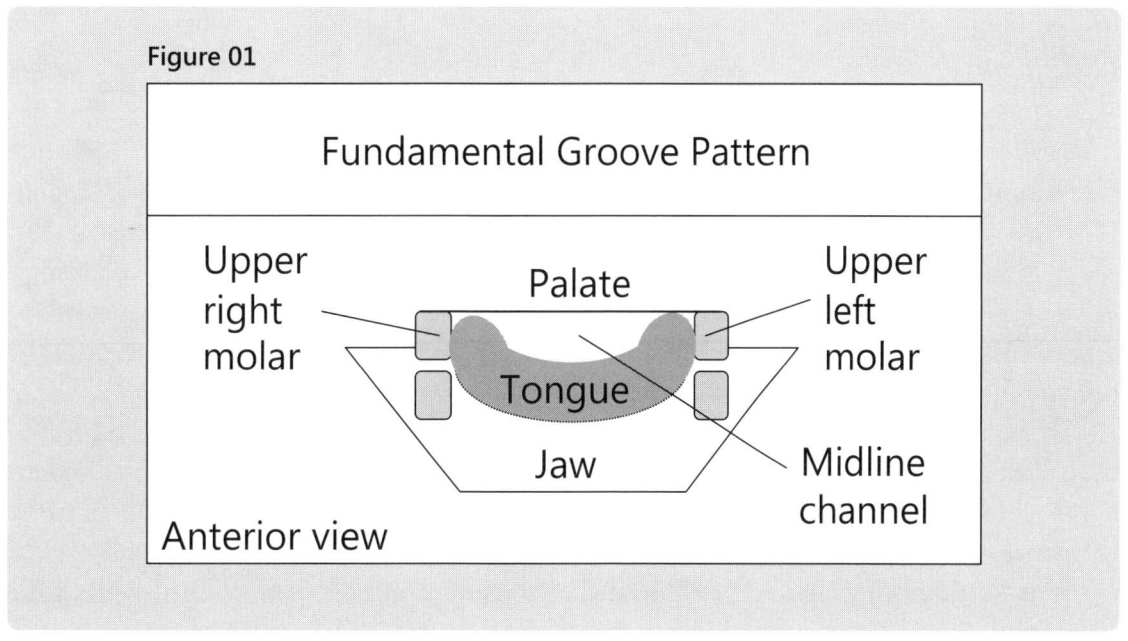

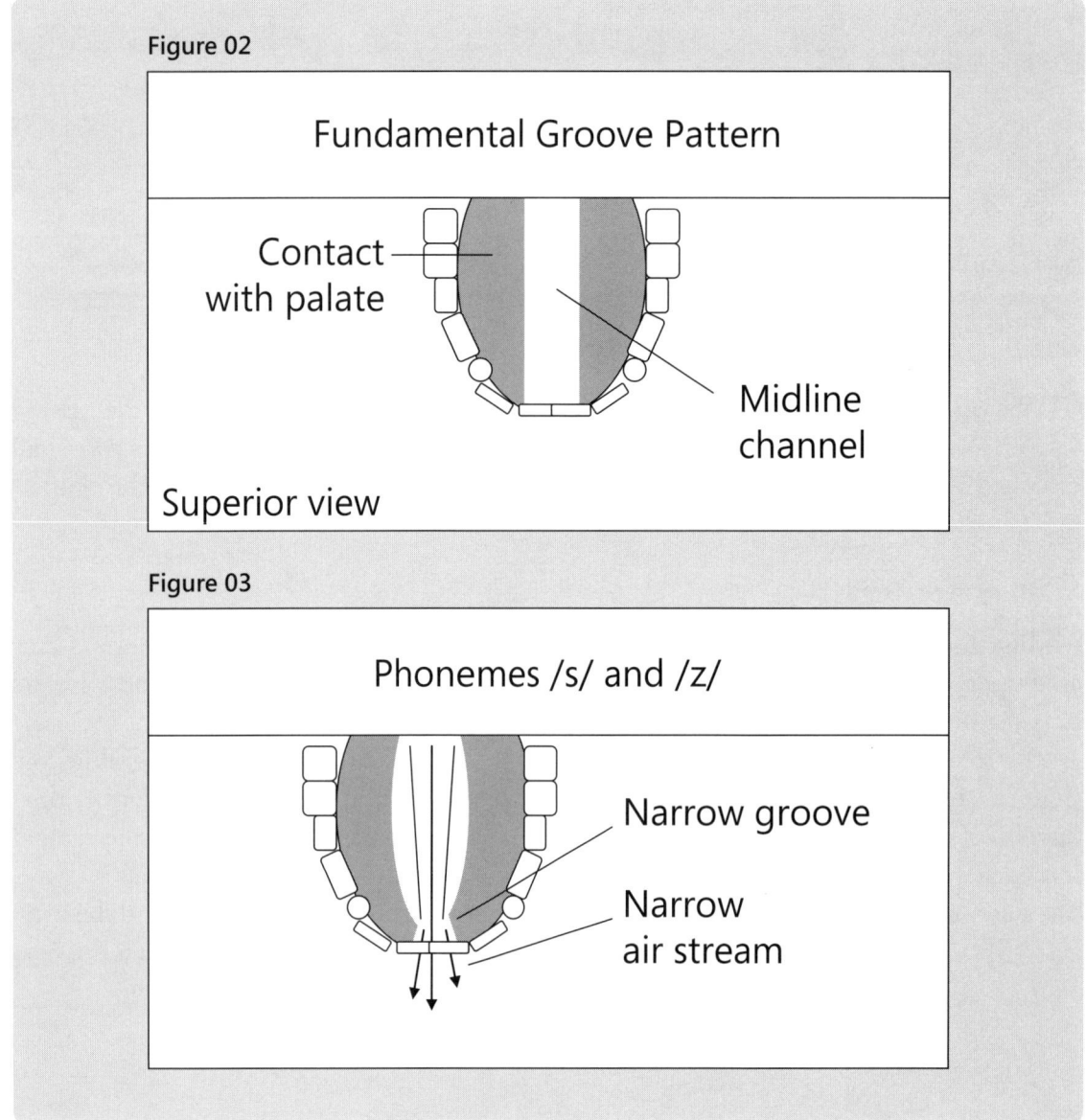

First Pair: /s/ and /z/

In the traditional phonetics literature, phonemes /s/ and /z/ were classified as "lingua-alveolar fricatives." That is because it was thought that the principle action necessary for production of these sounds occurred between the tongue-tip (lingua) and the alveolar ridge. As we shall see, this is partly correct. However, the tongue-tip is not the only part of the mouth that creates this ombissure (mouth position). The rest of the tongue, as well as the jaw and lips must be taken into consideration.

From an oral-motor perspective, phonemes /s/ and /z/ are produced with a specific modification of the essential tongue groove pattern introduced above. This tongue position is identical for both /s/ and /z/ (figure 03). Dark areas indicate where the tongue makes contact with the palate, and light areas mark where it does not (Zemlin, 1968).

In analyzing this drawing, first notice that the entire tongue is positioned behind the front teeth. No part of the tongue is positioned anterior to the front teeth. Next, notice that the tongue makes contact with the palate from back-to-front along both lateral margins. Positioning the sides of the tongue against the palate on both sides prevents air from escaping laterally. Also notice that articulation in the back and middle of the palate forms a wide channel of air while the position of the tongue at the alveolar ridge creates a very narrow channel at the blade of the tongue. Narrowness at the blade is caused by elevating the lateral portions of the blade while keeping its middle away from the palate.

The thin channel formed at the blade narrows the air stream, thus increasing its speed and strength. The distinct stridency of /s/ and /z/ is made as this forceful, swift and narrow channel of air strikes the back of the central incisors, rebounds, and then escapes from between the teeth. Narrowness at the blade is a critical factor for correct /s/ and /z/ production.

Tongue-tip placement is also a factor in production of /s/ and /z/, however, there is more than one position which can be used. The tongue-tip can be (1) elevated toward but not touching the alveolus, (2) lowered toward the floor of the oral cavity, or (3) kept in a middle position between the two extremes. The tongue-tip cannot be placed against the alveolar ridge at any time, however.

The lips also play a part in production of /s/ and /z/. The lips generally are slightly retracted (pulled away from midline into a slight smile) so that they stay out of the way of the escaping air stream. Having the lips retracted and pulled back away from mid line contributes to the acoustic quality of /s/ and /z/.

The jaw, as mentioned earlier, is a background figure to production of /s/ and /z/. It should be in a stabile and graduated position: low enough to allow air and sound to escape but high enough to support tongue-to-palate articulation.

The ultimate strident sound of /s/ and /z/ is created by air turbulence. The small, narrow and forceful air stream of /s/ and /z/ strikes the incisors and tumbles around between the incisors and the blade of the tongue where the channel is the most narrow. The sound is further enhanced as the air stream cuts between the upper and lower incisors, and as it passes between the lips. The area of air turbulence rather resembles a tiny ball of swirling air behind the teeth (figure 04 on next page). Learning Exercise 3 (on next page) will help the reader become aware of this phenomenon.

Second Pair: /ʃ/ and /ʒ/

In the traditional phonetics literature, phonemes /ʃ/ and /ʒ/ were classified as "lingua-palatal fricatives." That designation was chosen because of the important contact of the body of the tongue to the palate. But this description presents us with another limited view of tongue position for these sibilants. Again, one must consider the relationship between the entire tongue and palate, as well as jaw and lip position.

From an oral-motor perspective, /ʃ/ and /ʒ/ are produced with a second specific modification of the essential tongue groove pattern. This tongue configuration is essentially identical for both /ʃ/ and /ʒ/ (figure 05 on next page). In analyzing this drawing, first notice that /ʃ/ and /ʒ/ also are produced with the entire tongue positioned behind the front teeth. Next, notice that the tongue makes contact with the palate from back-to-front along both lateral margins. In this instance the central groove is wide throughout its length. This wide groove allows the air stream to remain broad as it strikes the teeth. As a result, the air stream is slower and less

Figure 04

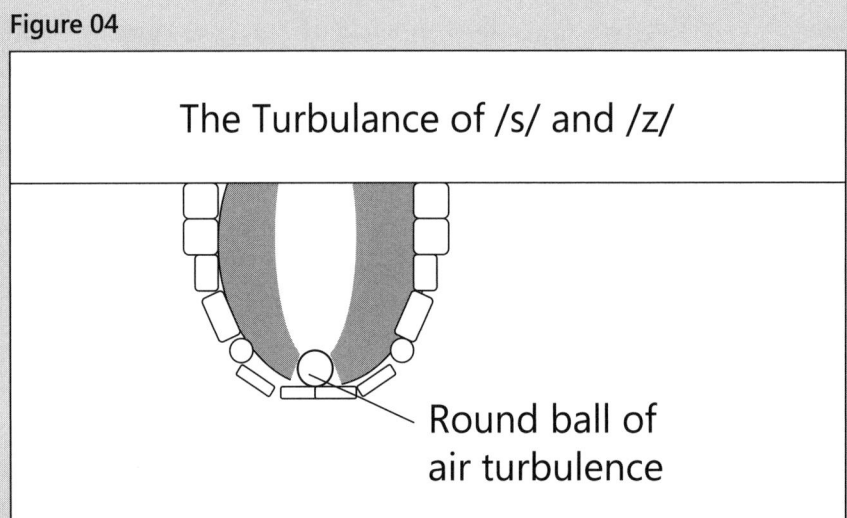

The Turbulance of /s/ and /z/

Round ball of air turbulence

LEARNING EXERCISE 3
The Ball of Air Turbulence

Sitting quietly, produce and prolong /s/ in isolation. Notice that your tongue maintains articulation with the palate along its lateral margins, thus preventing lateral air escape. Also notice that the entire tongue is positioned behind the front teeth. Notice that the tongue groove narrows at the blade, forcing the air stream into a very narrow channel there. Also notice the force with which the air stream strikes the anterior teeth. Observe that a small ball of air turbulence forms between the front of the tongue and the central incisors, and that, as it exits, this air can be felt with the skin of the lips, face or chin.

Repeat this activity for /z/. Notice the addition of voicing and the resultant pressure differences in the process.

Figure 05

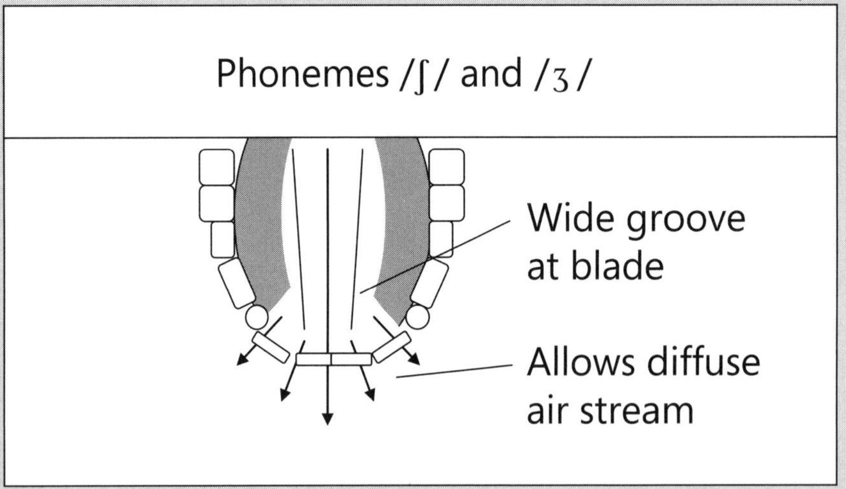

Phonemes /ʃ/ and /ʒ/

Wide groove at blade

Allows diffuse air stream

powerful than that for /s/ and /z/. The unique sibilant quality of /ʃ/ and /ʒ/ is created when this wide and slow-moving air stream strikes broadly across all the anterior teeth.

Tongue-tip placement also plays a part in production of /ʃ/ and /ʒ/. In essence, the tongue-tip needs to stay out of the way of the broad air stream. The tongue-tip can be held slightly higher or lower, but it can never be placed against the alveolar ridge. Such a move would force a lateral production of sound.

The strident sound of /ʃ/ and /ʒ/ is created by broad air turbulence as it (1) strikes the lingua surfaces of the incisors, (2) rushes around in the space created between the teeth and the tongue, and (3) escapes the mouth out between the upper and lower teeth.

The lips play an important role in the acoustic quality of /ʃ/ and /ʒ/. The lips are somewhat rounded or puckered, which causes a lengthening of the oral cavity and an anterior extension of the ball of air turbulence. The resultant shape of air turbulence is rather like football. It stretches from about the middle of the tongue groove to the most anterior point of the puckered lips before escaping from between them (figure 06). Learning Exercise 4 will help the reader experience and understand this phenomenon.

The jaw again is a background figure to production of /ʃ/ and /ʒ/. It should be in a graduated position: low enough to allow air and sound to escape but high enough to support tongue-to-palate articulation.

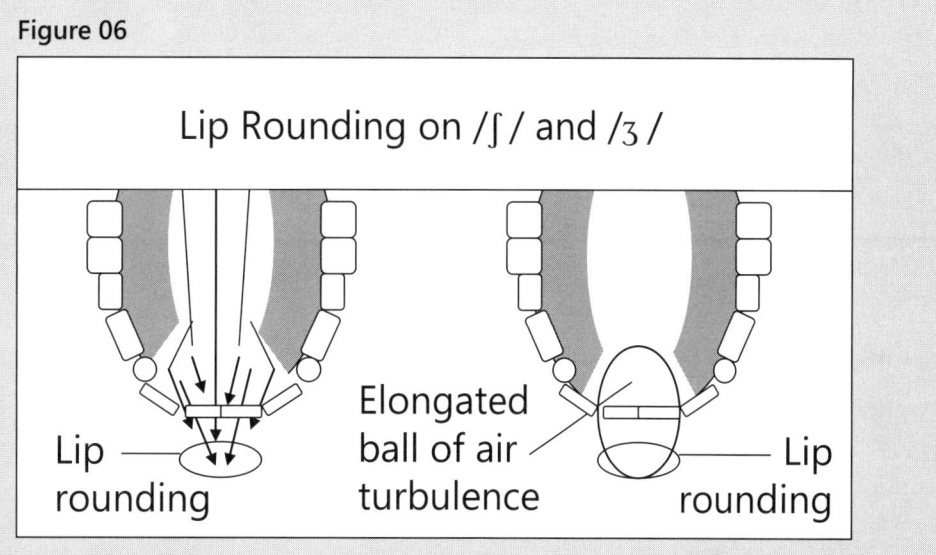

Figure 06

LEARNING EXERCISE 4
Lip Protrusion and the Ball of Air Turbulence

Produce and prolong /ʃ/ while sitting quietly. Notice that your tongue maintains articulation with the palate at its lateral margins, thus preventing air escape laterally. Also notice that the entire tongue is positioned behind the front teeth. Notice that the tongue groove remains wide throughout its length, allowing the air stream to remain wide throughout. Also notice that the air stream's force is reduced when compared to /s/. Observe that a longer football-shape of air turbulence is created. It stretches between the middle of the tongue toward the back to the lips that are slightly rounded in the front.

Alternate rounding and retracting the lips (pucker and smile) while prolonging /ʃ/ and listen to the acoustic changes that result. The phoneme should sound correct when the lips are somewhat rounded, and it should sound distorted when the lips are retracted. It also should be distorted if the lips are puckered so much that a very small lip opening is created.

Also, produce /ʃ/ and alternate it in sequence with /s/. Feel the slight difference in the tongue groove configuration in these two phonemes. Also notice the differences in lip rounding and retracting. Notice how slight these differences are.

Repeat all aspects of this exercise for /ʒ/, and compare it with /z/. Notice the addition of voicing throughout.

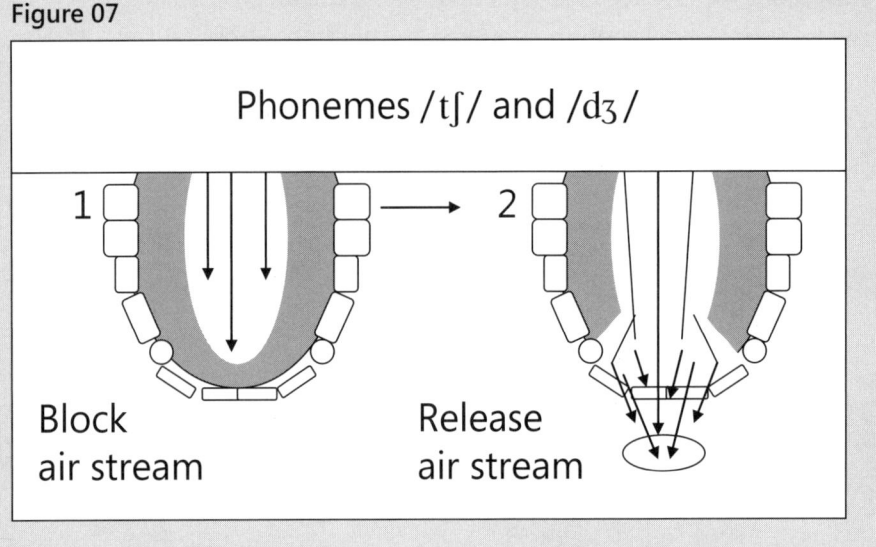

Figure 07

Third Pair: /tʃ/ and /dʒ/

In the traditional phonetics literature, phonemes /tʃ/ and /dʒ/ were classified as "linguapalatal affricates." Affricates are made in two phases. During the first phase, the air stream is completely occluded or held from being released – like a stop consonant. In the second phase, the air stream is swiftly released, and it is during this second phase that we hear frication or stridency. Learning Exercise 5 helps us perceive these phases. Let's analyze the oral movements and positions of these two phases for both /tʃ/ and /dʒ/ (figure 07).

- *First Phase:* During the stop phase the exhaled air stream is prevented from escaping the oral cavity by positioning the tongue as it does for /t/ and /d/. Blocking occurs because the tongue articulates with the palate in a horseshoe shape around its perimeter from the back lateral margin on the left to the back lateral margin on the right. This position is held just long enough for air pressure to build slightly behind the horseshoe.

- *Second Phase:* The second phase of the two affricates is comprised of a swift lowering of the tongue tip while the sides of the tongue remain articulated with the palate. As a result of tip lowering, the tongue assumes the same shape as that used for /ʃ/ and /ʒ/. Lowering the tip allows the air stream to escape medially and for stridency to be created. Tongue position and lip puckering create the same football-shaped air turbulence chamber as that created for /ʃ/ and /ʒ/.

Again, the jaw is a background figure to production of /tʃ/ and /dʒ/. It should be in a graduated position: low enough to allow air and sound to escape but high enough to support tongue-to-palate articulation.

The Jaw's Role in Sibilant Production

On the stage of sibilant production, the jaw plays a primary yet silent role. We hardly notice the jaw at all during correct articulation in mature speech. That is perhaps why most discussions of articulation and sibilant production ignore jaw function completely. But terrible things can happen to the acoustic quality of these sounds when jaw movement and position are incorrect.

Mature speech is produced with relative jaw stability. When the jaw is stabile, it moves up, down, left, right, forward, back and in rotation during speech, but it does so in a very tiny range. This is the *restricted range of movement* that defines stability. The jaw is not immobile or stiff. It is movable but restricted in its movement and thus stabile. This position also has been called a *slightly graded open position.*

Jaw stability allows for maximum articulation proficiency. Jaw stability keeps the jaw relatively high during speech. This allows for efficient articulation of the tongue to the teeth and palate, and the upper and lower lips to one another. As such, jaw stability supports rapid and precise speech movements that can be sequenced flawlessly in rapid conversational speech.

Jaw position is especially important in production of the sibilants. The jaw is positioned in such a way that it allows air to flow against the teeth for creation of stridency. Since the

---

LEARNING EXERCISE 5
Discover The Phases of Affricate Production

Produce /tʃ/ slowly in isolation in a quiet environment. Notice that the tongue first articulates in a horseshoe pattern against the palate to completely block the air stream. And notice that air pressure is allowed to build slightly as the tongue maintains this position. Next, release /tʃ/ slowly, and notice that the tongue-tip alone lowers away from the palate. The sides of the tongue remain elevated against the palate to continue the midline movement of air.

Further, say /ʃ/ and /tʃ/ in alternating sequence. Notice that the oral position for the second phase of /tʃ/ is the same as that for /ʃ/.

Now, compare /tʃ/ and /s/ in this way. Many differences will be noted in tongue and lip position. Repeat this exercise for /dʒ/. Compare it to /ʒ/ and then to /z/.

LEARNING EXERCISE 6
The Jaw's Role in Sibilant Production

Produce and prolong /s/ and attend to your jaw position. Watch yourself in a mirror so you can see its position and attend to the internal proprioceptive sensations. Also, place your hand on your chin to feel its position that way. Notice how your jaw position supports correct production of /s/. Also notice that it is positioned so that your central incisors are very close to one.

Now, continue to prolong /s/ as you slowly lower your jaw several millimeters. Do you notice that the stridency you need for correct production of /s/ vanishes? Alternate production of correct /s/ with the jaw held high and then incorrect production of /s/ with the jaw lowered too far. Listen to the acoustic changes that occur as the jaw moves in to and out of position. Make sure not to alter tongue position relative to the jaw. You want to hear the effects of jaw alteration only.

Now continue to prolong /s/ but this time shift your jaw to the left and to the right. Notice the acoustic variations that occur. Phoneme /s/ should become at least slightly distorted as the jaw lateralizes too far to the left or right.

Next continue to prolong /s/ but this time shift your jaw too far forward (protrusion) and too far back (retraction). Notice the acoustic variations that occur. Phoneme /s/ should become at least slightly distorted as the jaw lateralizes too far forward and back.

Repeat all the steps of this jaw exercise with the other sibilants – /z/, /ʃ/, /ʒ/ /tʃ/ and /dʒ/.

Figure 08

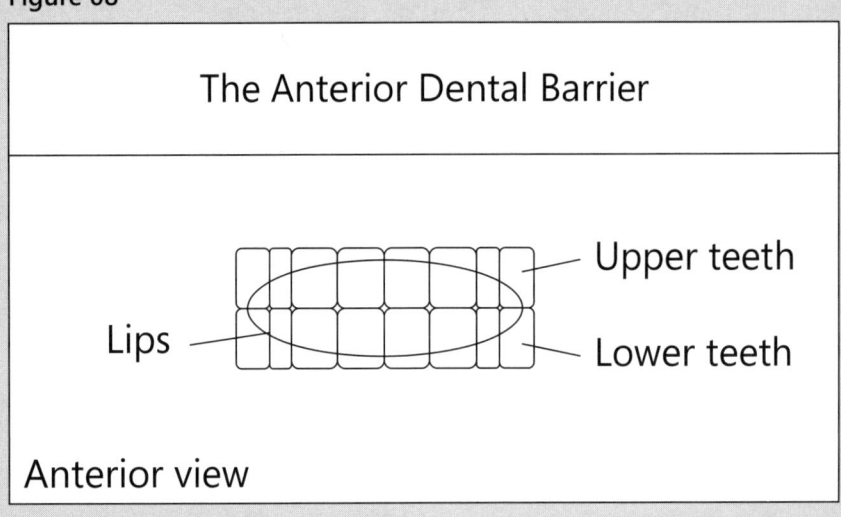

front teeth must nearly approximate during production of all the sibilants, the jaw must move into this position.

The movement pattern assumed by the jaw is dependant upon the position from which it begins its movement. It may lower, elevate or protrude depending on its starting point. Suffice it to say the jaw should lower, elevate or protrude just enough to allow the upper and lower central incisors to position themselves only a few millimeters apart. Too much shifting of the jaw to the right, left, forward or back causes phoneme distortion. Too much lowering or elevating also causes distortion. Learning Exercise 6 brings clarity to the concept of the jaw's role in sibilant production.

The Dental Barrier and Sibilant Production

As we have seen, the production of stridency is dependent upon a barrier created by loose articulation of the upper and lower incisors (figure 08). Problems in sibilant production occur when this barrier cannot be formed correctly. Malocclusion as well as missing, malformed or improperly positioned anterior teeth can cause the dental barrier to be too porous for good sibilant production. Distortion will be the result. The nature of the distortion will depend on the specific gaps caused by missing and misplaced teeth.

Adequate progress in articulation therapy for both the frontal and lateral lisp is destroyed when the anterior dental barrier cannot be formed. Therapy plans usually are postponed until the dental barrier is correct and stabile. This usually means postponing therapy until the permanent incisors have stabilized in position. It also can mean postponing treatment until certain stages of orthodontic treatment are complete. Compensatory techniques must be employed when the dental barrier cannot or will not be corrected.

Chapter 2 Summary
Oral Position for Sibilant Production

- The oral mechanism must be positioned in precise ways in order to achieve the hissing element necessary for correct production of each of our six target phonemes.

- Midline stridency is the most important element of sibilant production.

- The air stream of sibilant production is directed through the oral cavity along a mid line channel from back to front.

- The basic groove shape is created by elevating the sides of the tongue and by keeping its midline low.

- The fundamental grooved tongue pattern is essential for correct production of all six target phonemes because it ensures that the exhaled air stream will strike against the lingual surfaces of the incisors in such a way as to create air turbulence right at midline.

- Each of the sibilant phonemes is produced with a specific modification of the essential tongue groove pattern.

- All three sets of sibilant phonemes are produced with the tongue behind the anterior teeth.

- The sibilants are produced with relative jaw stability.

- Problems in sibilant production occur when the barrier formed by the anterior teeth cannot be formed.

Chapter 3

Deep Analysis of the Frontal Lisp

The frontal lisp is an oral-motor pattern seen in typically developing young children and in those with developmental impairment. The term applies when excessive interdental tongue placement is employed during production of one or more of the hissing sounds (figures 09 and 10). The client with a frontal lisp incorrectly slips the tip of the tongue between the upper and lower incisors while saying /s/, /z/, /ʃ/, /ʒ/, /tʃ/ or /dʒ/. The tongue tip may extend slightly to the left or right, but it generally stays at mid line. It is this mid line protrusion that characterizes the frontal lisp error pattern. The tongue may protrude all the way through the blade, but this more extensive protrusion occurs less frequently than simple tip protrusion. The jaw lowers enough to allow this protrusion. The jaw also may protrude somewhat as will be discussed below. A sloppy sound with limited true stridency results when our target phonemes are produced in this way. Sometimes the error results in a true /θ/ or /ð/ substitution for the sibilants.

The frontal lisp is an adorable fact of early childhood. But it usually becomes an affront to the eye and ear once a child is expected to outgrow it. The age at which a child crosses that line is blurry, however. For decades it has been widely accepted that children should outgrow this error by eight years of age, the time at which the average child leaves early

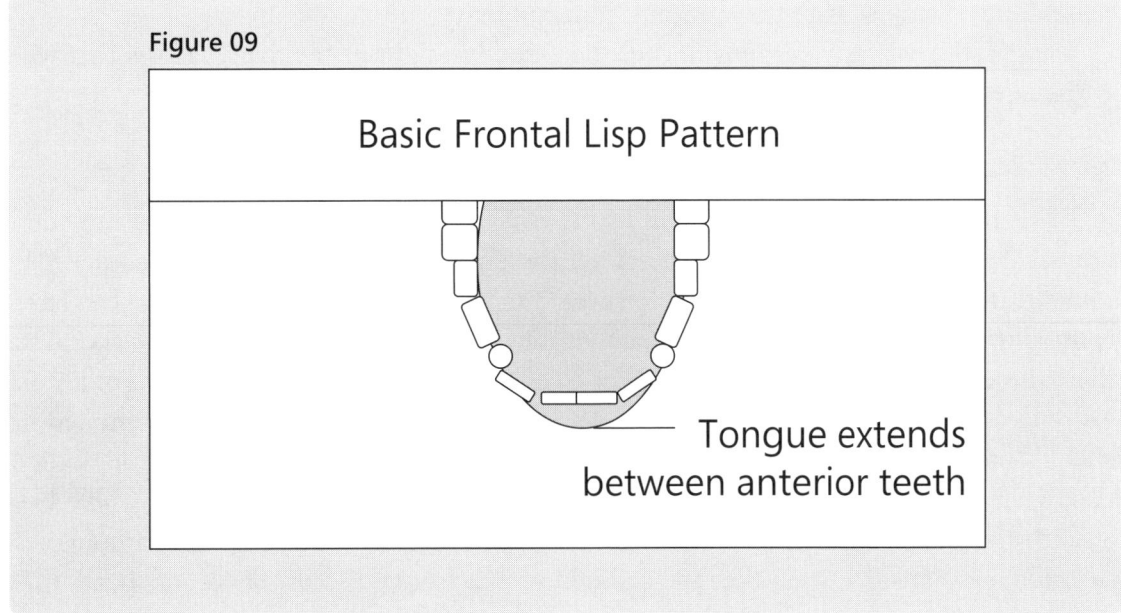

Figure 09

Basic Frontal Lisp Pattern

Tongue extends between anterior teeth

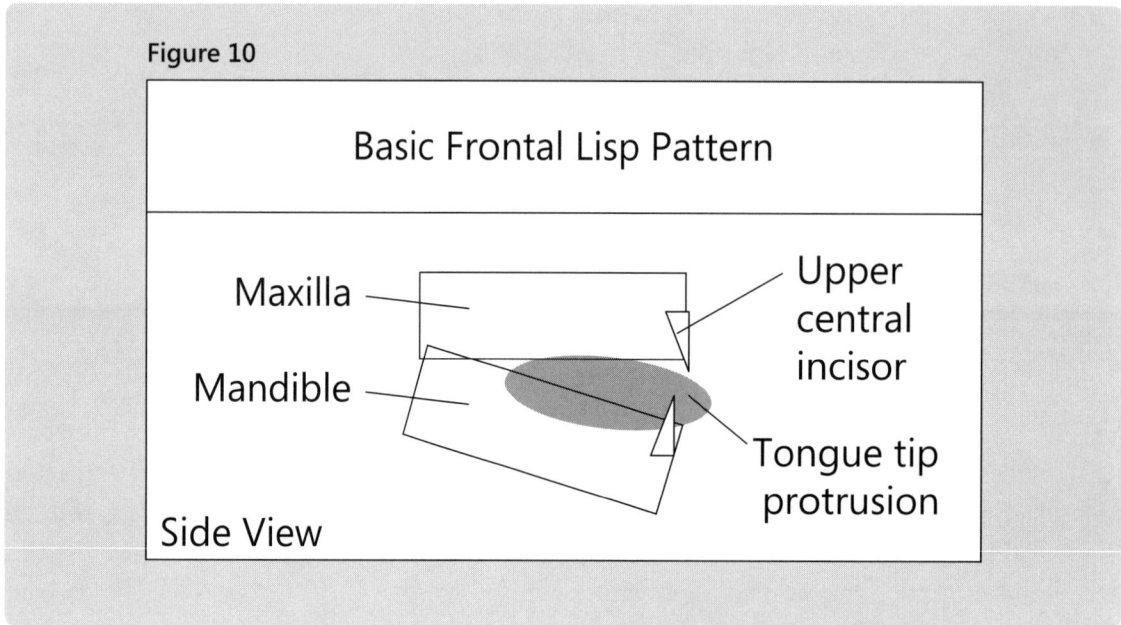

Figure 10

childhood. As a result, most speech-language pathologists in the United States withhold treatment of the isolated frontal lisp until a client is eight or nine years of age.

Some parents request that the frontal lisp be treated when their children are below eight years of age. Parents seeking early treatment are informed that correction of a frontal lisp below age eight years is possible. They also are informed that the therapy may be unnecessary because children often outgrow the frontal lisp. Sometimes a decision is made to give the child another six-to-twelve months of natural growth and development before deciding to begin therapy. Therapy may commence if the lisp does not go away during that time. And it may be addressed earlier if the client is uncomfortable with or distressed by the distortion. Lee Edward Travis' original criteria for enrolling a client in treatment is still a good decision-making process in this situation. Clients are enrolled if the error is troubling to the client, therapist, parents or other significant party.

The question of early enrollment must be viewed in light of the many factors that will be discussed throughout the rest of this chapter.

The Frontal Lisp and the Public School

In the United States today, the frontal lisp is regarded as having no impact on the educational development of children. Therefore, the error, when it occurs alone, sometimes is not treated in the public schools. However, hundreds of therapists across the US have reported to me over the past fifteen years that they try whatever means at their disposal to enroll these children in school therapy. For example, students who receive low grades on oral reports because the frontal lisp makes them difficult to understand can be enrolled in school therapy because the problem is one of both sibilant production and intelligibility. Also, when the lisp interferes with all six sibilants enrollment is sometimes possible because this can be categorized as a multiple misarticulation. Speech-language pathologists have told me that sometimes they see children with a frontal lisp at school "off IEP." This means that the child is not officially enrolled in therapy but is seen periodically to check his progress. These periodic visits to therapists' offices are not actually assessment sessions: they are mini-treatment sessions. Such is the heart of the speech-language pathologist. It is very hard to turn clients away even when school policy dictates something different. Of course, a frontal lisp that occurs along with other articulation errors or with other specific language or communication problems, can be addressed within the child's overall school speech and language program.

Limited school-based treatment of the frontal lisp has had certain results. First, the frontal lisp seems to be increasing in frequency of occurrence among educated adults. Second, the number of children receiving this service privately seems to have increased. These two general observations should be studied formally to determine if this apparent trend bears out statistically.

Distribution Patterns

The frontal lisp generally is viewed as a simple *delay* in the development of correct sibilant production. However the frontal lisp pattern is noted in a wide variety of clients including those with specific speech and language *delay* as well as those with *disorder*. The following patterns of occurrence are noted:

1. A frontal lisp can occur on one or more of our target phonemes, but the problem usually includes both members of the cognate pairs. In other words, (a) if the lisp occurs on /s/ it also occurs on /z/, (b) if the lisp occurs on /ʃ/ it also occurs on /ʒ/, and (c) if the frontal lisp occurs on /tʃ/ it also occurs on /dʒ/. There may be exceptions to this observation, of course, but I have not seen one in thirty years of direct clinical work.
2. A frontal lisp almost never occurs on the palatal sibilants (/ʃ/, /ʒ/, /tʃ/, /dʒ/) without also occurring on the alveolar sibilants (/s/ and /z/). The opposite does occur however.
3. A frontal lisp can occur along with interdental tongue placement on the other lingua-alveolars – /t/, /d/, /n/ and /l/. This combination of errors is a significant factor in therapy because it suggests a wider oral movement problem and a more urgent need for remediation.
4. A frontal lisp on certain phonemes can occur alongside a lateral lisp on other phonemes.
5. A frontal lisp can occur in clients with phonological impairment. Usually the phonological patterns are addressed earlier in the course of treatment, although the phonological patterns and the frontal lisp can be treated simultaneously. The frontal lisp is not viewed as a major factor in low intelligibility, however. Therefore it is considered of less importance than the phonological error patterns.
6. A frontal lisp can occur in clients with severe apraxia or dysarthria. In these cases the frontal lisp pattern is only one small result of the speech movement disorder.
7. The frontal lisp is common when typical children are gaining their first words and phrases during the toddler years. Thus the frontal lisp is considered a *developmental error* when it occurs during early childhood and the early elementary years.

Auditory and Visual Discrimination and the Frontal Lisp

The ability to discriminate one speech sound production from another is at the heart of all articulation development and treatment. Without the ability to hear and see the difference between speech sounds, one has no reason to produce different speech sounds. In the case of the frontal lisp, clients are ignoring the difference between the way they are saying sounds and the way most of the rest of us are. They are accepting allophones that shouldn't be. They are treating sibilants made with the tongue protruded as if they were the same as sibilants produced with the tongue kept behind the teeth. Their range of acceptable productions of the sibilants is too large. It contains too many examples because important visual and acoustic characteristics are being ignored. Therapy for the frontal lisp is designed to help clients begin to discriminate between correct and incorrect production of the sibilant phonemes. This training is done through visual and auditory discrimination training.

The Oral-Motor Continuum and the Frontal Lisp

The study of oral movement patterns in children with articulation and phonological disorders has been one of my major areas of clinical investigation throughout thirty years of clinical work. The information I present on the oral motor problems related to the frontal lisp comes exclusively from my own observations. All the patterns I shall describe need to undergo rigorous study in the research lab to satisfy the profession at large.

Oral-motor problems occur on a continuum in all clients with articulation and phonological delay and disorder, and that includes clients with the frontal lisp pattern. Some clients with frontal lisp display oral-motor problems and other do not. Let's look more carefully at this idea (figure 11).

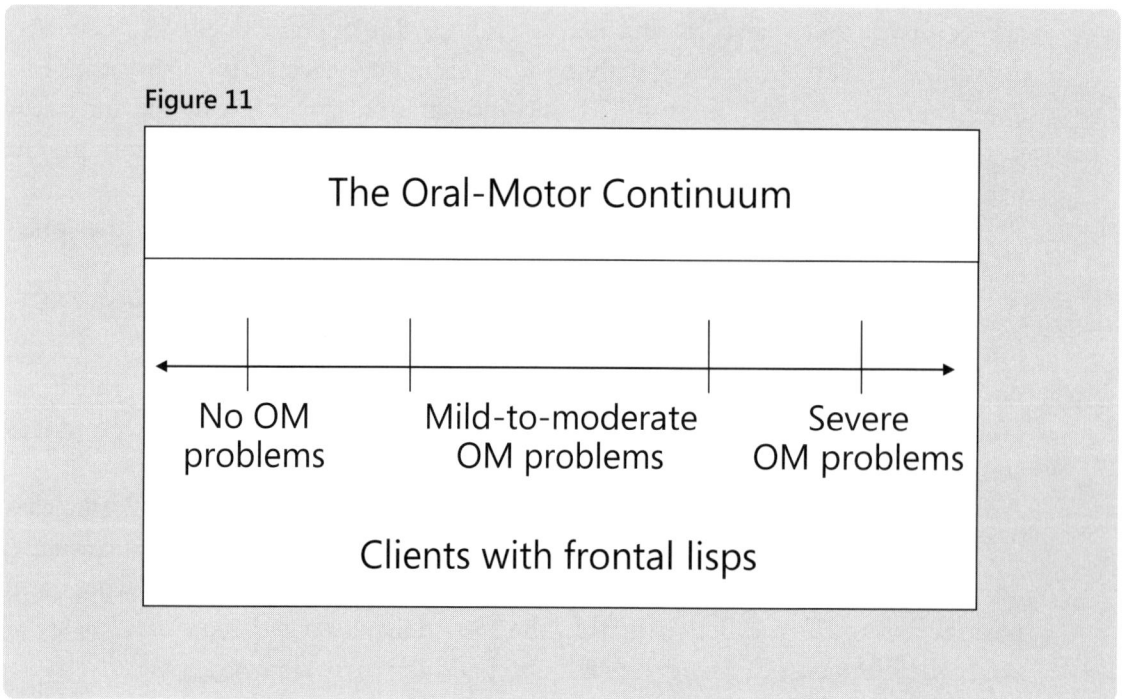

No Oral Motor Problems
Some clients with the frontal lisp pattern demonstrate no oral motor problems whatsoever. They are represented on the left-hand side of our continuum. These are clients whose articulation is excellent in all other ways except for the habitual interdental pattern they have retained for production of the sibilants. The frontal lisp error can be considered a habit. These clients fly through treatment and benefit quite well from traditional articulation therapy methods and procedures.

Severe Oral Motor Problems
Some clients demonstrate a frontal lisp pattern with severe oral-motor dysfunction. They are represented on the right-hand side of our continuum. These clients have a frontal lisp pattern that occurs amid a wide variety of phonological and phoneme errors including other interdental tongue placement problems. They have major phonological pattern errors, including significant sound and syllable omissions, and they have prosodic errors as well. These clients do not fly through treatment. This problem is much more than habit. The frontal lisp error pattern may be one part of a pervasive neuromuscular problem or an apraxia. These are clients for whom a combination of traditional articulation therapy, phonological therapy and oral-motor therapy including feeding therapy is most appropriate. They also are clients for whom the frontal lisp takes a back seat in the over all process of treatment.

In the Middle
Between these extremes are those clients who have a mild-to-moderate degree of oral-motor dysfunction along with their frontal lisp. These are clients who demonstrate interdental tongue placement on all the sibilants as well as the four lingua-alveolar sounds /t/, /d/, /n/ and /l/. These clients also may have other high-level substitution errors such as f/θ/, v/ð, w/l, w/r and so forth. These clients experience a certain degree of success in traditional articulation therapy. They can benefit from "show–and-tell" therapy: show them what to do, tell them about it and model correct sounds. But these are the kids who tend to stay in therapy for a long time. They need help with auditory, visual, tactile and proprioceptive awareness and discrimination.

Jaw Instability and the Frontal Lisp

As discussed above, the jaw must function in a finely graded open position to support the articulatory positions necessary for mature production of the sibilants. However jaw instability is a primary characteristic of the frontal lisp. This is true even when no oral-motor dysfunction is present and the frontal lisp pattern is simply a habit left over from early childhood.

The jaw destabilizes in one of two ways when the frontal lisp results: by lowering down too far or by protruding too far forward. Each has a different effect on the lisping pattern. I have labeled these the *classic frontal lisp* and the *jaw protrusion lisp*. Learning Exercise 7 (on next page) helps the reader understand the role of jaw function in sibilant production.

LEARNING EXERCISE 7
Experiment with the Classic Frontal and Jaw Protrusion Lisp

At a mirror, produce /s/ correctly and then with the tongue-tip protruding between the upper and lower central incisors. Repeat for /z/, /ʃ/, /ʒ/, /tʃ/ and /dʒ/. This is the classic frontal lisp. Notice that the tip protrudes and the jaw lowers.

Now produce /s/ while jutting the jaw forward so that the lower incisors are positioned anterior to the upper incisors. Then repeat for /z/, /ʃ/, /ʒ/, /tʃ/ and /dʒ/. This is the jaw protrusion lisp. Notice that the jaw protrudes but the tongue does not: the tongue is carried with the jaw. Pay careful attention to the acoustic and visual differences between the classic frontal lisp and the jaw protrusion lisp so you can differentiate them easily.

Figure 12

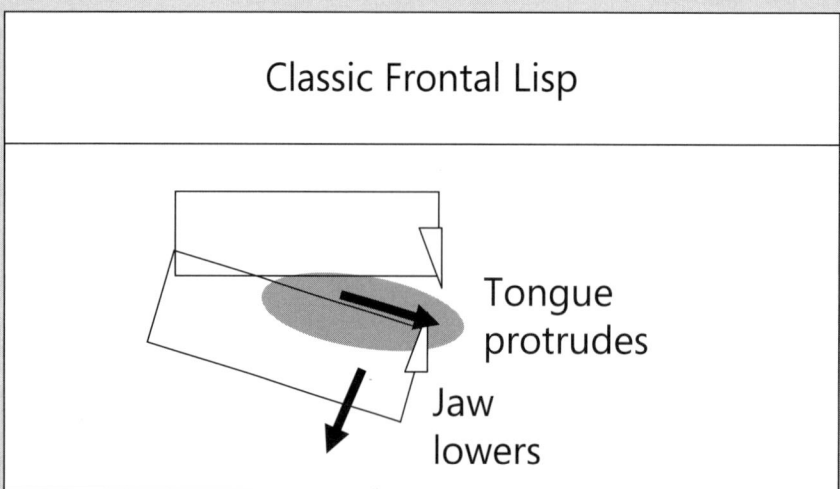

Figure 13

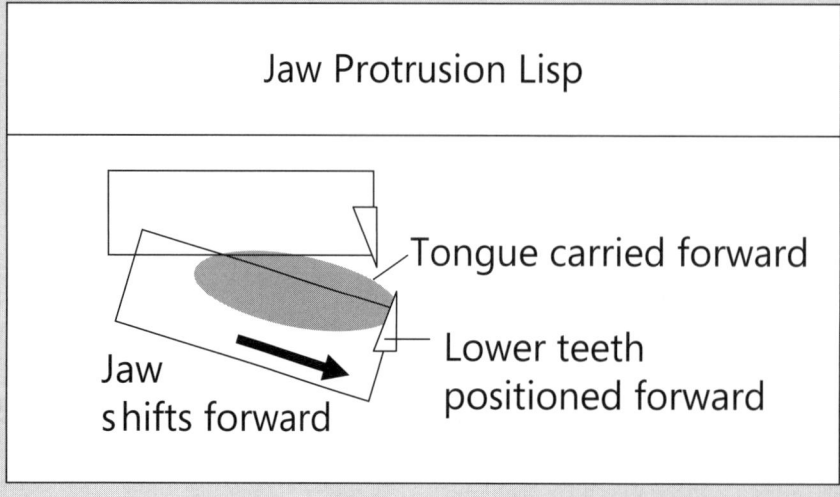

Classic Frontal Lisp
The classic frontal lisp pattern occurs when the jaw moves down too far and the tongue-tip is allowed to protrude between the upper and lower incisors (figure 12). This is the frontal lisp pattern expected in early childhood. Excessive downward movement is the way the jaw first learns to move. It is a form of gross and immature oral-motor control. Over time, these wide excursions of the jaw become more refined and a restricted range of movement appropriate to mature speech is developed. As the jaw begins to move with maturity in this more restricted range, the tongue begins to keep its movements inside the mouth. Mature sibilant production with the tongue-tip well placed behind the central incisors is one result of maturing jaw stability. Correct tongue-tip placement at the alveolar ridge for production of /t/, /d/, /n/ and /l/ is another.

Jaw Protrusion Lisp
The jaw protrusion lisp results when the jaw moves too far forward (it protrudes) during speech (figure 13). The result is that the lower incisors become positioned anterior to the upper incisors. The position assumed by the front teeth resembles an under bite. But this is not that kind of structural deficit. This is an oral-motor pattern of excessive jaw protrusion during speech. It is a problem of *function* rather than one of *structure*. As the jaw protrudes, it carries the tongue forward with it. Sibilant phonemes made under this condition are distorted as the tongue tip is carried forward and positioned under the upper incisors. The important aspect of this error is that the tongue itself is not protruding. The tongue remains positioned inside the mandibular arch, behind the lower incisors. The jaw protrusion lisp is a jaw movement problem and not a tongue movement problem *per se*. Treatment is directed toward jaw position.

The jaw protrusion lisp is NOT a typical pattern of early childhood because excessive jaw protrusion is not part of oral-motor development in the same way that excessive jaw lowering is. Jaw protrusion can be considered an aberrant oral-motor behavior. Therefore the jaw protrusion lisp should not be considered a developmental error. It does not occur on the normal developmental path of phoneme learning. Also, the jaw protrusion lisp should not be confused with a true structural (occlusion) problem. Referral to the dentist and/or orthodontist will need to be made in order to make a definitive diagnosis of this error in most cases. Input from the orthodontist will help you decide if this is an error of less-than-optimal jaw structure or one of inappropriate jaw movement.

Tongue Stability and the Frontal Lisp

Tongue mobility is dependent upon stabilizing factors. The first tongue stabilizer is the jaw, as we have discussed above. The second stabilizing factor occurs in the tongue itself. Tongue stability is accomplished by maintaining close approximation of the tongue's back lateral margins to the molars and palate (figure 14 on next page). I have called these the *stability zones* or *shoulders* of the tongue. The tongue's stability zones remain in relative contact with the palate and molars located directly above them during almost all aspects of speech production. These are the points of tongue stability. All movements of the tongue are based

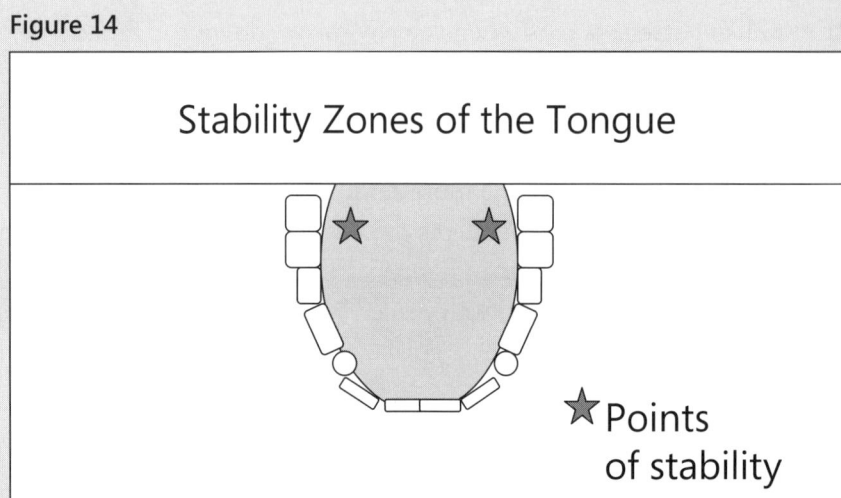

Figure 14

Stability Zones of the Tongue

★ Points of stability

LEARNING EXERCISE 8
Discover the Tongue's Stability Zones

Recite the alphabet aloud rapidly as if you were speaking in a quiet conversational style. Think about the back lateral margins of your tongue as you do so. Where are they? You should notice that the tongue's back lateral margins stay in relative contact with the molars and/or the palate near the molars during your recitation. Repeat several times until you can feel this contact. Notice that these places of articulation are consistent during this speech task. Repeat this process as you read this paragraph aloud. The shoulders of the tongue are the places from which all tongue movements are made.

LEARNING EXERCISE 9
Discover Tongue Stability in the Frontal Lisp

Count aloud from 60 to 80 in rapid conversational speech style. This will allow you to produce many /s/ sounds in sequence. Notice the relative stability of the tongue at the back lateral margins.

Now repeat this numerical sequence with a classic frontal lisp pattern. Pay careful attention to the stability zones. What happens? You should notice that tongue stability at the back lateral margins is lost as you produce a frontal lisp.

Now, say *sixty* several times in a row, alternating between correct production and production with a frontal lisp. Do you feel the shifting back lateral stability?

on these points of stability. Learning Exercise 8 helps the reader understand the tongue's stability zones.

The sibilants are produced by moving the lateral margins of the tongue toward and away from the palate while maintaining back lateral stability at the stabilizing zones. The tongue's points of stability at the back lateral margins remain intact when one pronounces the sibilants correctly. But stability is lost during the frontal lisp production as the tongue's lateral points of stability shift forward (Learning Exercise 9). When the back lateral mar-

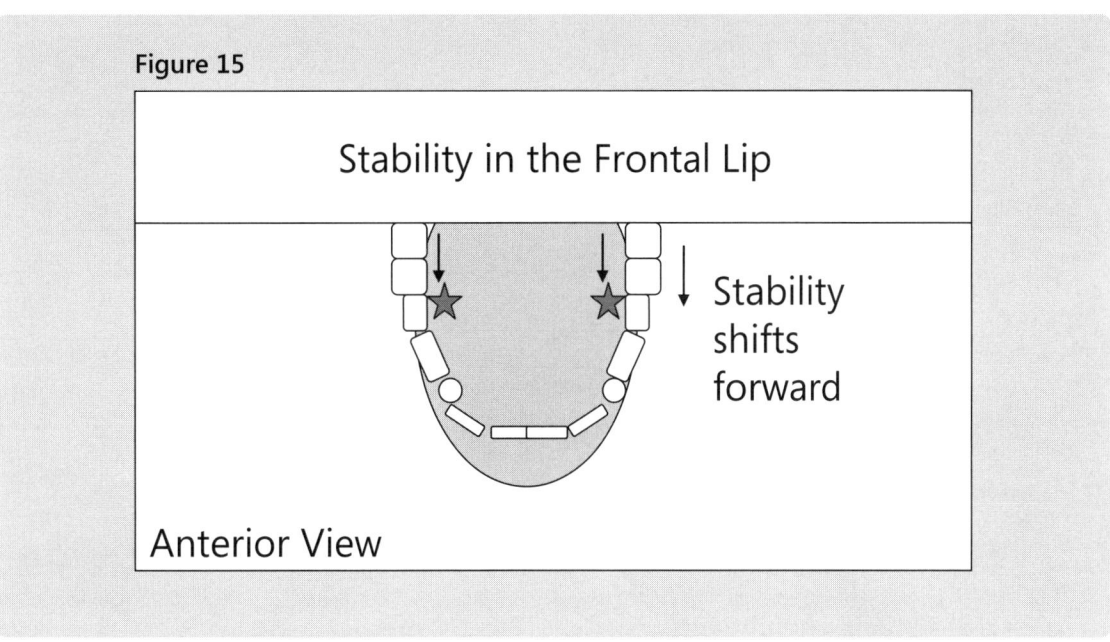

Figure 15

Stability in the Frontal Lip

↓ Stability shifts forward

Anterior View

gins of the tongue shift forward, so does the entire tongue (figure 15). In other words, from an oral-motor perspective, excessive anterior movement of the tongue-tip occurs because the tongue has lost its proximal stability in the rear. Loss of proximal stability causes incorrect distal mobility.

An oral-motor perspective reveals that the frontal lisp is the result of both jaw and tongue instability. Speech therapy that ignores this fact and attends only to the phonemes and/or the tongue tip may take a long time and may be met with limited success in the carryover phases. This does not occur when the frontal lisp is the result of simple habit. But it does when the client has an oral movement disorder related to the frontal lisp. Treatment for the frontal lisp is enhanced in these clients when activities designed to facilitate jaw and tongue stability are included. The development of appropriate tongue stability allows a client to speak in rapid conversational speech without shifting the tongue forward. It helps him produce his sibilants correctly during all levels of therapy.

Oral Tone and the Frontal Lisp

The jaw and tongue instability characteristic of the frontal lisp often can be attributed to low oral tone. *Tone* refers to a muscle's strength and speed of reactivity. Muscles that are low in tone tend to react slowly and in a weak manner. Low tone makes body parts lax and droopy, as if the muscles, skin and other soft tissues were hanging from the bones underneath them. When tone is low in the oral and facial muscles, the jaw and tongue tend to be carried lower and more forward. The mouth hangs open, the lower lip droops and is not very active, and the tongue slips forward out the mouth. Low tone in the muscles of the jaw, lips and tongue can have a negative effect on the production of all phonemes. The sibilants are especially affected since they require that the jaw be held high and that the tongue stay inside the mouth. The frontal lisp often is the result of low oral tone.

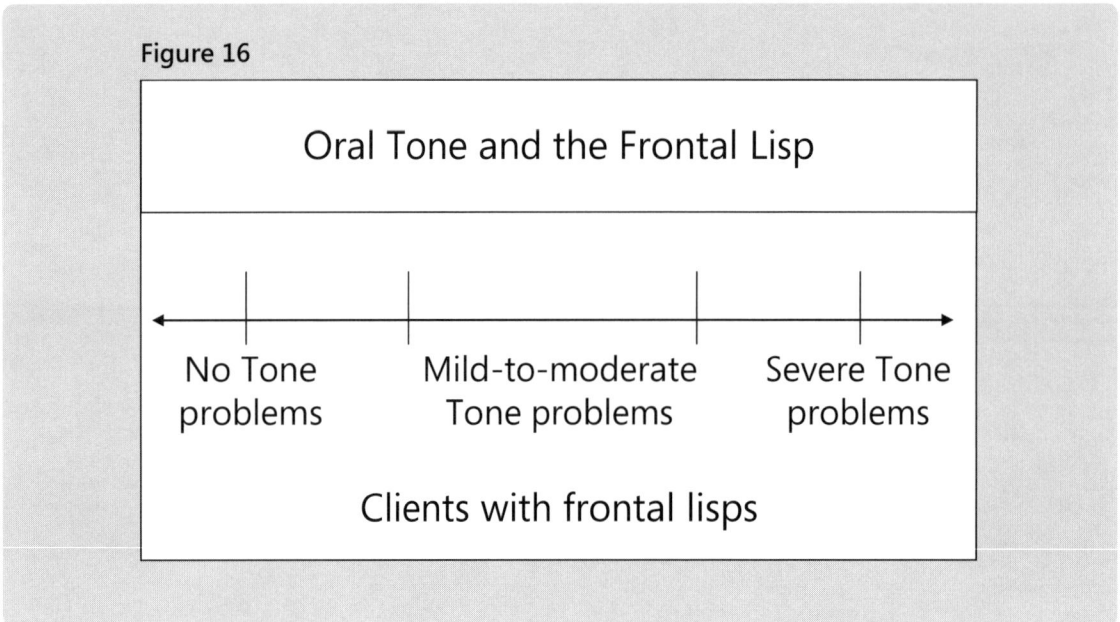

Figure 16

Readers should keep in mind that low oral tone is not always a characteristic of the frontal lisp. Remember, oral movements span a continuum from non-existent to severe in the frontal lisp. Thus, some clients have oral tone problems and others do not, and their problems also occur on a continuum (figure 16). A complete assessment of the frontal lisp includes an examination of oral and facial tone. Sometimes further assessment of whole body tone is obtained from occupation or physical therapy. This information helps formulate a thorough analysis of muscle tone and its relation to the frontal lisp pattern. An understanding of oral tone helps shape the treatment program. Clients with normal oral tone are likely to outgrow the developmental frontal lisp pattern. Clients with low oral tone are not.

Oral-Tactile Sensitivity and the Frontal Lisp

It is the author's experience that the frontal lisp can be associated with low oral-tactile sensitivity, or *hyposensitivity*. Oral sensitivity refers to the ability to perceive and discriminate tactile stimulation to the lips, gums, tongue, palate and oropharynx. When a client is hyposensitive in the oral mechanism, he under-reacts to tactile input given there. As a result, all the basic reflexive movement patterns of the mouth are under-rehearsed, under-experienced and under-developed. Clients with oral-tactile hyposensitivity know less about the physical structure of their mouths because they have not experienced responses to touch input in the same way as others. The "feel" in the mouth is different. These clients tend to move the mouth clumsily, and they are much less precise in their articulation. Their ability to discriminate place of articulation is impaired as a result. The sibilants require a high level of oral-tactile sophistication and position discrimination. The client with oral-tactile hyposensitivity almost always resorts to more primitive oral movement patterns, and the frontal lisp often is the result.

Like oral tone problems, oral-tactile sensitivity problems are not always present in the frontal lisp. Oral sensitivity also spans a continuum from non-existent to severe in the fron-

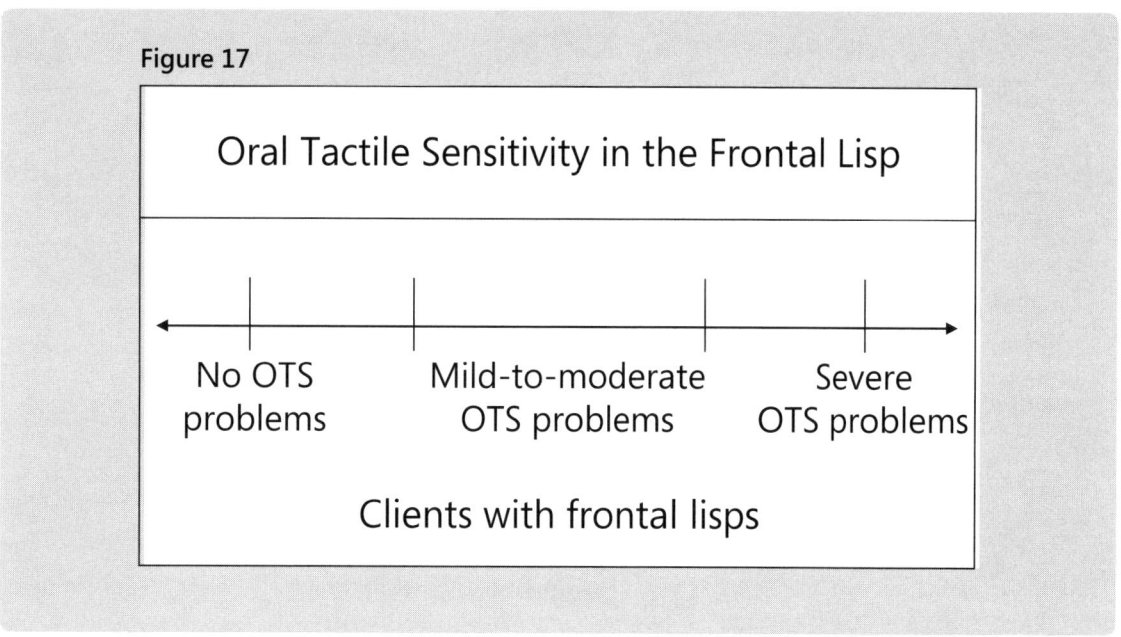

Figure 17

tal lisp (figure 17). Some clients have oral sensitivity problems and others do not. When a client has a frontal lisp with low oral sensitivity, movement patterns for other phonemes usually are similarly affected. Injury to the nerves of the tongue also can result in a frontal lisp pattern if the insult has resulted in reduced tactile sensation.

A differential diagnosis of the frontal lisp includes procedures for assessment of oral-tactile sensitivity. Results impact the treatment plan. Clients with normal oral tactile sensitivity are more likely to outgrow the developmental frontal lisp pattern. Those with oral tactile hyposensitivity are less likely to outgrow the problem and are more likely to need therapy for their lisp.

A Word About the Whole Body

Certain clients have poor oral control because they have development problems in motor control of the whole body. Jaw, lip and tongue movements are an outgrowth of and integral to head, neck, shoulder and hip movements. An occupational therapist (OT) or physical therapist (PT) can help the speech-language pathologist analyze the relationship between the client's neuromuscular control and his oral control. Treatment of jaw, lip and tongue position can be integrated together with treatment techniques for the rest of the body. Treatment procedures are designed by the motor specialist. Therapy incorporates methods to normalize tone, balance, sensitivity and the like. These methods are incorporated into speech therapy in order to maximize oral-motor learning. This process is absolutely necessary when designing an effective program for a frontal lisp in clients with significant sensorimotor or neuromuscular disorder.

Having said that, however, the average client with an isolated frontal lisp will need little of this work. He will not need a full evaluation by the OT or PT. The SLP who knows basic information about hip-trunk-shoulder alignment and its relationship to head and oral control can be mindful of small matters as they relate to the frontal lisp. An old-fashioned

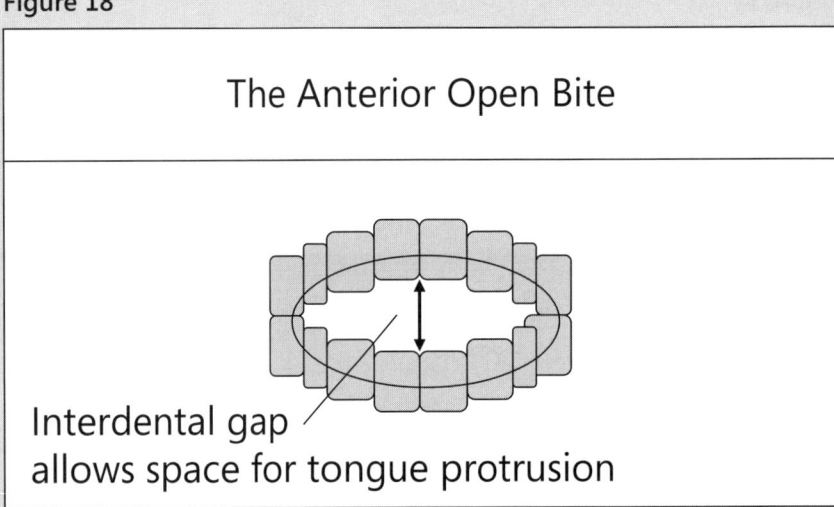

Figure 18

The Anterior Open Bite

Interdental gap allows space for tongue protrusion

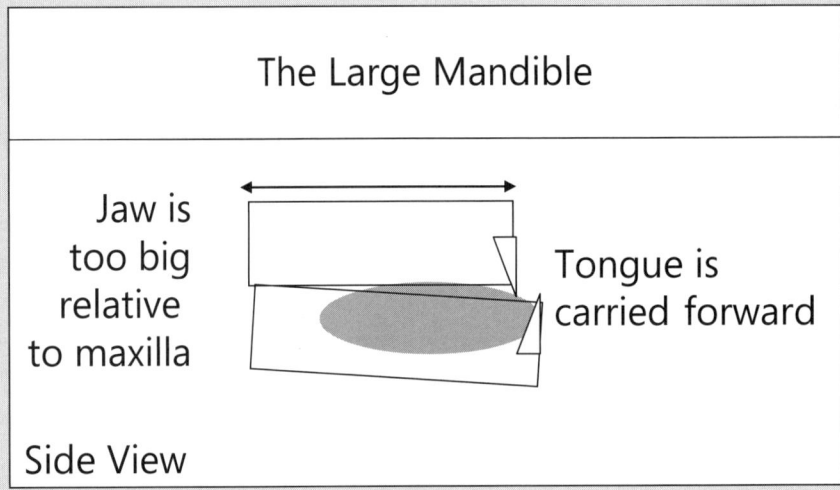

Figure 19

The Large Mandible

Jaw is too big relative to maxilla

Tongue is carried forward

Side View

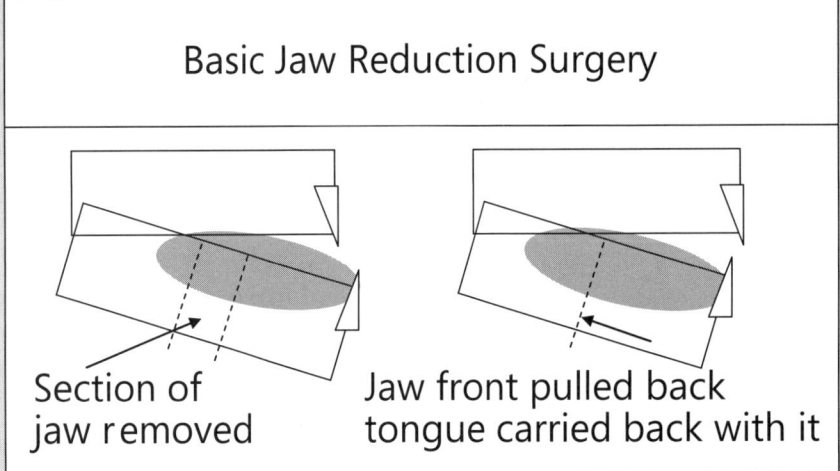

Figure 20

Basic Jaw Reduction Surgery

Section of jaw removed

Jaw front pulled back tongue carried back with it

direction to "Sit up straight," "Get your body ready" or "Show me good sitting" will be enough for these clients to get their head into a good position for control of the jaw, lips and tongue.

Oral Structure and the Frontal Lisp

A complete evaluation of the frontal lisp always includes a thorough assessment of oral structure. Oral structure has a direct impact on the pronunciation of all phonemes since the shape of the oral cavity literally comprises the walls of acoustic resonation during sound production. Several structural alterations in the oral cavity cause specific distortion to the sibilants that cause a frontal lisp. Other structural alterations force a client to use a frontal lisp pattern in order to compensate for the structural difference.

Structural differences related to the frontal lisp are described below. In the ideal situation, problems in oral structure are eliminated before or during treatment of the frontal lisp. In many cases, we must compensate for these problems and adjust our treatment plans accordingly.

Anterior Open Bite

An anterior open bite is characterized by a gap between the upper and lower incisors (figure 18). That gap can be narrow or quite wide depending upon many factors. The gap allows the tip of the tongue to slip out between the teeth.

There continues to be much controversy regarding the cause and effect relationship between the anterior open bite and the frontal lisp pattern. Does the frontal lisp pattern cause the anterior open bite, or does the anterior open bite cause the frontal lisp? Regardless of the view, the fact remains that an anterior open bite allows the tongue to slip forward and both problems need to be addressed. The refined stridency needed for production of the sibilants cannot be achieved when there exists such a gap.

Large Mandible

A mandible that is too large relative to the maxilla will cause the lower teeth and the tongue to be positioned anterior to the upper teeth (figure 19). The client may appear to be speaking with a frontal lisp because too much of the tongue is showing during speech. But this is not a classic frontal lisp or a jaw protrusion lisp. This is a distorted speech pattern related to a structural deviation of the mouth. We can train a client to pull the tongue alone back in behind the upper teeth as he speaks, but this is difficult work that requires near adult maturity. It also means learning to habituate a retracted tongue position which is an uncomfortable position for most people. Holding the tongue in retraction while speaking can cause aching in the jaw and tongue as well as tension headaches. Only a change to the actual structure of the jaw via oral surgery will change this pattern completely (figure 20). Without surgery the client must learn to keep the tongue back further or settle for the lisping pattern that results.

Missing Teeth

Missing central and lateral incisors can be a problem for sibilant production because stridency is reduced. A missing tooth allows a tremendous amount of air to escape through the front, thus eliminating the appropriate dental barrier necessary for production of the

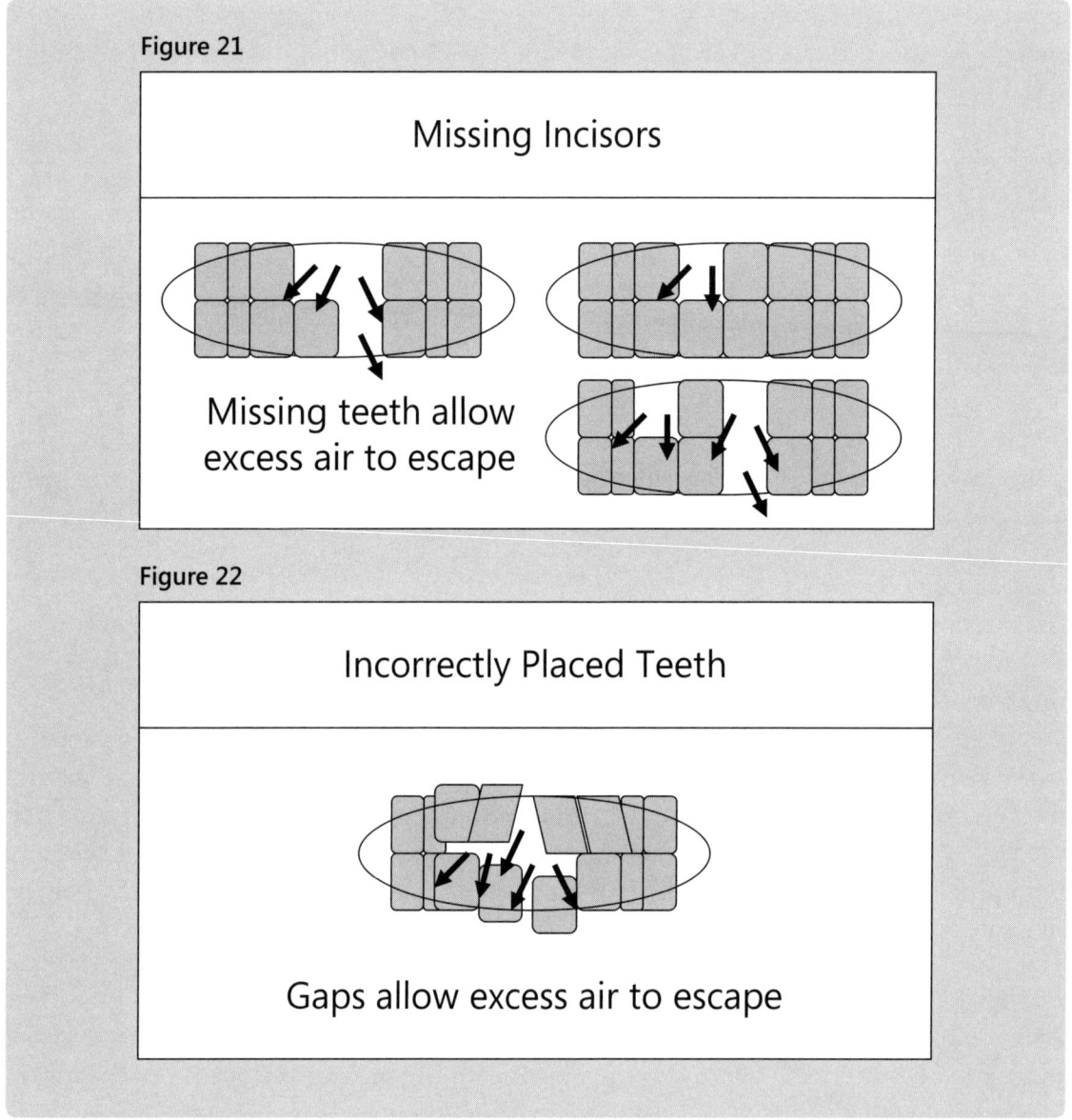

Figure 21

Missing Incisors

Missing teeth allow excess air to escape

Figure 22

Incorrectly Placed Teeth

Gaps allow excess air to escape

hissing quality (figure 21). Children who experience the comings and goings of their teeth during the childhood years tend to shift the position of the tongue groove in order to create the stridency they desire against the teeth that remain. Thus, the central groove of sibilant production tends to shift as baby teeth go missing and as permanent teeth erupt. Too many teeth missing in the front of the mouth at one time can result in the same problem as the anterior open bite: there are no teeth against which to create stridency.

If a frontal lisp did not exist before a child's anterior teeth fell out, and if the frontal lisp truly was created as a result of missing teeth, the lisp should be viewed as temporary. The lisp usually disappears as the new adult teeth emerge. This process takes place naturally and without speech therapy, but it can take a year or more depending upon the length of time it takes for the permanent teeth to settle. It is precisely for this reason that treatment of the frontal lisp often can and should wait until the permanent teeth are firmly in place. This is especially true if the frontal lisp exists in isolation. If, however, the client has missing anterior teeth, a frontal lisp, and other phoneme errors, therapy can and should commence with an early focus on the other phonemes that can be produced correctly even though the teeth are missing.

Tooth Position Problems
Teeth that are positioned incorrectly cause the same problems as teeth that are missing. This is because incorrectly positioned teeth create gaps in the dental barrier and appropriate stridency cannot be created once again (figure 22). Clients with cleft lip and palate are especially prone to problems in tooth position, and the extent and location of these short fallings depends upon their surgical and/or orthodontic management. Tooth position problems are treated with braces, spacers, oral surgery and other methods. A letter explaining the relationship between the tooth position problems and speech may be requested of the speech-language pathologist (appendix 9).

Supernumerary Teeth
Extra teeth sometimes cause a client to position the tongue in an anterior direction and a frontal lisp can result. For example, extra teeth behind the upper incisors can prevent correct stridency from being shaped. A forward shifting of the tongue can make the phoneme sound better in some of these cases. Removal of the supernumerary teeth may be used to stimulate correct tongue movement and position. A letter of support explaining the relationship between the extra teeth and the client's speech may be requested of the speech-language pathologist (appendix 10).

Large Tongue
A tongue that is too large for the oral cavity will protrude from between the teeth (figure 23 below and 24 on next page). A large tongue should not be confused with a tongue that is low in tone and thus protruding. Input from occupation or physical therapy and/or

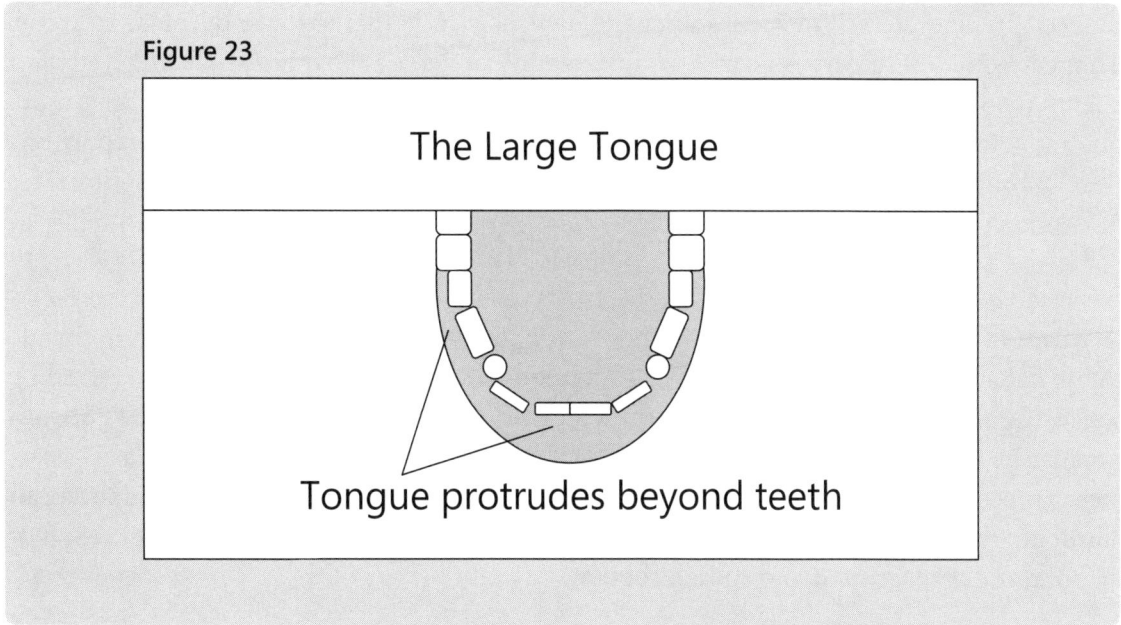

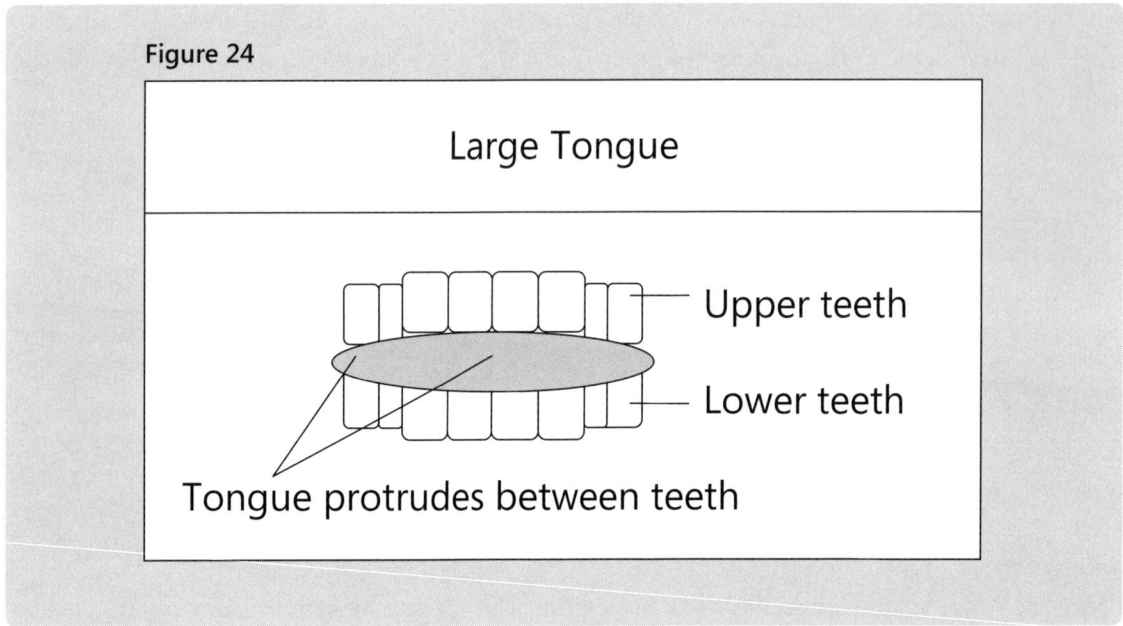

Figure 24

neurology will assist in the diagnosis of low oral tone. Evaluation by an otolaryngologist or oral surgeon may need to be made in order to determine if the tongue actually is too large.

Some clients with large tongues undergo surgery to reduce its size (figure 25 and 26). Tongue reduction surgery is an enormous decision made between the family and their physicians. The decision to undergo this procedure is discussed in relation to breathing, eating, speech and cosmetics. Safety is also a primary concern because a young child can fall and bite off the tongue tip. Speech-language pathologists will be asked to supply a letter or report (appendix 7) explaining the relationship between the client's tongue and his speech. Tongue reduction surgery allows the remaining tongue tissue to function inside the mouth and behind the teeth.

Tongue reduction surgery is not a cure for speech problems. The tongue that is now reduced in size creates an environment in which speech therapy can be most effective. Tongue reduction surgery is an area that constantly undergoes change. SLP's involved with clients who may be candidates for this surgery are compelled to investigate this area thoroughly before making recommendations for such an approach. ASHA's 1990 report entitled "Tongue Reduction Surgery, Efficacy and Relevance to the Profession" summarizes our concern.

Narrow Palate

A palate that is too narrow does not allow a tongue of normal proportion to fit up inside the maxillary arch for production of lingual phonemes unless the tongue narrows itself by squeezing medially (figure 27). Sometimes a client will allow the tongue to hang forward because he has not figured out how to do this. A frontal lisp pattern can result. Narrow palates can be widened with orthodontic appliances in most cases. Successful orthodontia can eliminate the need for speech therapy in some cases. Most clients require a combination of orthodontic management and speech therapy.

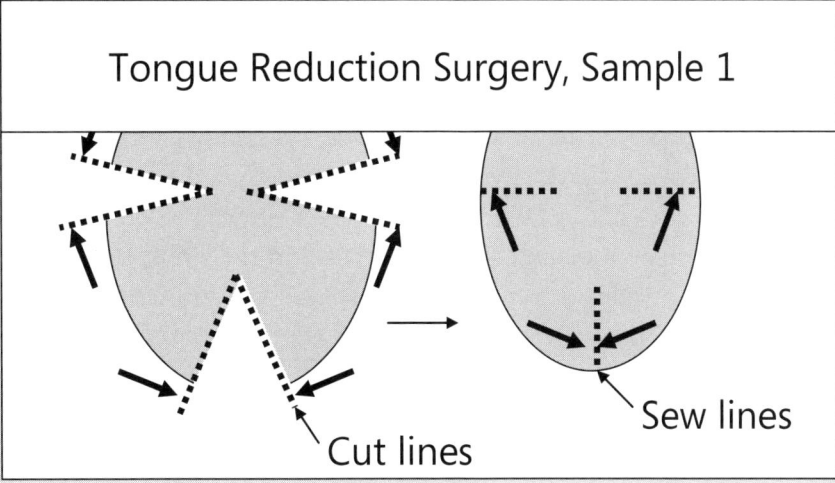

Figure 25

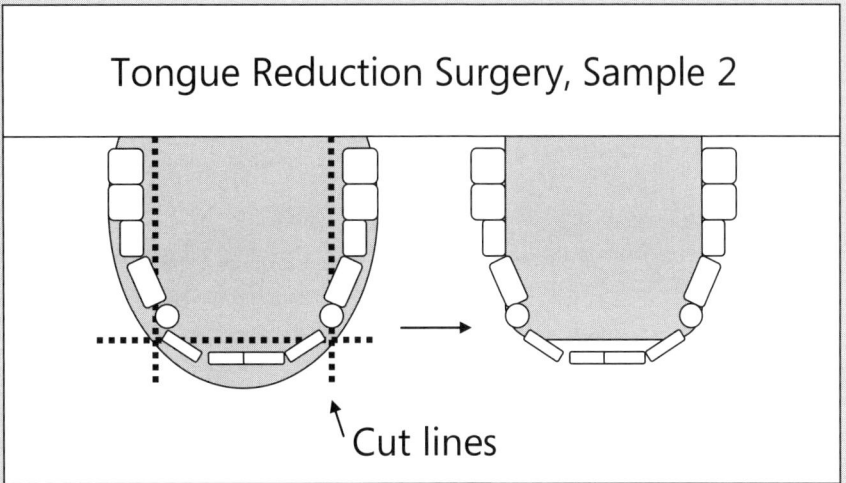

Figure 26

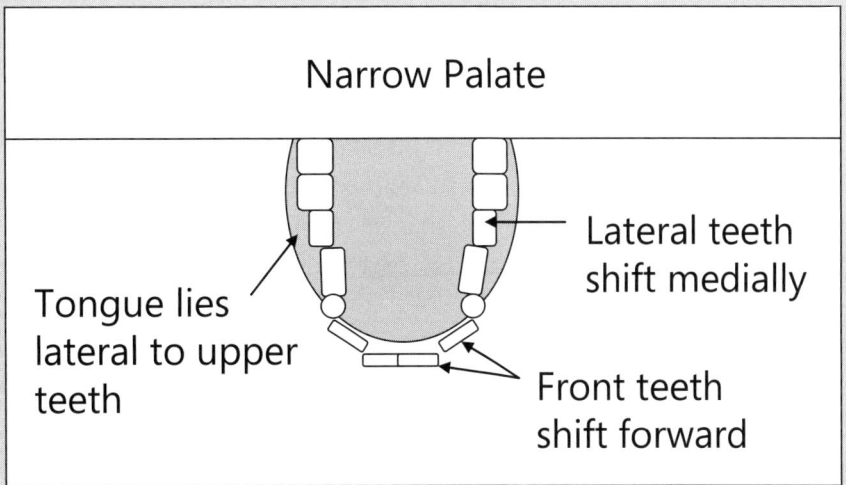

Figure 27

Tonsil and Adenoid Problems
Enlarged tonsils and adenoids can cause a client to shift the entire tongue forward in order to create a larger air passage in the oropharynx. A frontal lisp can result along with interdental tongue placement on the other lingua alveolar phonemes. Tonsils and adenoids can be reduced or removed. However medical practice today discourages this approach unless breathing problems such as snoring or sleep apnea are present. Some parents "shop" physicians until they find one who will remove their child's tonsils and adenoids. A letter of support (appendix 8) from the speech-language pathologist should be provided, however, this decision usually is a medical one made by the parents and their physician. DO NOT refer clients for tonsillectomy or adenoidectomy if hyper nasality is present. Refer the client for velopharyngeal evaluation instead and move forward cautiously.

Parts of the Tongue Removed
A frontal lisping type pattern can result in clients who have lost part of the tongue due to injury, illness or surgery. The role of the speech therapist is to help the client discover and habituate the speech pattern with the best visual and acoustic result that is possible given the structural condition of the tongue. This is usually short-term therapy that may need to be revisited during the course of subsequent surgeries. Pre- and post-operative evaluations will be required along with appropriate reports.

Unrelated Problems
There are a number of structural problems that generally do NOT result in a frontal lisp pattern. These include: the presence of palatal fistulas, the short lingua frenulum, velopharyngeal insufficiency, repaired cleft lip or palate, the small tongue, the small mouth, the geographic tongue, and scars on the tongue. This is not to suggest that the frontal lisp pattern cannot occur with these patterns. It means that if a frontal lisp pattern occurs in the presence of these structural differences, other causes should be sought.

Oral Habits and the Frontal Lisp

Excessive digit and pacifier sucking as well as other oral habits can be associated with the frontal lisp. Sucking habits that are frequent, long term and intense can perpetuate the infantile suckle-swallow pattern (see below). This in turn can extend the time during which the child lowers the jaw and protrudes the tongue in speech and feeding. All the lingua-alveolar phonemes can be impacted resulting in interdental tongue placement on all. Further, excessive digit or pacifier sucking can cause malocclusion, and malocclusion can impact speech as described above. Other oral habits also can have a detrimental effect on teeth position and speech including the frontal lisp pattern. These include excessive nail biting, skin biting, shirt chewing, and so forth.

A complete differential diagnosis of the frontal lisp includes questions about oral habits present or past. Treatment of the frontal lisp is enhanced when oral habits are eliminated either before or during the speech therapy program. Oral habits that go unrecognized and untreated can cause a program for the frontal lisp to fail. Clients with a frontal lisp and NO oral habits are in the best position to outgrow their lisp. Those with oral habits are less likely to outgrow their frontal lisp in my experience.

Eating and Swallowing Patterns and the Frontal Lisp

Oral-motor therapy began as an outgrowth of the research on feeding development that Suzanne Evans Morris began in the 1970's. Her work revolutionized the way we viewed oral movements because she demonstrated the intimate steps a baby takes as he learns to move his mouth while learning to eat. It is this data that contributed the most to my early understanding of the oral movement patterns of the frontal lisp.

Morris demonstrated that jaw, lip and tongue movement progress through a highly predictable sequence during infant feeding development. This is to be expected because the oral mechanism, just like all parts of the body, develops movement in highly stylized ways. All children progress through the same sequence of movement development. Of particular interest to us is the way in which jaw and tongue movements develop over time.

Morris instructs us that the earliest way in which the jaw and tongue function is the *suckle-swallow* pattern. In the suckle-swallow, the jaw and tongue function together as a unit. The jaw moves down as the tongue pushes forward, and the jaw moves upward as the tongue pulls back in (figure 28). This pumping action draws liquid from the nipple during bottle or breast-feeding.

The suckle-swallow pattern is particularly obvious when babies are introduced to spoon-feeding. An infant of about six months of age opens his mouth as the spoon approaches, he closes his mouth after the spoon is placed in and when it is withdrawn, and then he suckle-swallows the puree in his attempt to draw it into the oropharynx for swallowing. Basically, an infant tries to eat puree with the same suckle-swallow pattern he uses to draw liquid from a nipple. But this action is not very efficient for eating purees and the result is that just as much food gets pushed back out the mouth as gets swallowed. Parents patiently scrape the food off the child's lips and face, and then they spoon it back in. The suckle-swallow pattern dominates for many months.

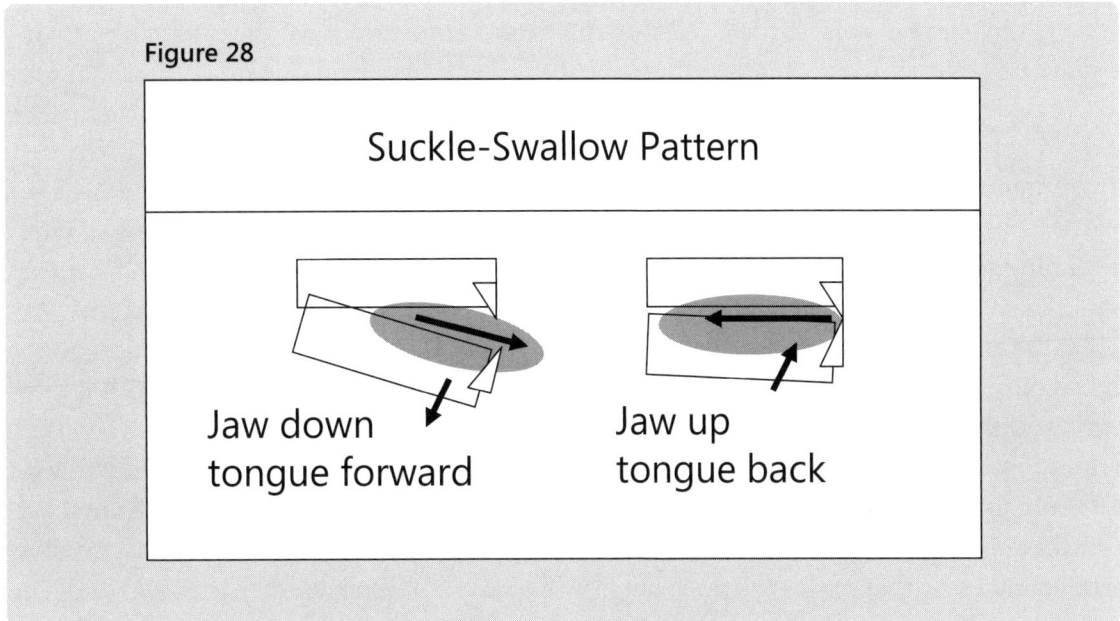

Figure 28

With time and practice, a child's swallow begins to change and become more efficient. It gradually evolves into a mature swallow pattern. The strong downward push of the jaw during suckling begins to fade in favor of upward positioning during sucking. But a suckle-swallow pattern can persist into childhood. A suckle-swallow that persists into childhood has been called a *reverse swallow*, an *infantile swallow* or a *tongue thrust swallow*. The jaw and tongue movements of the suckle-swallow are the same as those of the frontal lisp pattern. The pattern of jaw-down-tongue-forward and jaw-up-tongue-back are the same in both. In essence, both the suckle-swallow pattern and the frontal lisp pattern are the result of an oral mechanism that is functioning immaturely. Oral-motor immaturity causes the suckle-swallow to dominate feeding movements and it causes interdental tongue placement to dominate speech movements.

The question might be asked: If the tongue and jaw are functioning immaturely, why are the sibilants the only phonemes affected? The answer is this: They are not always the only phonemes affected. Remember, sometimes we also see interdental tongue placement on the lingua-alveolars /t/, /d/, /n/ and /l/. I believe that there are two things going on here, one related to oral-motor immaturity and the other related to a perpetuating habit. Consider:

1. A frontal lisp on the sibilants which occurs ALONG WITH interdental tongue placement on the lingua-alveolars – /t/, /d/, /n/, /l/ – occurs because the oral mechanism is still functioning immaturely. Oral-motor delay is widespread and it is affecting phonemes broadly. Immaturity of oral movement may also affect eating, swallowing and oral rest position.
2. A frontal lisp that occurs on the sibilants ALONE may be the result of simple habit. The habit is a perpetuation of the tongue movement patterns of early childhood. General oral-motor skills are appropriate for age. Production of the other phonemes is not affected. Swallow and oral rest likewise are not affected. This client simply has not attended to the different motor pattern necessary for production of mature sibilants. In addition to simple habit, this pattern may be a familial one, or the client may have poor auditory discrimination skills for these phonemes. In any case, the sibilants are the only phonemes affected because this is not an oral movement problem, per se. This is a phoneme production problem.

A complete differential diagnosis of the frontal lisp includes an assessment of oral-motor patterns in feeding. We are not talking about a full dysphagia evaluation here. A simple screening test comprised of eating a cracker and drinking a few swallows of water will reveal the swallowing skill of most clients with a frontal lisp pattern (See appendix 6).

A frontal lisp pattern that occurs along side an infantile suckle swallow pattern suggests a broad oral-motor dysfunction or delay. Treatment of the frontal lisp can be met with limited success if the infantile suckle swallow pattern is ignored. Treatment is enhanced when both are addressed together or when a mature swallowing pattern is facilitated first. Children with a frontal lisp and NO eating or swallowing problems are likely to outgrow their frontal lisp. On the other hand, children with a frontal lisp AND a persistent infantile suckle-swallow pattern are those that are less likely to outgrow their frontal lisp pattern.

Medical Influences on the Frontal Lisp

The evaluation of a frontal lisp includes a thorough medical review. Upper airway, specifically nasal breathing problems can contribute to a frontal lisp. A client who cannot breath consistently through the nose is forced to breathe through the mouth, and he will lower the jaw and part the lips in order to do so. Some clients position the tongue forward so that it extends out the front of the mouth to create a larger oral-pharyngeal air space. This forward tongue position can become a strong habit directly related to the frontal lisp pattern. Treatment of the frontal lisp is enhanced when the medical problems are eliminated before or during the treatment process. Problems in medical condition that cannot be reduced or eliminated must be compensated for. Again, children with a frontal lisp and NO upper respiratory problems are more likely to outgrow their frontal lisp while those with upper airway problems are less likely to outgrow the frontal lisp pattern.

Oral Rest Position and the Frontal Lisp

The differential diagnosis of the frontal lisp includes an assessment of oral rest position. Oral rest position is the habitual position assumed by the oral mechanism when the individual is not talking, eating or engaged in any other oral movements.

Correct Oral Rest
Correct oral rest position is characterized in very specific ways (figures 29, 30, 31).
1. The lips are lightly articulated
2. The teeth are slightly apart
3. The tongue tip and sides rest against the alveolar ridge and palate
4. The middle and back of the tongue are low and relaxed away from the palate

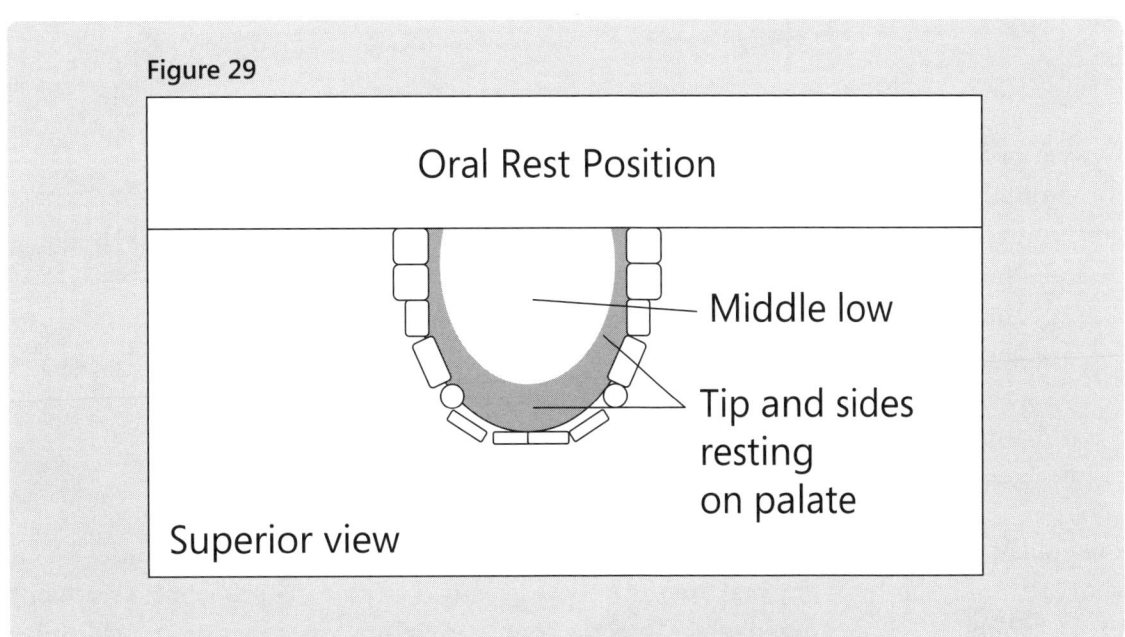

Figure 29

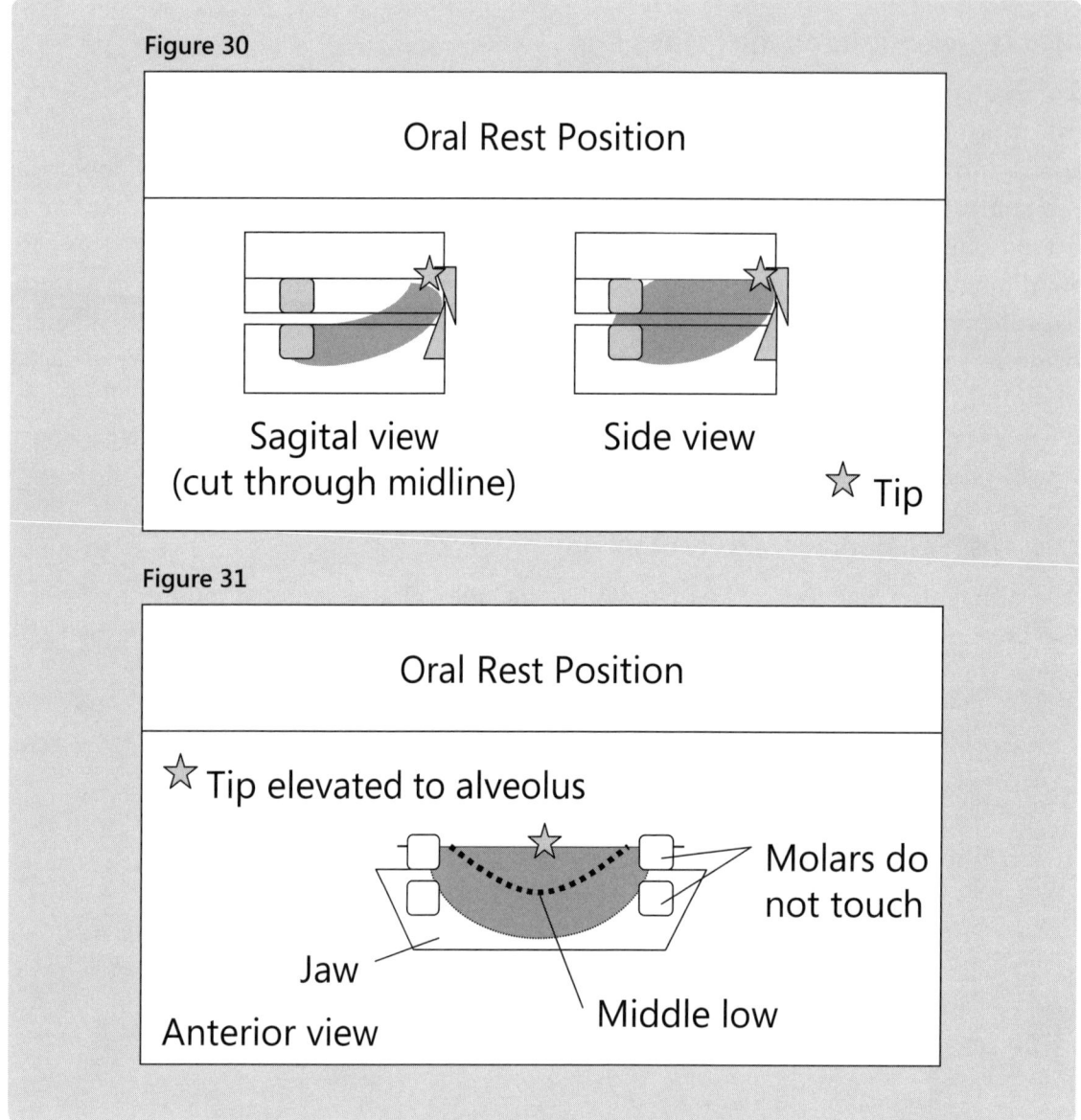

Figure 30

Figure 31

Open Lips Rest Posture
The frontal lisp often is associated with a habitual oral rest position that has different characteristics. This position has been called the *open lips rest posture* (figures 32, 33, 34).
1. The lips are apart
2. The teeth are too far apart (the jaw is too low)
3. The tongue tip is positioned anterior to the alveolar ridge, usually between the teeth
4. The blade of the tongue may rest against the upper anterior teeth
5. The back of the tongue is pushed forward

Obviously, the open lips rest posture is directly related to any and all of the causes listed above. It can result from low oral tone as well as structural or medical problems. Treatment of the frontal lisp is facilitated when it stems from correct oral rest position. Establishing

Figure 32
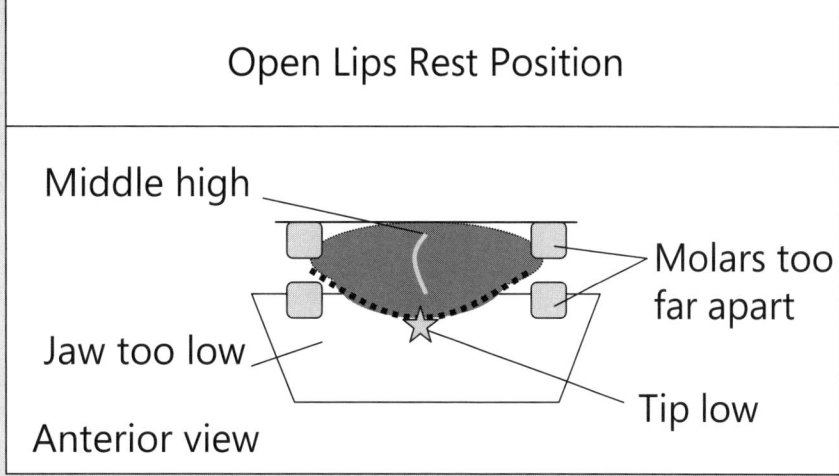

Figure 33
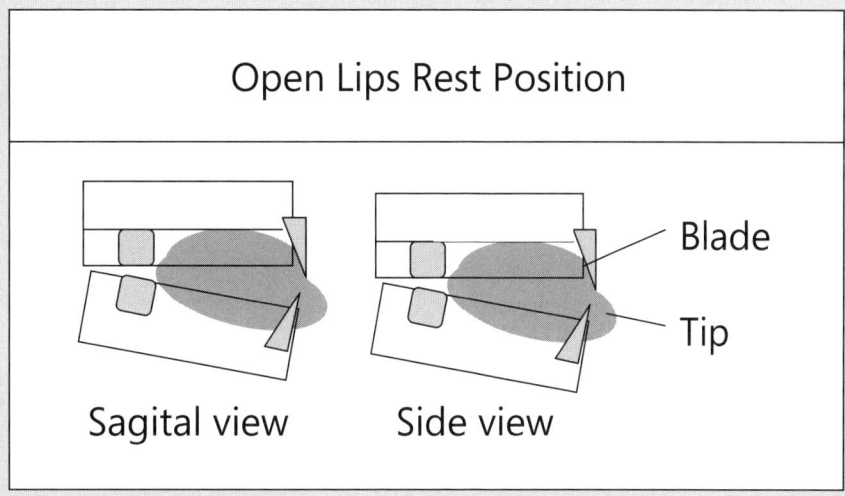

Figure 34
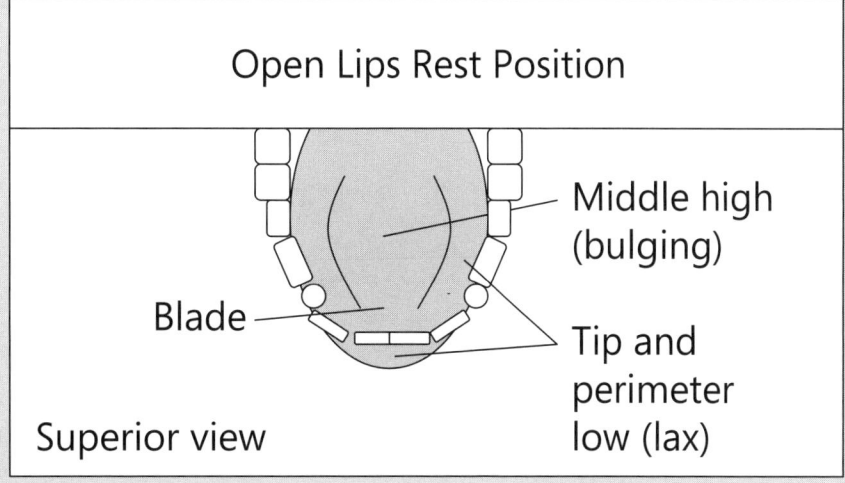

and habituating correct oral rest position is an integral part of treatment either before or during treatment of the frontal lisp.

Personality, Lifestyle and the Frontal Lisp

It must be noted that some adults with a frontal lisp do not consider it to be a problem and do not always want to eliminate it. This group includes those who believe "This is who I am" and those who want to stay "Natural." This group also includes those who want to use their frontal lisp to make their speech stand out or to be identified with a particular social group.

It also should be noted here that the public at large sometimes views the frontal lisp as a feminine speech pattern when it is seen in males. However, there is no research of which I am aware that supports this view: girls do not use a frontal lisp at a higher rate than boys. The view from an oral-motor and speech development perspective suggests that the frontal lisp is an immature speech pattern, not a feminine one.

Chapter 3 Summary
A Deep Analysis of the Frontal Lisp

- The frontal lisp is an oral-motor pattern seen in typically developing young children and in those with developmental impairment.

- Speech-language pathologists typically withhold treatment of the frontal lisp until a client is eight or nine years of age.

- Parents seeking early treatment are informed that correction of a frontal lisp below age eight years is possible but that their child may outgrow it naturally and on his own.

- A child's ability to outgrow a frontal lisp depends upon many factors.

- Clients with a frontal lisp are ignoring the differences between correct and incorrect production of the sibilants.

- Oral-motor problems occur on a continuum in clients with a frontal lisp pattern. Some have oral-motor problems and others do not.

- The classic frontal lisp pattern occurs when the jaw moves down too far and the tongue-tip is allowed to protrude between the upper and lower incisors.

- Tongue mobility is dependent upon tongue stability. The frontal lisp occurs when tongue stability is forfeited.

- The frontal lisp can be related to hypotonicity, hyposensitivity, specific deviations in oral structure and incorrect oral rest position.

- The frontal lisp can be related to persistent oral habits, eating and swallowing problems and medical conditions.

- Some adults prefer to keep their frontal lisp due to personality or lifestyle considerations.

Chapter 4

Deep Analysis of the Lateral Lisp

The term *lateral lisp* is assigned when air escapes laterally instead of medially during production of one or more of the sibilants. The client with a lateral lisp incorrectly positions the tongue and/or jaw so that the midline air stream is blocked while saying /s/, /z/, /ʃ/, /ʒ/, /tʃ/ or /dʒ/. A characteristic sloppy or slushy sound results when these phonemes are produced in this way. The lateral lisp is not seen in young children who are developing in a typical way. In other words, the lateral lisp is not a part of the normal process of speech development. From an oral movement and speech development perspective, therefore, the lateral lisp is considered an *aberrant* or *deviant* speech movement pattern. It is the author's experience that the pattern will not be outgrown. Speech therapy is always recommended.

When a client with a lateral lisp will be enrolled in treatment is a matter of debate. In earlier decades, children with a lateral lisp were placed into therapy in the public schools by third or fourth grade. In the United States now, however, many of these children are excluded from public school therapy because it is believed that the error does not impact the child's education in a negative way. School therapy sometimes is provided if the lateral lisp detracts from overall intelligibility. Many children with lateral lisps receive private speech therapy to remediate the problem. Still there is much confusion about the right age for enrollment. Most therapists seem to prefer to wait until these children are eight years of age or older. And this is a good plan for many students. However, there are methods that can be used with younger children as we shall see in chapter ten.

Tongue Position and the Lateral Lisp

Either tongue or jaw position can be the primary problem when the lateral lisp is diagnosed. We shall discuss tongue problems here and jaw problems below. During production of the lateral lisp, the tongue situates itself in such a way that air escapes laterally instead of at the midline. Air can escape to the right, left or both sides simultaneously and are named accordingly. The terms *right unilateral, left unilateral* and *bilateral lisp* are classic terms. The term *omni lisp* is my own.

1. *Right Unilateral Lisp:* the left side of the tongue articulates with the palate. This allows the air stream to escape to the right (figure 35).
2. *Left Unilateral Lisp:* the right side of the tongue articulates with the palate. This allows the air stream to escape to the left (figure 35).
3. *Bilateral Lisp:* some part of the middle of the tongue articulates with the palate. This allows the air stream to escape simultaneously to the right and left (figure 36).

Figure 35

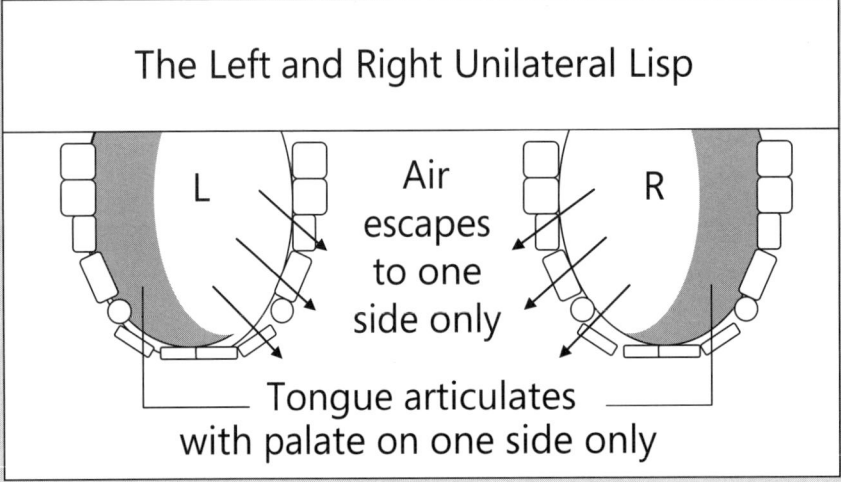

The Left and Right Unilateral Lisp
Air escapes to one side only
Tongue articulates with palate on one side only

Figure 36

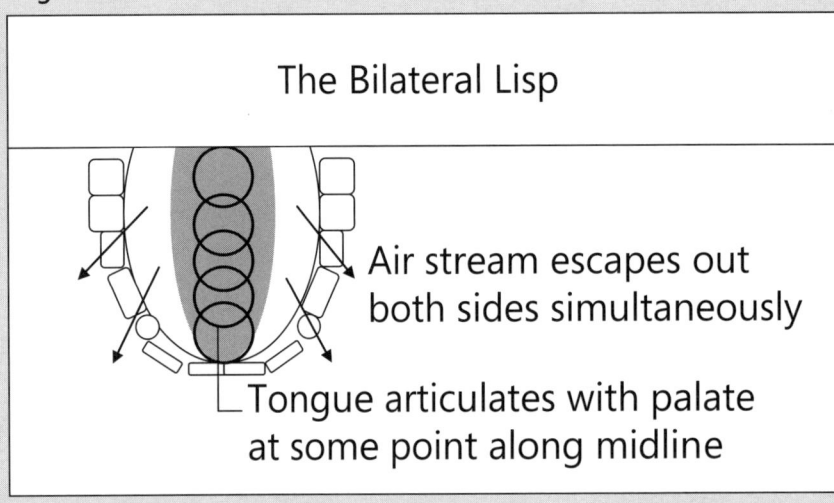

The Bilateral Lisp
Air stream escapes out both sides simultaneously
Tongue articulates with palate at some point along midline

Figure 37

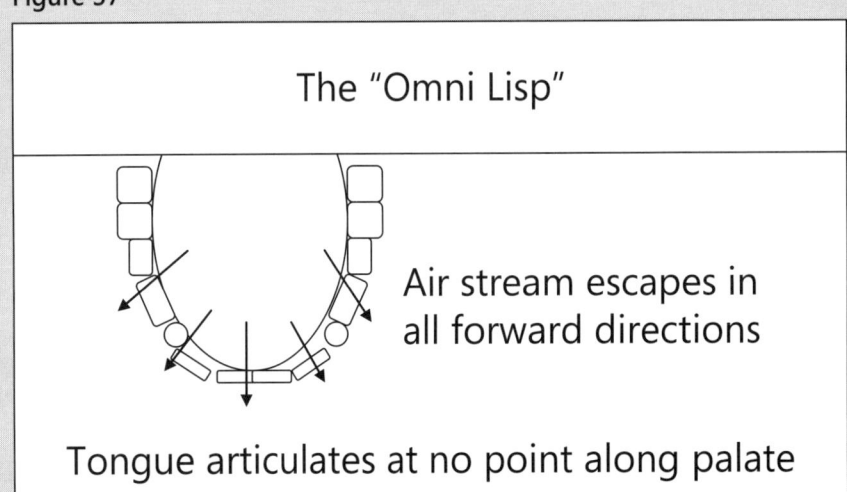

The "Omni Lisp"
Air stream escapes in all forward directions
Tongue articulates at no point along palate

4. *Omni Lisp:* no part of the tongue articulates with the palate. This allows the air stream to escape across the entire surface of the tongue (figure 37).

Testing for Direction of Air Channel

> **LEARNING EXERCISE 8**
> Tongue Position and the Lateral Lisp
>
> Produce /s/ correctly. Then attempt to produce it with the tongue positioned in each of the positions described in Figures 35-37. Note the acoustic changes. Repeat the same for /z/, /ʃ/, /ʒ/, /tʃ/ and /dʒ/.

The lateral escape of air that occurs with the lateral lisp makes stridency diffuse, and thus it sounds sloppy or slushy. This imprecise sound quality can make it quite difficult to determine where the air is escaping, and listening with the ear alone often is not enough to determination the air's direction. Another method is needed to make this assessment.

The easiest way to assess the direction of airflow is to use a straw. A regular soda straw with approximately a ¼-inch diameter works best. The following procedures can be employed:

1. Place one end of the straw at the teeth (figure 38). The end should be at midline, right at the point where air should be exiting the mouth at midline. Tip the straw down slightly as illustrated to catch the air stream.
2. Ask the client to produce /s/ in isolation while the straw is held in place. If the air stream is directed correctly down the midline of the tongue, it should amplify as it rushes into the straw. However, if the client is producing a lateral lisp, no air will enter the straw at midline and the sound will not be amplified.

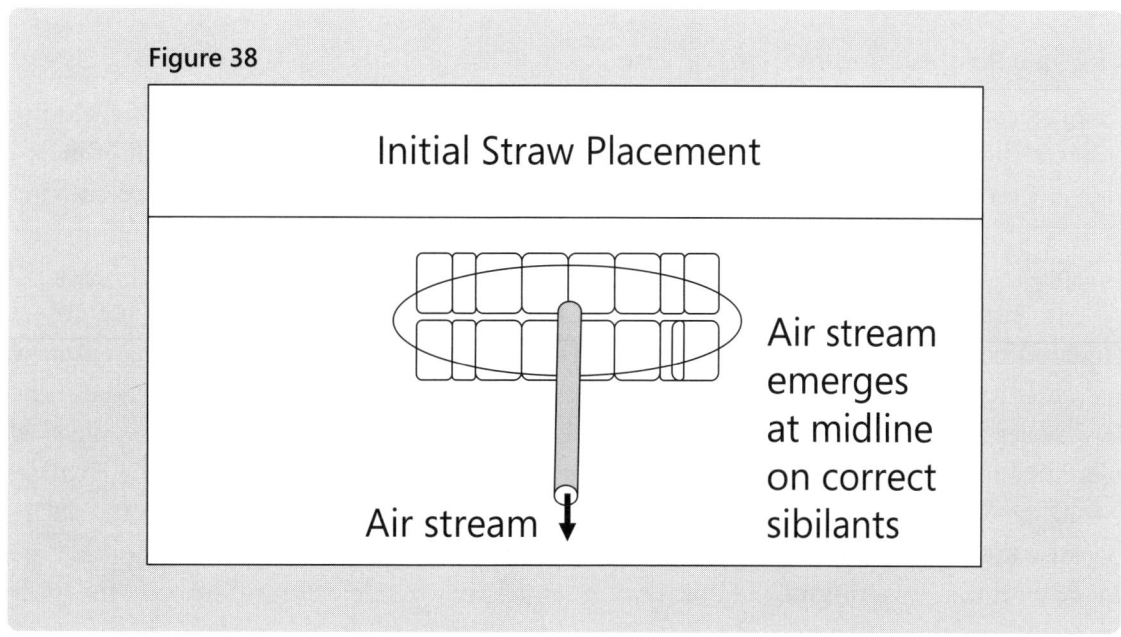

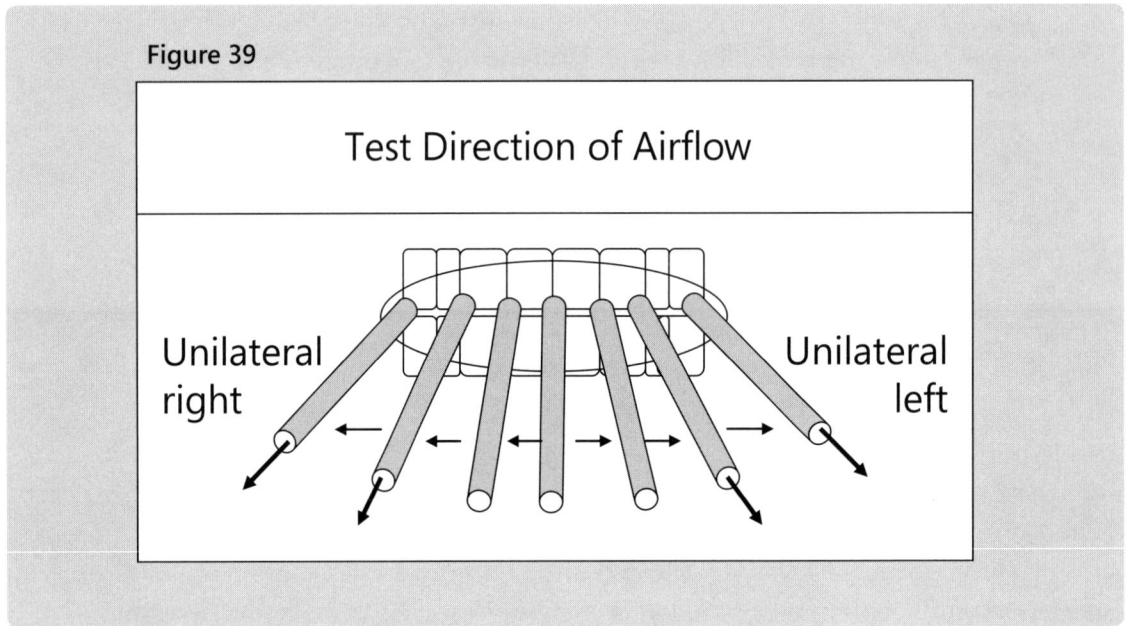

Figure 39

3. Slowly shift the position of the straw to the left and to the right along the teeth (figure 39). Listen carefully to determine if air is escaping anywhere along this line. Air will amplify at the point where it escapes from between the teeth.

Amplification of air as it moves through the straw will be obvious to the examiner as well as the client. This test of airflow is an excellent way to introduce treatment concepts to the client and his family. They will discover the core of the problem – that air is escaping laterally instead of medially.

A long flexible tube of ¼-inch diameter also works very well for this task. The flexible tube can be held with one end at the client's teeth and the other at the examiner's or the client's ear. Air will be amplified nicely and directly into the ear. This makes detection quite easy.

The Jaw Position and the Lateral Lisp

The jaw can cause a lisping pattern that usually is called a lateral lisp, but this one is quite different in oral position from those described above. This lateral lisp is the result of incorrect jaw movement and position. In this case, the jaw shifts to the right or left. Jaw shifting causes airflow to escape laterally. Air escapes to the left as the jaw shifts to the left, and air escapes to the right as the jaw shifts right.

As stated earlier, a correct sibilant is produced with the jaw functioning at midline (figure 40). This midline orientation allows the tongue to create a medial channel with the palate. If the jaw moves left, however, then the tongue is carried to the left with it, and if the jaw moves right, the tongue is carried to the right (figures 41 and 42). The tongue's physical relationship to the palate shifts left or right with the jaw. The tongue still may be creating a midline channel, but the channel itself has been moved left or right relative to the palate because the entire tongue has moved left or right with the jaw. Sibilant phonemes that are made with the jaw positioned left or right become lateralized left or right because the mid-

Figure 40

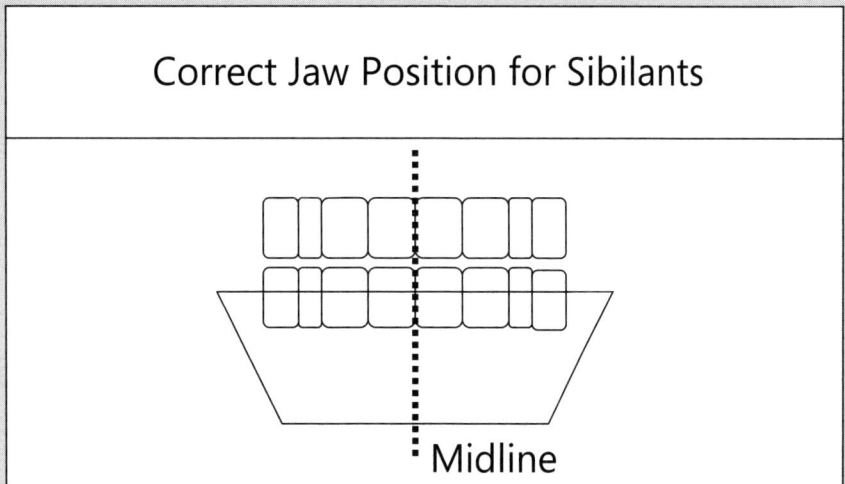

Figure 41

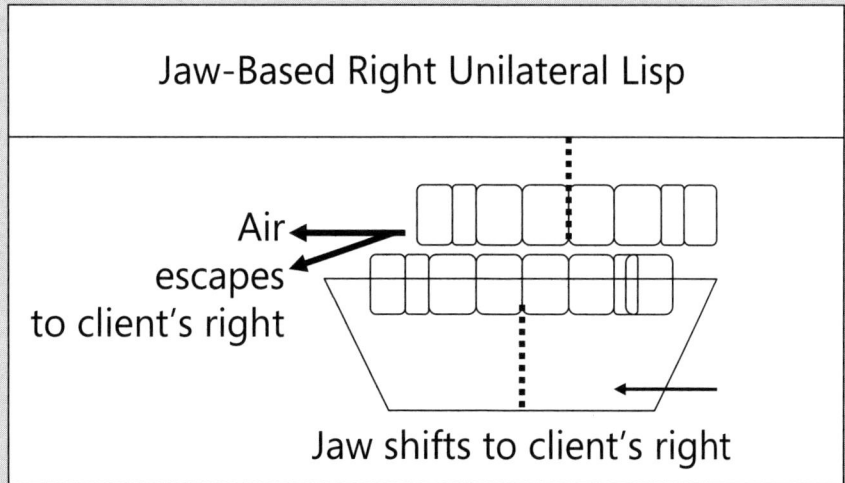

Figure 42

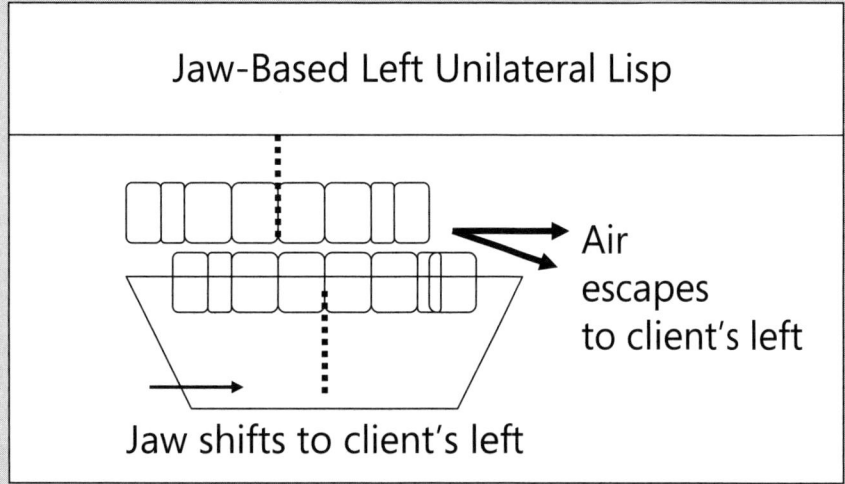

line air stream is directed lateral to the midline position as a result of jaw position. Learning Exercise 9 helps the reader understand this idea.

We shall call this lisp the *jaw-based unilateral lisp*. It is important to differentiate between the jaw-based unilateral lisp and the unilateral lisp that is the result of incorrect tongue grooving because treatment will be different for each. If tongue position is in error, then therapy is directed toward the tongue. If jaw position is incorrect, then therapy is directed toward the jaw. These differences will become clear as our treatment procedures are described.

Testing for Jaw Stability

There is a simple procedure for determining if the jaw is shifting right or left during sibilant production. Ask the client to bite down gently onto a coffee stirrer, swizzle stick, toothette handle or straw. Have him bite gently with the molars on one side. Then ask him to produce several isolated productions of his deviant sibilants. If the jaw is stationary, the biting tool will remain stationary. If the jaw shifts right or left, the biting tool will jerk or even fall out.

> **LEARNING EXERCISE 9**
> Discover the Jaw-based Unilateral Lisp
>
> At a mirror, produce and prolong /s/ in isolation with your jaw in a correct midline position. Then shift the jaw to the right as far as it will go while you continue to produce the phoneme. Listen to the acoustic changes that result as you watch your jaw move out of midline. Make your shifting movement slowly so you can hear the changes clearly. Notice that air begins to escape to the right at some point, and that the acoustic quality changes, becomes sloppy and distorted. Also notice the visual changes. Repeat this procedure to the left. Then repeat these procedures with /z/, /ʃ/, /ʒ/, /tʃ/ and /dʒ/.

Lip Position and the Lateral Lisp

Lip rounding and retracting is affected when a client produces a bilateral or unilateral lisp. In essence the following patterns are noted:

1. Right side retraction: the right side of the lips tends to retract during production of the right unilateral lisp. This allows air to escape to the right.
2. Left side retraction: the left side of the lips tends to retract during production of the left unilateral lisp. This allows air to escape to the left.
3. Bilateral lip retraction: both sides of the lips tend to retract during production of the bilateral lisp. This allows air to escape to both sides.

Lip retraction is the most visually distracting characteristic of the lateral lisp. Lip retraction during production of the sibilants can be the diagnostician's first clue about incorrect airflow direction. However, lip retraction is not the principle problem. Lip retraction does not cause a lateral lisp. Instead, lip retraction is a secondary effect of the lateral lisp. The lips pull out of the way to allow the air stream to escape left, right or bilaterally because the tongue or jaw are causing air to be channeled that way. The tongue and the jaw are the real culprits in this airflow problem. Therapy for a lateral lisp will include some measures to reposition the lips. However, this is done secondarily to repositioning the tongue and the jaw.

The False Lateral Lisp

There is one more error pattern that is worthy of mention in this chapter. This is an error on /s/ and /z/ that masquerades as a lateral lisp but actually isn't one. This is the lisping pattern heard when a client makes an anterior channel that is too deep and large. As such, too much air strikes the alveolar ridge and the upper incisors. The result is a production that sounds like a lateral lisp. But it is not. The air stream is still midline: there is just too much of it. The result is an enormous slushy sound, especially on /s/.

Upon first hearing, one can easily assume that this error is lateral. But careful analysis of the air stream done with the assistance of a straw or tube will reveal that the air stream actually is midline. Also, try to produce the client's sound yourself. If you can imitate it exactly, you should be able to figure out what he is doing wrong. This is a demonstration of how important is the analysis of the air stream. An air stream that is medial but simply too big needs a simple adjustment of its size accomplished through slight adjustments of tongue position guided by auditory discrimination.

The Lateral Lisp in Speech

Any of the lateral lisp patterns described above can occur alone or in conjunction with other phoneme errors. Several common patterns are noted:

1. A lateral lisp can occur alone with no other speech sound errors.
2. A lateral lisp can occur alongside other developmental errors on later-developing phonemes such as /l/, /r/, /θ/, /ð/, /f/ or /v/.
3. A lateral lisp can occur in clients with severe articulation disorder.
4. A lateral lisp can occur on some of the sibilants while the others are left unaffected. For example, some clients demonstrate a lateral lisp on the palatal sibilants – /ʃ/, /ʒ/, /tʃ/ and /dʒ/ – but correct midline air stream on /s/ and /z/. Sometimes this pattern is the result of client's quitting therapy before the treatment program has been completed.
5. The same lateral lisping pattern seems to be used on all affected sibilants. For example, one never encounters a client with a left unilateral lisp on one phoneme, a right unilateral lisp on another, and a bi-lateral lisp on still another. The lateral lisp he uses on one sibilant will be the same as that used on the others. I have seen no exceptions to this rule in 30 years.

Etiology of the Lateral Lisp

The causes of a lateral lisp are unknown. However, I have had one opportunity to observe first hand the emergence of a lateral lisp in a very young child, Sarah, whose story follows. A single sample does not reveal all the possible reasons for the emergence of a lateral lisp, but it may shed some light on the factors that should be investigated.

Sarah

Sarah was the infant daughter of personal acquaintances of mine. I first saw her at the age of five months when the family moved back to my area. At the time, Sarah was cooing and gooing and producing midline raspberries made with the lips and tongue. Sarah was a bright and happy child who was anxious to stand, so at five months she began to stand regularly with her parent's help. She stood on their thighs as they held her hands. The parents thought that early standing was a sign of Sarah's great intelligence, so they encouraged it often and willingly held her in this position for extended periods of time.

I noticed an interesting thing as Sarah held this position. She held the position very stiffly, her knees were locked in position to hold her legs stiff and straight, her hips were thrust forward, her shoulders were elevated and her tongue protruded stiffly out the mouth. It was this last characteristic which held the most fascination for me. In this position Sarah's raspberries shifted from a midline airflow to a bi-lateral one. The tongue was narrow and somewhat box-shaped and it moved very little in this position. Sarah began to blow laterally as her tongue was held stiffly and in a boxy configuration.

As the months passed, I watched Sarah's bi-lateral raspberries change into bi-lateral sibilants. I was mortified but found myself in that awkward position with friends who have children with speech problems. Do you say something or not? I was only in my twenties and was a young therapist at the time. I actually did not know if Sarah would retain this lateral lisp as she grew into her preschool and school years. And the advice from my former professors was that we should wait. It was believed at the time that most children outgrow a lisp, and no differentiation was made between a frontal and a lateral one. The feeling other professionals had was that she should outgrow it. So I said nothing.

The parents and I were not especially close friends and I had no children at the time, so I began to lose touch with them as Sarah approached her third birthday. I did not see her again until she was seven years of age, and I am sorry to report that she retained her bi-lateral lisp. The father told me that he thought Sarah might need therapy, but they were waiting another few years to see if she would outgrow the error. By that point I knew she wouldn't.

The story of Sarah demonstrates how one child developed a bi-lateral lisp by exercising a stiff and forward tongue position during early standing. Sarah had habituated a tongue position that allowed air to escape laterally as she made raspberry sounds and then sibilant phonemes. She did not outgrow the error because it was not an immature oral motor pattern to be outgrown. It was a deviant oral motor pattern learned early, encouraged often, and exercised regularly. It became an oral movement pattern that would have to be unlearned.

This experience early in my career convinced me that we could understand the etiology of the lateral lisp if we would begin to observe the emergence of sibilants in a wide variety of infants and toddlers. Thirty years later this is still an area that begs for good research.

Oral Tone and the Lateral Lisp

A complete evaluation of the lateral lisp includes an assessment of oral tone. Deviations in oral tone have been noted in my clinic when the lateral lisp is present. The following patterns have been noted:

1. Unilateral Low Tone: Oral tone that is too low on one side of the oral mechanism can cause that side of the tongue to be lax. A lax side can be unable to elevate its lateral margin in order to establish back lateral stability and a lateral seal with the palate. A unilateral lisp in which air escapes to that side can occur.
2. Unilateral High Tone: Oral tone that is too high on one side of the oral mechanism can cause that side of the tongue to be stiff and immobile, and retracted toward midline. A stiff side can have a negative effect on all lingual movements, rendering it difficult to move for many phonemes. A unilateral lisp can be one result. Either side can be chosen for escape of air.
3. Overall High Tone: Overall high tone in the oral mechanism often causes a tongue to move with a dominant high midline pattern and lax sides. In motor terms, we call this *proximal fixing* with limited distal mobility. The body of the tongue also may be retracted toward the back (more proximal fixing). The result can be a bi-lateral lisp as well as distortion on other phonemes.

Oral-Tactile Sensitivity and the Lateral Lisp

The unilateral or bilateral lisp can occur with no problem in oral sensitivity. If oral tactile sensitivity is a problem, however, the most common one seems to be a problem of tactile hypersensitivity (figure 43). Children who are overly sensitive in the oral area tend to hold the tongue in what has been called a *high guard position*. The high guard position is the client's unconscious attempt to prevent a gag response, and it is another example of proximal fixing. In order to prevent the gag, the tongue is held stiffly, it is retracted toward the back of the mouth, and it is high in the middle. The result is a tongue that is stiff and limited in movement as if it had high tone. If the tongue is held in this position during production of sibilants, a bilateral lisp can result. High tone and oral-tactile hypersensitivity often go hand-in-hand.

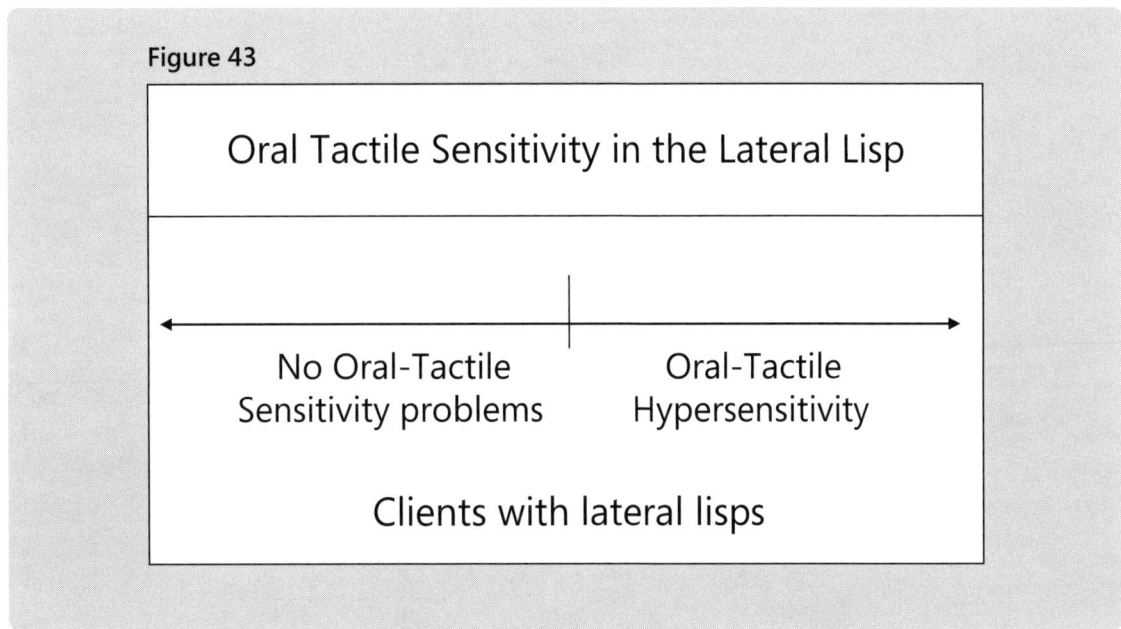

Figure 43

Tongue Stability and the Lateral Lisp

In chapter four we discussed the role of tongue stability in sibilant production. It was stated that tongue stability is accomplished by maintaining close approximation of the tongue's back lateral margins to the molars and palate. These stabilizing zones remain in relative contact with the palate and molars located directly above them during almost all aspects of speech production. These are the points of tongue stability. All movements of the tongue are based on these points of stability. The important thing to note about this is that *back lateral stability is lost during lateral lisp production*. Midline stabilization replaces it (figure 44). The midline point of stability occurs at whatever parts of the tongue articulate with the palate during sibilant production. Learning Exercise 10 reveals this to the reader.

An oral-motor perspective reveals that the lateral lisp that is not jaw-based is the result of tongue instability. Speech therapy that ignores this fact and attends only to the phonemes and/or the tongue tip may take a long time and may be met with limited success especially when the client has a clear oral movement disorder or dysfunction. Treatment for the lateral lisp is enhanced in these clients, however, when activities designed to facilitate appropriate tongue stability are included. The development of appropriate back lateral tongue stability allows a client to speak in rapid conversational speech without stabilizing along midline or one side only. It helps him produce his sibilants correctly during the ballistic movements of speech at all levels of therapy.

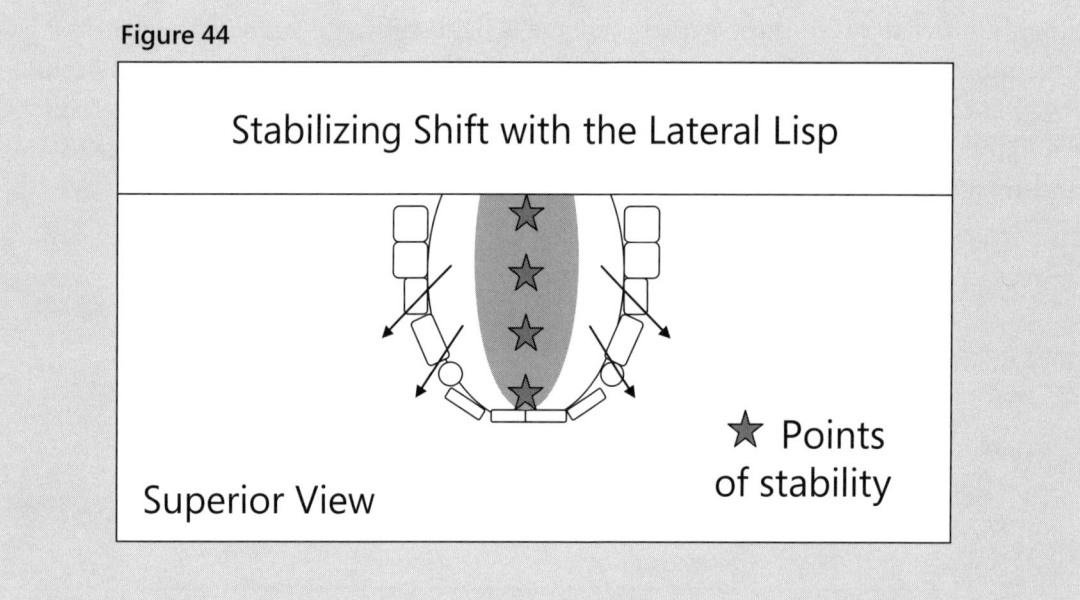

Figure 44

LEARNING EXERCISE 10
Discover Shifting Tongue Stability in the Lateral Lisp

Produce and prolong /s/ in isolation and pay attention to the points of stability at the back lateral margins. Then produce /s/ with a right unilateral lisp, a left unilateral lisp, and a bi-lateral lisp. Notice the ways in which stability shifts. Repeat for /z/, /ʃ/, /ʒ/, /tʃ/ and /dʒ/.

Oral-Structure and the Lateral Lisp

A complete evaluation of the lateral lisp includes a thorough assessment of oral structure. Again, oral structure has a direct impact on the pronunciation of all phonemes since the shape of the oral cavity creates the acoustic quality of sound. The following structural differences have been noted in children and adolescents with lateral lisps of one type or another. Please keep in mind that no correlation will be made between these structural deviations and the lateral lisp. Every client is different. A deviation in one of these areas may cause or contribute to a lateral lisp in one client but not another. A thorough evaluation will reveal the nature of the structure and function relationship in each individual case.

Narrow Palate

A narrow palate with a high vault can contribute to or confound a lateral lisp. The hard palate that is too narrow to accommodate a tongue of normal length and width can impede creation of the midline channel (figure 45). This can occur because the tongue cannot assume its normal wide position with lateral stability. Also the high palatal vault alters the height of the midline channel and distorts the sound quality. The tongue narrows itself to fit up against the palate. A lateral lisp of one sort or another can result. Treatment is enhanced when the palate is widened and lowered with orthodontic appliances. Work on the sibilants should wait until the palatal spreading process is complete and the appliance is removed.

Cleft Lip and Palate

A lateral lisp can be related to a cleft lip or palate, however, this certainly is not always the case. The nature of sibilant distortion will be directly related to position of the teeth and alveolar ridge, as well as to the integrity of the palate. Often the distortion that results can be very difficulty to classify as any specific type of lisp. The straw technique will help you analyze where air is emerging, and treatment will depend on where the client is in his process of surgical and orthodontic management.

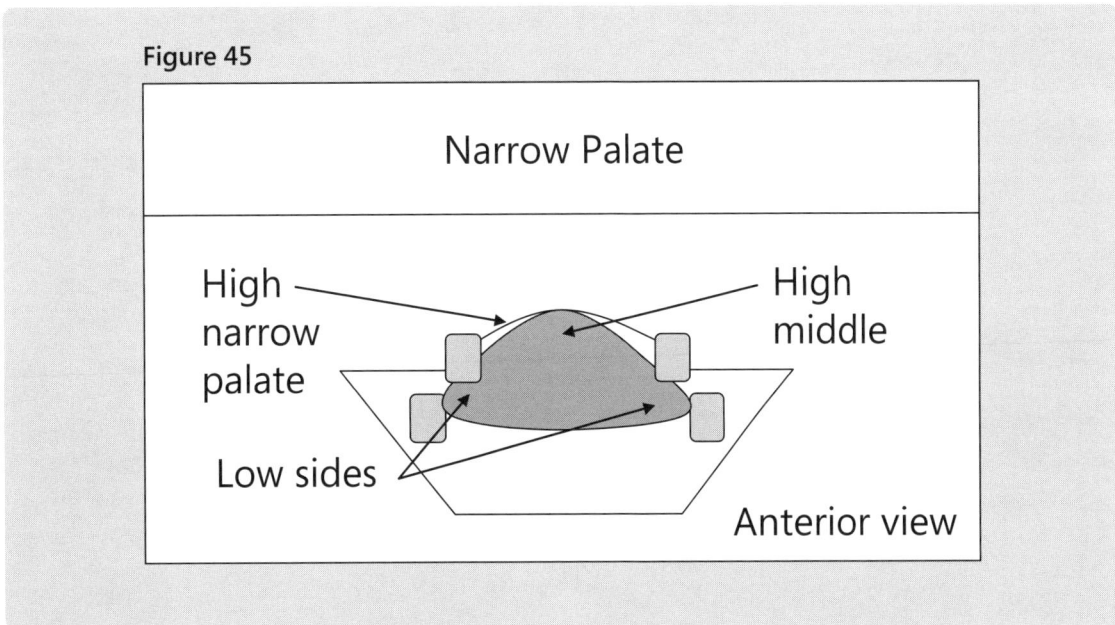

Figure 45

Missing Teeth
Missing teeth change the characteristics of the oral cavity and thus have an impact on oral movements in speech as described in the last chapter. Sometimes children settle into a unilateral lisping pattern during their production of the sibilants in order to compensate for missing teeth. This pattern can come-and-go during the childhood years as the deciduous teeth slough off and the adult teeth emerge. Most children straighten out these sounds as the adult teeth stabilize. Therapy usually is not necessary unless the lateral pattern settles in. These clients should be monitored through the process.

Large Tongue
As described in the last chapter, a client with a tongue that is too large for the oral cavity usually produces sibilants with a frontal lisp. However, there can be occasion when a lateral lisp results. In these cases, the client lifts the midline of the tongue, often the blade, in order to achieve tongue-to-alveolar articulation. The bi-lateral lisp results. Oral surgery is the only option for a client with a tongue that is too large. Again it must be stressed that surgery this radical is not to be approached lightly. Only in the most extreme cases does tongue reduction surgery become an option and the lateral lisp usually does not qualify as such. Tongue reduction surgery usually is scheduled only when the client's safety is at risk because of breathing or eating problems. The decision for tongue reduction surgery is one made by the parents and their physicians. A client with a lateral lisp associated with a large tongue can learn to substitute a frontal lisp for it and can learn to keep his tongue inside the mouth during speech. But this process requires tremendous effort and conscious control on the part of the client.

Restricting Lingua Frenulum
A severely restricting lingua frenulum can contribute to a lateral lisp (figure 46). This is especially true if the frenulum pins the tip of the tongue to the floor of the mouth, although

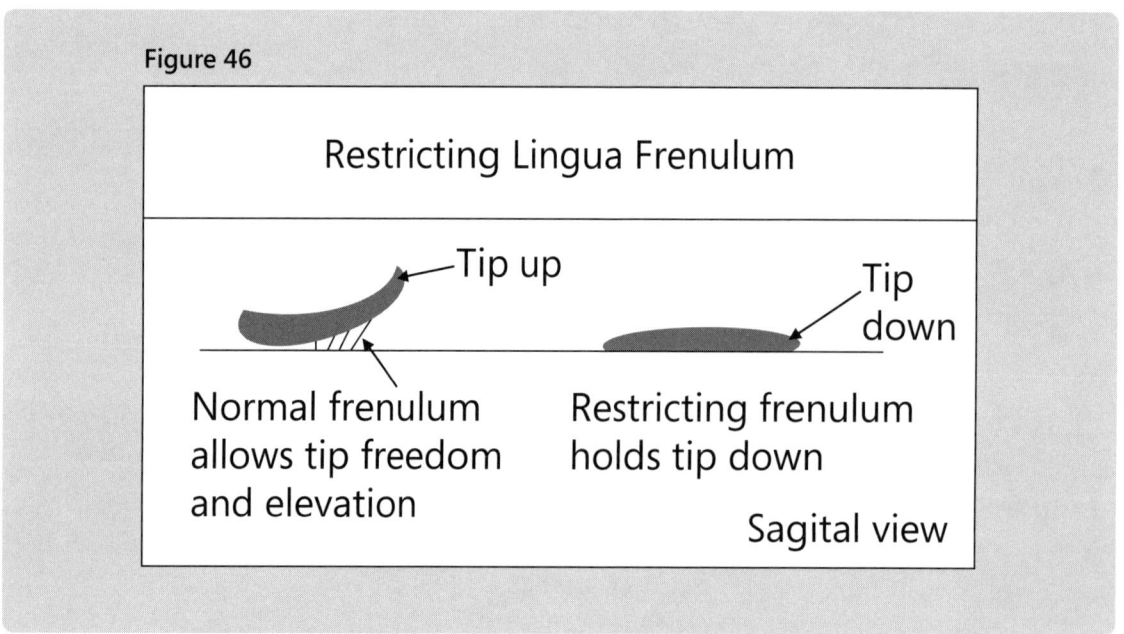

not always so. A severe restriction in tip mobility forces the tongue to lead its upward movements with the blade. A bi-lateral lisp can result. Eliminating the restriction in the frenulum is the first step in the remediation process. We are not saying that a restricting lingua frenulum causes a lateral lisp. We are saying that in some cases there is a relationship between the two.

Missing Tongue Tissue
Missing tongue tissue can cause an error that sounds like a lateral lisp. The type of lisp that results depends on the location and extent of the missing tissue. SLP's can teach mature clients of normal intelligence to reposition their tongue to create the best look and sound quality possible given the integrity of tongue tissue.

Oral Rest Position and the Lateral Lisp

Correct oral rest position was described in chapter four. The lateral lisp that is associated with mature oral movements (the lateral lisp that is the result of simple habit) typically will be associated with correct oral rest position. However, when oral tone, oral structure, oral-tactile sensitivity or medical problems are present, oral rest position can be altered. For example, I have seen many children with bilateral lisps who had difficulty in nasal breathing. These children propped their mouths open by pressing the middle of the tongue up against the roof of the mouth. In this way they were able to breath through the mouth without lowering the jaw too far or allowing the tongue to hang forward. The type and degree of alteration in oral rest position due to medical conditions is client specific and the treatment plan will be highly individualized. Some medical problems can be ignored while treatment of the lisp ensues. In the ideal situation, treatment begins by training a correct oral rest position. Correct production of the sibilant phonemes stems from this good neutral position.

Eating and Swallowing Patterns and the Lateral lisp

In my experience, an eating or swallowing problem may or may not be associated with a lateral lisp. Of course this depends on whether the lateral lisp is the result of simple speech habit or is the result of incorrect oral-motor development. A lateral lisp that is the result of simple speech habit will have no eating or swallowing problem associated with it. But a lateral lisp that is the result of oral motor dysfunction often does have an eating and swallowing problem associated with it. The eating and swallowing problem associated with the lateral lisp is not one of simple immaturity as it is in the frontal lisp.

Oral tone, oral tactile sensitivity and habitual oral movement patterns dictate how the oral mechanism will function for eating, swallowing and speech. In the case of the lateral lisp, the eating and swallowing movement problem usually is identical to the lisping pattern. In essence, whatever the jaw, lips and tongue do on the lateral lisp, they also do on eating and swallowing if the speech, eating and swallowing problems are intertwined. We could call this a "co-occurring speech-eating-swallowing problem." In other words, it is my experience that the same oral movement patterns are observed when there is a co-occurring speech-eating-swallowing problem. In essence, if the middle of the tongue is overused for speech, it will be overused for eating and swallowing. And if one or both of the sides are weak in speech, they will prove to be weak in eating and swallowing.

These kinds of eating and swallowing problems are very subtle and difficult to see by the untrained eye. It takes specific schooling in the normal and abnormal aspects of stage one and stage two of the swallow to spot these differences (See appendix 4). This skill cannot be taught in the few short paragraphs devoted to this subject in this book. Suffice it to say that there is a "normal" eating and swallowing pattern, and there are "abnormal" ones. The reader of this text is encouraged to begin to explore this information via other avenues so that a correct analysis can be made. It must be stated here, however, that the average lateral lisp in children with no other speech problems seems to be the result of simple habit. Speech therapy can ensue without attention to swallowing.

Oral Habits and the Lateral Lisp

Excessive digit and pacifier sucking as well as other oral habits can be associated with a lateral lisp. Further, excessive digit or pacifier sucking can cause malocclusion, and malocclusion can impact speech as described earlier. A complete differential diagnosis of the lateral lisp includes questions about oral habits present or past. Treatment of the lateral lisp is enhanced when oral habits are eliminated either before or during the speech therapy program. Oral habits that go unrecognized and untreated can cause a program for the lateral lisp to fail.

Chapter 4 Summary
Deep Analysis of the Lateral Lisp

- The term *lateral lisp* is assigned when air escapes laterally instead of medially during production of one or more of the sibilants.

- In earlier decades, children with a lateral lisp were placed into therapy in the public schools by third or fourth grade.

- Today many children with a lateral lisp are excluded from public school therapy because it is believed that the error does not impact the child's education in a negative way. The author disagrees with this perspective.

- The lateral lisp can occur alone or in conjunction with other phoneme errors.

- The cause of a lateral lisp is unknown.

- A lateral lisp can be the result of incorrect tongue movement and position. The tongue situates itself in such a way that air escapes laterally instead of at the midline.

- Lip rounding and retracting is affected when a client produces a bilateral or unilateral lisp.

- A lateral lisp can be the result of incorrect jaw movement and position.

- Deviations in oral tone have been noted when the lateral lisp is present.

- The lateral lisp can occur with no problem in oral sensitivity, however, hypersensitivity has been noted.

- An oral-motor perspective reveals that the lateral lisp that is not jaw-based is the result of tongue instability.

- Certain relationships between the lateral lisp and oral structure, oral rest, eating and swallowing have been noted.

Chapter 5

Developmental Considerations in Sibilant Acquisition

Developmental patterns can be observed as children gain the ability to produce the six sibilant phonemes. The process begins shortly after birth and extends to approximately eight or nine years of age. This chapter begins our discussion of treatment for the frontal and lateral lisps because these developmental patterns have an influence on our organization and design of the treatment procedures. The topic of treatment shall be our focus in the balance of our chapters.

Raspberries

The underpinning of stridency is the raspberry, a pre-speech vocalization gained by infants between four and six months of age. A raspberry is made by fricating grossly. Infantile raspberries are produced in at least five different locations along the vocal tract: (1) bi-labial, (2) lingua-labial, (3) lingua-velar, (4) tracheal, and (5) glottal. Babies produce raspberries as they are learning how to attain and maintain a loose but fixed oral position while exhaling air. In producing raspberries, children learn to stabilize the jaw. The result is a pre-speech vocalization made with loose vibration of the soft tissues located in each area as the jaw is stabilized. The most important aspect of these sounds as they relate to the sibilants is that they are made with midline air stream. The lingual raspberries can be considered gross motor foundations of the sibilants. They are made in voiced and voiceless pairs just like true consonants.

Application to Treatment
Raspberries lay the foundation for stridency to emerge. With them children learn to hear and feel gross frication, and they learn to make airflow travel medially down through the oral cavity. Raspberries provide strong vibratory stimulation to the lips and tongue thus helping to increase awareness and control of the lips and tongue. The raspberries can be used in treatment to teach voicing and voicelessness. They also can be used to "wake up" the oral mechanism in cases of oral tactile hyposensitivity. The raspberries can be contrasted with the sibilants for ear and oral discrimination training.

Inhaled Sibilants

Infants produce primitive fricative sounds while exhaling and while inhaling. Inhaled sounds are called *ingressive* sounds. Exhalation on phonemes stabilizes some time before a child reaches one year of age, so that when first words emerge they are produced almost exclusively upon exhalation. However, sometimes this pattern of inhaling sibilants persists into childhood and therapy must ensue.

Application to Treatment
Children can learn to exhale instead of inhale on sibilants fairly easily in most cases if given direct instruction. This requires a certain level of intellectual skill. The inhalation/exhalation process can be taught using blow toys. Especially effective are those that can be sounded upon inhalation and exhalation. This set includes harmonicas, sirens and whistle straws. Teach the exhalation process with the toys, then move on to raspberries and fricatives.

Midline Air Stream

Midline air stream dominates throughout normal development as children gain the ability to add raspberries and stridents to their expressive speech repertoires. The lateral escape of air is not seen typically in raspberries or in sibilants. As such, the lateral lisp does not qualify as a developmental error.

Application to Treatment
The lateral lisp should not be considered a developmental speech error and therefore is not expected to be outgrown. Lateral escape of the air stream should be considered a deviant speech pattern. In producing a lateral lisp, a child's oral motor development has begun to veer away from the normal developmental path. The child is developing and habituating an incorrect oral movement pattern. Specific training must be initiated to put the child's development of oral skills back on the normal path.

Sometimes we train a client with a lateral lisp to produce a frontal lisp instead. This puts his oral movements on the normal developmental path. Once the frontal lisp pattern is habituated we then teach him to keep the tongue inside the mouth. This is an old traditional technique that still makes sense today in light of what we know about oral motor development. We shall discuss this method in chapter ten.

Tongue Protrusion

Stridency often is added to a child's speech sound repertoire while the tongue protrudes. In other words, it is normal to learn to produce stridency with the tongue protruded. Think about an infant who, at eight or nine months of age, produces a raspberry while spitting out spoon-fed rice cereal or applesauce. Where is his tongue tip when he produces this raspberry? It is interlabial, of course. This pattern of tongue protrusion often persists as a child's early raspberries mature into sibilants. Tongue protrusion that persists into later childhood eventually is called a frontal lisp. We have called it a *tongue protrusion lisp*.

Application to Treatment
Interdental tongue position on raspberries and sibilants is so common in infants and toddlers that the average person barely notices it. This is why the frontal lisp is considered normal throughout childhood. And this is why we sometimes train a client with a lateral lisp to produce a frontal lisp instead. Exchanging a lateral lisp with a frontal one puts his

error on the normal path of sibilant development. It puts his oral control back on track at the point at which he veered off track.

Honoring Stridency

Stridency is honored above place during sibilant acquisition. This means that as stridency is added to a child's speech repertoire, the strident sounds will be substituted one for another. This is confusion about place, not manner. Over time the child straightens these phonemes out by place. As such children freely interchange /f/, /v/, /s/, /z/, /θ/, /ð/, /ʃ/, /ʒ/, /tʃ/ and /dʒ/ for a long time during the toddler and preschool years. The full set of hissing sounds emerges together and children spend many months, even years, sorting through them.

From an oral-motor development perspective, presence of the frontal lisp is a sign that differentiation of these phonemes by place is incomplete. It means that sense of place is not fully developed. This is a tactile discrimination skill that interfaces with the child's auditory discrimination skills. The child must learn to hear and feel the difference between all the sibilant phonemes.

Application to Treatment
When the frontal lisp is present, therapists should determine how many of the full set of these phonemes have emerged or are being attempted. Correcting a frontal lisp before all of these phonemes have begun to emerge often is a mistake if many of the sounds still are missing from the client's speech sound repertoire. Work to develop all the sounds will be needed for a while. Treatment of the interdental tongue placement may be intertwined with treatment to facilitate emergence of all the sibilants.

Final Position

Strident phonemes often emerge in the final position of syllables and words before they emerge in the initial position. Words like: *kiss, bus, off* and *ouch* with final stridents can emerge very early and even can be part of a child's first few words.

Application to Treatment
The traditional way of approaching phoneme training by addressing the initial, medial and final position in that order may need to be reconsidered for many clients. The final or postvocalic position often is the easiest and best way to begin. Placing a correct strident phoneme on the end of a syllable or word seems to be easier for many children.

Final Cluster

Word-final sibilants often emerge as a /ts/ cluster. Consider the following examples:

- *house* pronounced /hoʊts/
- *fish* pronounced /pɪts/
- *catch* pronounced /kæts/
- *knife* pronounced /naɪts/

Application to Treatment
I have found that teaching /s/ as an extension of final /t/ often is the easiest way to teach correct tongue position for both the frontal and lateral lisp (see Chapter 6). Also, inappropriate tongue placement on /t/ as well as the other lingua-alveolars – /d/, /n/ and /l/ – cannot be ignored when a lisp is present. Interdental tongue placement on the lingua-alveolars as well as the hissing sounds suggests a more pervasive delay in oral movement development. Trying to change a frontal lisp without changing oral position for the other lingua alveolars can be futile because the underlying oral movement pattern is not being addressed. In other words, we often have limited success in the remediation of a frontal lisp when we ignore interdental tongue position on the other lingua-alveolars. Treatment is going to be more successful when the underlying cause of the extensive interdental tongue position pattern is addressed, and when all lingua-alveolars are targeted.

Phoneme and Morpheme

Phoneme /s/ is the most frequently occurring sound in the English language due in part to the fact that it is used as both phoneme and morpheme. Morphemes begin to emerge between eighteen and twenty-four months of age. They occur in word-final position in the following forms:

1. Plural – *two cups*
2. Possessive – *the cat's meow*
3. Third person regular tense verb marker – *he walks*
4. Copula forms of to be – *that's right*
5. Auxiliary forms of to be – *the boat's floating*

Application to Treatment
This consideration is further evidence for the tremendous importance of word-final /s/ practice. A rich assortment of practice fodder can be developed using this wide range of /s/ opportunities. Including all the /s/ morphemes in treatment extends the practice into practical and very common occurrences of /s/.

It is important to note that morphemes marked with orthographic symbol "s" are produced as either a voiced /s/, a devoiced /z/, or /z/ itself when the preceding consonant is voiced. Consider the following words: *cabs, pods, bags, moms, pans, sings, cows, balls, boys* and *cars*. Say these words aloud and notice the amount of voicing that occurs on the final hissing sound. The use of /z/ and devoiced /z/ points to the importance of working on /z/ as well as /s/ early in treatment.

Teeth

The comings and goings of the deciduous and permanent teeth cause changes in airflow all throughout childhood. Children often shift the direction of their air stream away from baby teeth that go missing and toward the baby teeth that are remaining and the new permanent teeth that are emerging. This means that children naturally change tongue and lip position in order to gain the acoustic quality they desire for their hissing sounds as their dental barrier changes over time. This can occur on a conscious or unconscious basis.

Application to Treatment
The treatment of the frontal and lateral lisps is impeded when deciduous teeth are shed. Therapy may have to be postponed depending upon the number and position of missing teeth. Likewise, anterior permanent teeth that have come out due to mouth injury or decay necessitate adjustment and compensation of oral movement until dental work can replace them. Compensation for missing teeth will be the entire plan if missing teeth will not be replaced.

Voiced and Voiceless Sibilants

The voiceless sibilants /s/, /ʃ/ and /tʃ/ are more frequently occurring than their voiced counterparts /z/, /ʒ/ and /dʒ/ in children's words. In my experience, the voiceless cognates also seem to be easier to produce among young children. This seems to be because it is easier to constrict the vocal tract at one place at a time. The voiced cognates require that constriction occur at the glottis and in the oral cavity simultaneously. If you have ever watched a young child while he is learning /z/ or /v/, you know what I mean. When trying to say /z/ for the first time, for example, many children produce either the strident element or they produce the voicing element, but they don't do both at the same time. It takes them several days, weeks or even months to figure out how to voice and produce stridency at the same time.

Application to Treatment
The voiceless sibilants usually are targeted earlier and more often in treatment. Sometimes only the voiceless sibilants are taught and generalization is automatic to the voiced cognates. Many therapists work on the voiceless phonemes only and figure that the voiced counterparts will take care of themselves.

Early Stridency

If your education in articulation is based primarily on the early articulation research of the 1950's, you may have a concept that the sibilants emerge late. This is a false belief. The sibilants emerge during the infant and toddler years. Perfect articulation of all the sibilants is not achieved until seven or eight years of age. But stridency itself emerges very early and thus the concept for it emerges early.

Application to Treatment
The concept of stridency can be added very early to treatment, months or even years before the phonemes themselves will be used in words. This means that we can help children gain the ability to produce good midline sibilants in isolation long before they are ever ready to use them in words.

We usually introduce these sounds by producing them in isolation and assigning them a specific meaning designed to capture the young child's imagination. Commonly therapists assign:

- The hiss of a snake for /s/
- The buzz of a bee for /z/
- The sound meaning "be quiet" for /ʃ/

- The sound of a motor for /ʒ/
- The sound of a train for /tʃ/
- The sound of jumping for /dʒ/

Chapter 5 Summary
Developmental Considerations in Sibilant Acquisition

- Developmental patterns can be observed as children gain the ability to produce the six sibilant phonemes.

- The underpinning of stridency is the raspberry. Raspberries are produced with exhalation.

- Midline air stream dominates throughout normal development.

- Stridency often is added to a child's speech sound repertoire while the tongue protrudes.

- Stridency is honored above place during sibilant acquisition. As a result, children interchange /f/, /v/, /s/, /z/, /θ/, /ð/, /ʃ/, /ʒ/, /tʃ/ and /dʒ/ for a long time during the toddler and preschool years.

- Stridency often emerges in the final position of syllables and words.

- Phoneme /s/ is the most frequently occurring sound in the English language due to the fact that it is used as both phoneme and morpheme.

- The comings and goings of the deciduous and permanent teeth cause changes in airflow all throughout childhood.

- The voiceless cognates seem to be easier to produce among young children.

- Stridency emerges very early and thus the concept for it emerges early.

Chapter 6

The Long T Method

Thirty years of clinical work have taught me to do as little as possible in every therapy session. This does not mean I have become lazy. It means I have learned to be efficient. Every session of articulation therapy should contain just as much technique as necessary to elicit the responses we want. The correct way to begin therapy for both the frontal and lateral lisp is to take a traditional articulation therapy approach. That means that we begin with phonemes. We do not begin with fancy oral-motor techniques to improve jaw, lip and tongue function. Instead, we begin with phoneme production to see where it takes us.

The reason we begin with a tradition approach is because it is the simplest and most efficient thing to do. Many of our clients with frontal or lateral lisp can correct their error by working directly on phonemes, and they can do so right from the start. They just need to learn what to do to make their phonemes correctly. That is where we will begin. A client who does not respond well to a simple phoneme approach obviously needs more, but we shall save those ideas for later chapters. In this present chapter we shall concern ourselves with phonemes.

We shall begin in this chapter with a traditional approach that contains a new twist. The traditional approach taught us to work phonemes in the following order: isolation, syllable, word, phrase, sentence and then conversation. We shall roughly follow that schedule, but we shall use our knowledge of oral-motor development to alter and shape the process to more directly reflect the way little children learn the sibilants through the natural course of time. I call it the Long T Method.

The Long T

In choosing a phoneme with which to begin, most therapists start with /s/ because it is the most frequently occurring phoneme in the English language. To change /s/ will have a profound influence on correct overall articulation. The Long T method is a process of using /t/ to shape oral position for /s/. We move on to other phonemes once oral position for /s/ is in place.

Many clients can produce a correct /s/ by using /t/ as a springboard. I discovered this myself in my early years of therapy after reading Neilson V. Smith. In *The Acquisition of Phonology*, Smith wrote on the development of phonological skills in his son during the toddler stage. Careful study of this work reveals that the child began to use /s/ in the final position of words *after* he had acquired /t/ in the final position (appendix 12). This idea struck me as important because I had noticed this trend in many of my own clients. Highly unintelligible clients with no stridency in their speech consistently began to gain the hissing element *after* acquiring /t/ in the final position. When first learning the word "house," for example, a client may pronounce it as "hout." With time and maturity, "hout" changes to "houts," and then eventually to "house." This does not occur in all cases, of course, but it occurs often enough to be recognized at least as a tendency.

I began to experiment with this idea with older clients who had mild articulation problems, and I discovered that if a client had a final /t/ with correct tongue placement, I could use it to teach final /ts/ with correct tongue placement. I also recognized, of course, that /ts/ does not occur in the initial position of English words, so I switched my focus to final position. This allowed me to begin to work /s/ as a plural (e.g., *two cats*), possessive (e.g., *the cat's paw*), contracted copula (e.g., *the cat's big*), contracted auxiliary (e.g., *the cat's running*), and third person regular tense verb (e.g., *the cat hits*).

For nearly thirty years I have used /t/ as a springboard for /s/ with hundreds of clients. I have found that my clients with severe expressive speech delay or disorder learned to infuse stridency into their speech in this way months before they used strident phonemes in the initial position of syllables or words. I also have found that using /t/ as a springboard to /s/ has great value in working with clients with frontal and lateral lisp. Phoneme /t/, when produced correctly, sets the jaw and tongue into correct position. Stridency added to this phoneme subsequently can be produced with correct jaw and tongue position. Unfortunately, this is not a pattern recognized today by the research community. However, as I have talked with other seasoned speech-language pathologists across the United States and Canada, I have found dozens of other SLP's who have made this same simple discovery. They have found that working with /t/ is a solid way to train the tongue for /s/ and other sibilants.

Oral-motor Perspective

An oral-motor perspective reveals that /s/ is an outgrowth of /t/. There are many reasons for this involving the coordination of airflow and oral movements. But put most simply, this is because of the gross-to-fine principle.

All movements of the whole body develop from gross to fine. For example, the process of learning to walk begins in a gross and clumsy way. Toddlers who are beginning to walk use a wide gait, keep their arms in an elevated position, hold their bodies stiffly, and rock side-to-side instead of rotating through the trunk. We are all familiar with this adorable Frankenstein-like walking pattern of the toddler. This is walking that is still immature and under gross-motor control.

Over time, a child's walking pattern becomes much more refined. The feet position closer as the hips become strong enough to maintain the upright position. Balance reactions improve and a more natural forward-and-back loping of the legs becomes possible. The arms lower and begin to swing appropriately in a reciprocal pattern with the legs. Over time, a child can walk in rotary fashion without thinking about it. Then he can do other things with his arms and head at the same time that he is walking. Ultimately, a child learns to accelerate walking and to run without falling over. In sum, the process of learning to walk begins with gross movement patterns, and these patterns become refined in time as strength and stability improve and as mature movement patterns evolve.

This same process occurs as speech movements develop. Like all body movements, speech movements begin clumsily, and they become more refined with time. Sibilant phonemes are some of the most refined phonemes that humans produce. They require a high level of respiration, phonation, resonation and articulation control and coordination. The difference between the position and the sound of each of the sibilants is quite specific and very narrow in scope. The sibilants are delicate. That is why the sibilants are some of the last phonemes to mature in the natural development of expressive speech.

The emergence of stridency from final /t/ is one developmental pattern seen in the process of phoneme emergence and maturation. Phoneme /t/ is a more gross phoneme. It requires less refined oral control than /s/ or the other sibilants. To produce /t/, a child can bang the tongue against the roof of the mouth, and he can lower it clumsily to produce the plosiveness needed for a gross /t/. In fact, a child needn't move the tongue at all for /t/ - the jaw can do all the work of raising and lowering the tongue toward and away from the palate. A /t/ grossly produced is not considered defective because the allophonic variations for /t/ are wide.

However, the sibilants, especially /s/, require much more refined oral control. One cannot produce the sibilants with clumsy and immature oral movements. To do so causes these acoustically precise phonemes to sound in error. Slightly forward carriage of the tongue classifies the error as a frontal lisp. Slightly lateral emission of air causes these phonemes to qualify as a lateral lisp. A /t/ that is produced with these slight movement errors goes unnoticed. But these slight movement variations cause a stir when they are produced on the sibilants.

Application to Treatment
Movement professionals like occupational and physical therapists work from gross to fine. That is, when first introducing new movement, they expect their clients to move with gross patterns. For example, when first teaching a child to walk, an OT or PT would expect the child to use a wide gait, a stiff trunk and arms elevated. They would expect the child to toddle before he walks. Therapy would be designed to facilitate motor control in such a way that the more refined walking pattern emerges over time. We can do the same thing in speech. Using /t/ as a first step toward /s/ is like teaching a child to toddle before he walks.

Oral Position and Movement for /t/

Phoneme /t/ (figure 47 on next page) is produced correctly with articulation of the tongue against the palate in a horseshoe shape configuration created by the tongue's perimeter. The tongue articulates in this way in order to completely block the air stream. Once the air stream is blocked, the tongue lowers its tip in order to release the plosive sound of /t/. The back lateral margins stay in their stationary position against the palate and molars. The result is a midline release of air. This midline air stream is just like the one needed for a correct sibilant except that it is released plosively. (Learning Exercise 12)

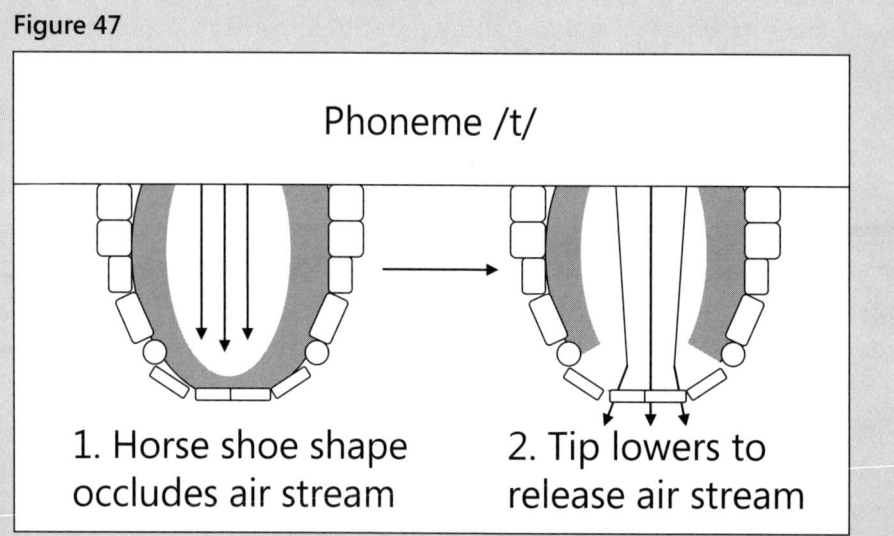

Figure 47

LEARNING EXERCISE 12
Discover the movement and position similarities of /t/ and /s/

Produce /t/ in isolation slowly three times in a row. Say, /t/-/t/-/t/. Feel how the tongue tip and the sides of the tongue elevate in a horse shoe pattern to the palate during the on-glide. Then notice how the tongue maintains this position briefly while inter oral air pressure builds. Then notice how only the tongue tip lowers to release the air in a plosive fashion. Notice that the lateral margins of the tongue remain in continual contact with the palate throughout. Only the tip moves down. The lateral margins remain stabile; the tip is mobile.

Now say /t/-/ts/-/s/ three times. Feel the similarities and differences between all three sounds. Notice that all three sounds are produced at the same location. Notice that the lateral margins of the tongue are in contact with the palate at all times. But notice that the tip alone does all the lowering.

The Long T Method

We can use the oral movements of /t/ to teach correct oral position for /s/ in the following way:

1. Instruct the client to say /t/ several times so he becomes familiar with its movement pattern. Talk about the up-and-down movement of the tongue tip. Talk about how the sound of /t/ emerges in the very front and center part of the mouth. Use a straw or tube to amplify the sound of /t/. Make sure the client understands that the sound of /t/ occurs as air rushes out the front of the mouth from behind the teeth. Talk about how the tongue is positioned behind the teeth.
2. Then ask the client to "blow more air through the T" in order to produce a "Long T." By blowing more air through /t/, the client will produce a /t/ with strong and long aspiration. We can write this as /tᶜ/. Please note that this excess air is not an /s/ nor is it an /h/. It is simply excessive aspiration on the /t/.
3. Rehearse /tᶜ/ until the client can produce it consistently.

4. Begin to shape /tᶜ/ into /ts/ by helping the client to make the excess air "tinier," or "thinner," or by telling him to "squeeze the air" or "put your front teeth together." This means elevating the jaw so that the front teeth stay in contact. Tell the client to bite the front teeth together gently and to say /tᶜ/. It should sound more like /ts/ with the front teeth together. Model the sound of /ts/ for your client. Modeling the sound is a critical step here. It lets the client know what he's aiming for. Help him listen carefully and use his powers of auditory discrimination to shape his aspiration into /s/. The result should be a slightly distorted /ts/ blend.
5. Throughout, do not ask the client to produce /ts/ because he will slip into his frontal or lateral lisp pattern. In fact, tell him NOT to produce /s/. Say, "Don't say S."
6. A good /ts/ will result if the client focuses on the oral position for /t/. Make sure he does not lose control of jaw and tongue in producing /t/. Keep the tongue in position behind the teeth for both the /t/ and the extra air. Allow for the /s/-part to be a little sloppy as long as it is not protruded or lateral. In other words, focus on keeping the tongue behind the teeth and the airflow midline, but do not worry if the /s/-part sounds sloppy at this point.
7. If the client cannot shape this sound into an acoustically correct /ts/ through the process just described, it can help to keep the air channel wide so more air escapes. It is more important to rehearse sloppy sounds with a wide midline channel of air formed behind the teeth than it is to make any sound with the tongue protruding or with air escaping laterally. Over time the sibilant sound will become more /ts/-like as the client learns to control this movement.
8. If the client cannot narrow the channel to get a true /ts/-like blend, try switching to /tʃ/ It is a wider sound to begin with and thus may come more naturally to the client. Some clients make a sound that is so much more like /tʃ/ that it is best simply to switch the entire approach to /tʃ/.

Rule

The "Long T" will work only if the client can produce /t/ correctly. If your client cannot produce /t/ correctly, then he is not ready to work on his frontal or lateral lisp. His problem is bigger. Work on /t/ and the other early-developing sounds for a while before attempting work on the frontal or lateral lisp. Work on maturing the oral-motor system and improving auditory awareness and discrimination. Save work on the frontal or lateral lisp until later in the program. Stimulate for early development of stridency as suggested in chapter five.

Drill

Like practicing scales on the piano, learning to speak a phoneme in a new way takes rehearsal and drill. Do not be afraid to drill your clients on the Long T and other aspects of this program. If your client says a sound well once, have him say it twice. If he says it well twice, have him say it three times, and so forth. Simply, say, "Perfect! Say it again… Say it again… Again… One more time… Very nice." This allows the client to drill fast, getting many repetitions in during a very short period of time.

Success

The Long "T" method will allow a client to produce /ts/ or /tʃ/ by itself with good oral control. Two characteristics should be noted:

1. The tongue should be positioned behind the anterior teeth. This means that the client with a frontal lisp has learned an oral motor pattern that allows him to produce stridency with the tongue behind the teeth. This is an excellent starting place for a client with a frontal lisp if he can do it.
2. The air stream should be midline. This means that the client with a lateral lisp has learned to produce his air stream with a midline channel. This is an excellent starting place for a client with a lateral lisp if he can do it.

Failure

Be aware that the Long T method will not work for all clients. Use the following guidelines to make decisions about pursuing the work of this chapter.

1. If your client with either a frontal or lateral lisp CAN produce a /ts/ or a /tʃ/ correctly by using the above method, then he is ready to move on to chapter seven.
2. If your client with either a frontal or lateral lisp CANNOT produce /ts/ or /tʃ/ correctly by using the above method – if he resorts to a frontal or lateral lisp on the sibilant – then you should skip chapter seven and read on in chapters nine and ten.
3. If your client CANNOT MAINTAIN a good /ts/ or /tʃ/ production at any point throughout this chapter, then he is not really ready to move on to chapter seven. Stay at the level you are at until he achieves more success. Discontinue this work and read ahead in chapters nine and ten if the client consistently fails.
4. If the client PROTRUDES THE TONGUE during production of /t/, and if he also does so on /d/, /n/ and /l/, then this is a clear indication of a more pervasive oral-motor delay. Jaw instability, low tone and hyposensitivity should be suspected. Oral-motor techniques as discussed in chapters nine and ten should be pursued.

Moving On

With the Long T in place, your client is ready to begin the Cornerstone Approach discussed in the next chapter. Celebrate with him the skill he has accomplished. Make sure your client knows he is doing very well.

Chapter 6 Summary
The Long T Method

- Every session of articulation therapy should contain just as much technique as necessary to elicit the responses we want.

- The correct way to begin therapy for both the frontal and lateral lisp is to take a traditional articulation therapy approach. That means that we begin with phonemes.

- In choosing a phoneme with which to begin, most therapists start with /s/ because it is the most frequently occurring phoneme in the English language.

- The Long T Method is a process of using /t/ to shape oral position for /ts/ or /tʃ/.

- An oral-motor perspective reveals that /s/ is an outgrowth of /t/ because of the gross-to-fine principle.

- Like all body movements, speech movements begin clumsily, and they become more refined with time.

- One cannot produce the sibilants correctly with clumsy and immature oral movements. To do so causes these acoustically precise phonemes to sound in error.

- Using /t/ as a first step toward /ts/ or /tʃ/ is like teaching a child to toddle before he walks.

- The Long T Method will work only if the client can produce /t/ correctly.

- If successful, the Long T Method will allow a client with either a frontal or lateral lisp to produce /ts/ or /tʃ/ with correct oral position.

- The Long T Method will not work for all clients. Other oral-motor and auditory discrimination methods must be employed when the Long T Method fails.

Chapter 7

The Cornerstone Approach

The Cornerstone Approach also is a new twist on traditional articulation therapy. The cornerstone method is a process of locking in on one perfect sound the client can make, and then gradually helping him use it in increasingly more complex oral-motor patterns. I first described this approach as it can be used to train /r/ in my earlier book *Successful R Therapy*. The Cornerstone Approach can work with a frontal or lateral lisp as well.

The Cornerstone Sound

A client with a frontal or a lateral lisp who can produce /ts/ successfully using the Long T Method described in the last chapter has created what I call a *cornerstone sound*. The cornerstone sound is the first target sound the client can produce correctly. It is his first correct oral movement pattern on the path of phoneme remediation. It is the sound upon which the rest of his program can be built. In this case, the cornerstone sound is /ts/. The client should rehearse this first sound until he can produce it consistently and easily. In the case of either a frontal or a lateral lisp, the cornerstone sound should be produced with the tongue behind the teeth and the air stream midline.

With /ts/ in place as the client's cornerstone sound, we can use it to create a full program for both the frontal and lateral lisp. In other words, the cornerstone sound becomes the foundation for the rest of the work we do. Notice that this production is not a phoneme in isolation as would be required in a traditional articulation therapy approach. This is a CC combination that will serve as our starting point. That's what makes the work different from a traditional approach. A traditional approach begins with the individual consonant. We will begin with a /ts/ cluster. And we will not jump from the sound to lists of random words. We shall build the client's repertoire of words around very specific oral movement patterns.

Cornerstone Syllables

With the cornerstone /ts/ sound in place, we move on to cornerstone syllables by rehearsing /ts/ after a vowel in a VCC syllable shape. The VCC is chosen: (1) because /ts/ does not occur in the initial position of syllables or words in English, and (2) because children naturally learn /s/ this way. Ask the client to practice /ts/ after each vowel in the English quadrilateral. He will say:

/its/	/ɪts/	/ets/	/ɛts/	/æts/
/uts/	/ʊts/	/ots/	/ɔts/	/ɑts/
/ʌts/				

Or have him practice /ts/ after each orthographic vowel. He will say:

A – Ates	E – Etes	I – Ites	O – Otes	U – Utes

Make sure the client is saying /ts/ as we have discussed. Do not allow him to slip into his frontal or lateral lisp. Remind him not to say /s/, but to blow a Long T. Also, allow the client to pause between the vowel and /ts/. This gives him time to produce an excellent /ts/.

What if /ts/ is not perfect?

The VCC syllable can be rehearsed even if the client can only produce a Long T and cannot produce a real /ts/. In other words, the syllable can be practiced even if the client is merely blowing excessive air after his /t/ and not yet producing true stridency. Rehearsal at this level allows him to practice the correct oral-motor pattern even though he cannot achieve perfect sound quality. The idea is to have him practice the motor pattern: to produce a Long T in sequence after a vowel. This trains him to control the oral-motor pattern carefully in a simple syllable that is void of meaning. Using a syllable instead of a word helps break his old pattern of frontal or lateral lisp. It disassociates the sound from his habitual ways of saying it in words.

Cornerstone Words

After syllables we move on to the oral movement patterns of words. The best way to begin work on words is to use five words that mirror the VCC syllable patterns rehearsed above. This keeps the oral movement pattern consistent and very simple. The words to use are:

Eights	Its	Oats	Outs	Eats

Help the client work at a pace that allows him time to produce each /ts/ correctly. Allow him to produce a Long T instead of /ts/ if necessary. Also, allow the client to pause between the vowel and /ts/ if he needs to. These five words will become his first words with a correct /s/! They should be celebrated! They are his *cornerstone words*.

Cornerstone Phrases and Sentences

After words we move on to phrases and sentences that contain the same simple oral movement patterns. Rehearse phrases and simple sentences with the cornerstone words. Keep the /ts/ sound consistent and true, and allow the client to pause after the vowel and before /ts/. Do not allow error. Use the following or devise phrases and sentences of your own. Keep your phrases and sentences void of other strident phonemes.

Short Phrases and Sentences

Good eats	Eats a lot	He eats.
It's okay.	It's fun.	It's raining.
I think it's here.	Five eights	The eights have it.
Rotten oats	Oats and corn	I eat oats.
Three outs	Make the outs	Two more outs

Sentences

He eats at noon every day.	I think it's that one.
I put the eights in the bucket.	He ate oats out of the bucket.
He made three outs.	Dad eats a burger there.
I wonder what it's all about.	Two eights are in my phone number.
Barley, oats and rye are in the bread.	Two more outs and the game will be over.

Cornerstone Paragraphs

Cornerstone paragraphs contain the motor patterns of the same simple cornerstone words and phrases but are void of any other sibilants.

Target Word: Eats

My family <u>eats</u> a lot on the Fourth of July. My dad <u>eats</u> a hotdog and a hamburger. My mom <u>eats</u> potato salad. David <u>eats</u> watermelon like there will be no tomorrow. And my baby <u>eats</u> baby food. I eat everything, too.

Target Word: It's

I think <u>it's</u> good when people help other people. <u>It's</u> better than not helping people. I think <u>it's</u> fun to help people, to take out their garbage or to help them open a door. Mom told me <u>it's</u> really good to help older people. <u>It's</u> polite and older people like that. I think <u>it's</u> good to help old people and young people.

Target Word: Eights

My old phone number had four <u>eights</u>. I remember it, and it had four <u>eights</u>. I think it went: 425-828-4883. That is a lot of <u>eights</u>. How many <u>eights</u> do you have in your phone number? It would be cool if a phone number had eight <u>eights</u>. Can a phone number have eight <u>eights</u>?

Target Word: Oats

Did you know that oatmeal is made from <u>oats</u>? <u>Oats</u> are the main ingredient. In fact, <u>oats</u> are the only ingredient. To make oatmeal, you put <u>oats</u> into a pan with water. Then you bring it to a boil. Then you lower the heat and cook it a little while. I like to eat my <u>oats</u> with milk, butter and honey.

Target Word: Outs

I remember who made all the <u>outs</u> in our game. Dave, Jacob and Lee made the early <u>outs</u>. Michael, Ron and I made the middle <u>outs</u>. And Daniel, Matthew and Brian made the final <u>outs</u>. Only nine <u>outs</u> and the game had to be called for rain.

Conversations with the Cornerstone Words

Talk about the words of this section. Have a conversation in which short comments go back and forth between you and your client. Speak slowly and over-exaggerate the target words. Teach your client to do likewise. Say a quick and quiet, "Good!" or nod with approval each time your client says one of these words correctly. Also stop and correct him each time he speaks one of these words incorrectly. Ignore all other sibilant phonemes he produces incorrectly. Learning to dialogue this way can be difficult for the novice therapist. Study the sample conversation in appendix 13 for assistance. It will show you how to initiate articulation work at a conversational level.

Moving Beyond the Cornerstone Words

As the Long T program unfolds, we can move beyond the motor patterns of the cornerstone words. We can begin to use words that are constructed with a slightly more difficulty combination and sequence of phonemes. We begin with the CVCC and the CCVCC pattern in words such as *bats, coats, kites, mutts* and *treats*. These words will be fairly easy for the client to assimilate because they are only slightly more difficult than *eights, eats, its, oats* and *outs*.

Sets of CVCC words organized around the main vowel are presented below. Many clients will need to produce these words in two parts in order to maintain control of their /ts/. Therefore, we can allow these clients to pause between the vowel and /ts/. For example, a client can practice *bats* as "ba-(pause)-ts." This gives the client a moment to prepare for the oral movements of /ts/. Pausing gives him ample opportunity to achieve his target. Do not worry about the precise acoustic quality of /s/ on these words. Remember, you are focusing on correct jaw and tongue position and not perfection of acoustic quality. The main requirements are that the tongue is positioned behind the teeth and the air stream is midline. The client can produce /ts/ or a Long T. Only rehearse these words if the client can produce /ts/ or a Long T as required.

Words with /æts/
Bats	Brats	Cats	Fats	Gnats
Hats	Mats	Pats	Rats	Vats

Words with /ɪts/
Bits	Fits	Hits	Kits	Knits
Mitts	Pits	Quits	Sits	Wits

Words with /ɑits/
Bites	Fights	Heights	Kites	Lights
Nights	Rights	Sights	Tights	Writes

Words with /ots/
Boats	Bloats	Coats	Floats	Goats
Moats	Notes	Quotes	Totes	Votes

Words with /its/
Beets	Bleats	Cleats	Feats	Fleets
Greets	Heats	Meets	Seats	Treats

Words with /eits/

| Baits | Crates | Dates | Fates | Gates |
| Grates | Hates | Mates | Rates | Waits |

Words with /ɑts/

| Cots | Clots | Dots | Jots | Knots |
| Lots | Pots | Plots | Rots | Tots |

Words with /ɑuts/

| Bouts | Doubts | Louts | Pouts | Touts |

Phrases with Final /ts/ Words

After words we move on to the motor patterns of phrases. Begin with phrases that contain /ts/ in the final position of the final word of the phrase. This allows the client to pause briefly before /ts/ and produce it as a separate syllable. For example, "The fat ca-(pause)-ts."

The fat cats	The black bats	The tiny gnats
The old hats	The warm mitts	The witty wits
The high kites	The brave knights	The beautiful sights
The book of quotes	The old goats	The deep moats
The yummy oats	The uncomfortable cots	The big dots
The red beets	The track meets	The parking lots
The tight knots	The many doubts	

Phrases with Embedded Final /ts/ Words

Continue with phrases that contain /ts/ in the final position of the first word of the phrase. This makes the motor patterns slightly more difficult because the client must say more after the produces his /ts/. Again, allow the client to pause. For example, "Ca-(pause)-ts who purr."

Cats who purr	Bats in the attic	Gnats that bothered me
Hats on the rack	Mitts for the team	Kites of blue and yellow
Knights in armor	Dates in April	Quotes of mine
Goats on the hill	Oats in the bag	Cots at camp
Dots on the blanket	Lots of cabbage	Knots in her hair

Sentences with Final /ts/ Words

Next, move on to sentences that contain the same motor pattern. Use /ts/ in the final position of the final word of the sentence. Again, allow the client to pause as in, "Look at the ca-(pause)-ts."

Look at the cats.	I hear bats.	I hate gnats.
He wore old hats.	Wear the warm mitts.	Fly the kites.
Here come the knights.	Turn on the lights.	He fed the goats.
He ate all the oats.	I bought the cots.	It had tiny dots.
We had many doubts.	I cannot undo the knots.	We went to all the track meets.

Sentences with Multiple /ts/ Words

Progress to sentences that contain several /ts/ words. This makes the motor pattern even more challenging. Allow pausing again as in, "Ca-(pause)-ts eat ba-(pause)-ts and ra-(pause)-ts on ma-(pause)-ts."

Cats eat bats and rats on mats.
The goats wore coats in boats on moats.
He waits at gates for mates with dates.
He writes about kites, lights and knights.

She knits mitts in bits and then quits.
She put beets in seats at meets. Yuck!
The tots tied lots of knots on the cots.
He doubts the sprouts had bouts of pouts.

Paragraphs with Final Position /ts/ Words

After words, phrases and sentences, move on to paragraphs with the same oral movement pattern. Read aloud paragraphs that contain words with final /ts/. Use paragraphs void of other sibilant phonemes like those found below. Have your client read slowly the first time and allow the pauses. Ask him to read slightly faster with each reading.

Paragraph with /æts/

Did you know that cats like to eat rats, play with bats and wear hats? Well, maybe not that part about the hats. I'm kidding. But I am telling the truth about the rats and bats.

Paragraph with /ɪts/

It's my grandma who sits and knits mitts. I love her mitts. It's my brother who hits in snits and fits and then quits. I hate it when he quits. It's the pits. And it's me who out wits them both when I make my kits in bits.

Paragraph with /ɑɪts/

I took a trip with my Uncle Mike. We climbed a hill north of town. We talked to two men flying kites. The kites were really cool and they flew very high. When it got dark, the town lights came on. It looked cool. We went there because my uncle writes about kites. He writes about the fights of medieval knights too.

Paragraph with /ots/

Do you hear the goats? I think they are on the boats in the moats. Will they eat oats? Do they wear coats? Do they get votes? Do they carry totes? I think not!

Paragraph with /its/

My dad greets people at an apartment door all day long. He meets them in front of the building, and he seats them in a cab on the way out if they need one. Great feats they are not, but he never cheats and people often give him a tip. My dad told me it beats having no job at all.

Paragraph with /eits/

The rates were high at the gates to the game. I forgot to get my ticket beforehand. My friend waits all day in line to get one. We're good mates, but he didn't know I needed one too. He hates to wait for them, but he did anyway. On Friday we will take dates to the big game.

Paragraph with /ɑts/
Let me tell you about the tots at the day care. They nap on cots and they play with toy pots. They don't know how to tie knots. And they draw dots on everything. I like tots lots.

Paragraph with /ɑuts/
He doubts that he will get a good grade in math and he pouts about it all day long. I told him not to worry about it. He touts about the good grade he got in P.E. though. I told him, "I don't care. Go eat broccoli." He won't eat broccoli and he doubts that I will eat it if I don't have to.

Conversation with Cornerstone /ts/ Words
Talk about the words of this section. For example talk about *cats, bats* and *rats*. Have a conversation in which short comments go back and forth between you and your client. Speak slowly and over-exaggerate the target words. Teach your client to do likewise. Say a quick and quiet, "Good!" each time your client says one of these words correctly. Also stop and correct him each time he speaks one of these words incorrectly. Ignore all other sibilant phonemes he produces incorrectly. Learning to dialogue this way can be difficult for the novice therapist. Study the sample conversation in appendix 13 for assistance. It will show you how to initiate articulation work at a conversational level.

Moving On: Medial Position /ts/ Practice

After establishing final /ts/ with the tongue behind the anterior teeth and the air stream midline, we can expand into words in which /ts/ occurs in the middle of a word. Again, do not worry about the precise acoustic quality of /s/. Even allow the client to produce a Long T. Focus instead on the tongue position behind the teeth and the air stream produced midline. Allow the client to pause before and after the /ts/. For example, pronounce *Betsy* as "Be-(pause)-ts-(pause)-y." This gives the client time to think through the required movements.

Words - /ts/ mid word

Betsy	Datsun	Gutsy	Itself	Outsell
Outside	Patsy	Pizza	Pretzel	Ritzy

Phrases - /ts/ mid word

The new Datsun	A gutsy guy	All by itself
Cannot outsell	Outside the room	My friend Patsy
Hot and peppery pizza	A big pretzel	The ritzy hotel
An old yaughtsman		

Simple Sentences - /ts/ mid word

Betsy came through the door.	I put ketsup on my hamburger.
He will drive the Datsun home at ten.	He can be a gutsy guy.
It payed for itself.	I am not in the jetset.
Go play outside today.	Eat pizza every day!
Get me a pretzel.	That might be a ritzy party.

Complex Sentences – /ts/ mid word
Betsy ate a pretzel with ketsup.
We found the gutsy yaghtsman outside.
The ritzy black evening bag will outsell the blue one.

Patsy drove the Datsun to get the pizza.
That gutsy guy went outside to eat a pretzel.

Paragraphs with Medial /ts/
Move on to paragraphs with the same oral movement pattern. Read aloud paragraphs that contain words with medial /ts/. Use paragraphs void of other sibilant phonemes like those found below. Have your client read slowly the first time and allow pauses. Ask him to read slightly faster with each reading.

My aunt Betsy made a huge pretzel. I ate it today. Betsy told me to put ketsup on it, but I didn't. Yuck! That was too gutsy for me. I went outside when I heard that.

My dad bought an old Datsun at the auction today. He told me it could be ritzy if we cleaned it up and repaired the big dent on the left. But I don't think that old Datsun could ever look like a car a jetsetter would drive.

My neighbor, Patsy, can make a real pizza. Patsy told me that a pizza practically can make itself. "It ain't hard," Patsy told me. Patsy might work on her grammar while working on that pizza.

Conversation
Talk about the words of this section. For example talk about a *pretzel* and *pizza*. Have a conversation in which short comments go back and forth between you and your client. Speak slowly and over-exaggerate the target words. Teach your client to do likewise. Say a quick and quiet "Good" each time your client says one of these words correctly. Also stop to correct him each time he speaks one of these words incorrectly. Ignore all other sibilant phonemes that come up and are he produced incorrectly. See appendix 13 for an example.

Rehearse /ts/ Across Words
The Long T Method also allows us to work on phrases in which /ts/ spans across two words. For example, the silly phrase *bat soap* meets this criteria. The final /t/ of *bat* and the initial /s/ of *soap* can be treated as a Long T. This will work well if the client can read and if he will accept this premise. Rehearse the following silly phrases and sentences. Allow the client to pause before and after the /ts/ that spans the words in the phrase.

Phrases
Bat soap	Cat sap	Hat soup	Kite sink	Coat sand
Boat sail	Right side	Bright side	Night seat	Light saw

Sentences
I bought a bar of bat soap.
I will never eat hat soup.

The tree gave off fat sap.
Wash the kite in the kite sink.

I got coat sand in my pocket.
The right side came off.
I like the night seat.

The boat sail broke.
The bright side came on.
Take the light saw to the back yard.

Non-standard Initial Position /ts/ Practice

In English, we do not use /ts/ in the initial position of syllables or words. But some clients cannot produce /s/ without /t/ for a long time. They need that /t/ to help keep the tongue back and to keep their air stream midline. However, their lack of skill need not stop us from marching forward. We do so by practicing words with a ts/s substitution.

I tell clients to pretend that their words have a /t/ in front of them, and I write a little "t" in front of the "s." Any words that begin with /s/ can be used as long as there are no other /s/ sounds in the words. Single-syllable words that do not contain s-blends work best at first.

Words – initial /ts/

ᵗSad	ᵗSail	ᵗSaint	ᵗSand	ᵗSank
ᵗSap	ᵗSave	ᵗSaw	ᵗSeat	ᵗSeek
ᵗSeen	ᵗSeep	ᵗSet	ᵗSew	ᵗSick
ᵗSide	ᵗSign	ᵗSin	ᵗSing	ᵗSoak
ᵗSoap	ᵗSob	ᵗSold	ᵗSound	ᵗSoy
ᵗSue	ᵗSung	ᵗSub	ᵗSuch	ᵗSurf

Phrases – initial /ts/ – first word

ᵗSad man	ᵗSail home	ᵗSaint Paul	ᵗSand pail	ᵗSank low
ᵗSeek more	ᵗSeep down	ᵗSet right	ᵗSign up	ᵗSing along
ᵗSoak up	ᵗSoap bar	ᵗSold out	ᵗSound off	ᵗSoy bean

Phrases – initial /ts/ – second word

| Wet ᵗsand | Hot ᵗseat | Not ᵗseen | My ᵗset | Can ᵗsew |
| Other ᵗside | Neon ᵗsign | Can't ᵗsing | Loud ᵗsound | Good ᵗsurf |

Sentences – initial /ts/

I am ᵗsad about it.
He bought ᵗsand and rock.
Tree ᵗsap flowed into the bucket.
We ᵗsaw the people.
What ᵗside do you want?

Get the ᵗsail ready.
We ᵗsank and called for help.
ᵗSave the paper.
ᵗSet the food on the table.
The ᵗsign fell down.

Reading with /ts/ in Initial Position

We can work toward carryover of correct tongue position by reading aloud using the ts/s substitution. Select a passage of reading material, highlight the initial /s/ sounds, and then have the client read the passage aloud using ts/s each time. Do not concern yourself with words that contain /s/ in other positions, only focus on the initial /s/ words. Have the client read slowly at first, and increase speed over time. Use bland reading material at first so the client can concentrate on his tongue position. Gradually work toward more interesting and amusing reading material that will draw the client's mind away from his productions. Challenge him to keep his mind on tongue position while he is enjoying the material. Use riddles, rhymes and jokes. The following passages are constructed with initial /s/ words but without any other sibilant phonemes. There are a few consonant clusters with /s/ here and there for a little more challenge. They will work nicely for you in this task.

ˈSam will not ˈsee the ˈsun today. It might be cloudy all day. ˈSam could be ˈsad, but he won't be. A football game will keep him occupied. ˈSam can't play well, but it won't matter. ˈSam will play for ˈSandfield High, and the game will be played with ˈSouth High. I hope ˈSandfield will come out on top. They are ˈso cool.

I bought ˈsoap for my mom. I did not know where to find the ˈsoap, but a clerk named ˈSally took me to it. I ˈsaw the kind we needed right away, ˈso I picked it up and brought it to the counter. ˈSue, another clerk, knew my mom. ˈSo ˈSue ˈsaid, "ˈSay 'Hi' to your mom for me." I ˈsaid, "Okay, I will." Then I went home. When I got home, I told mom, "Sue ˈsaid, "Hi." But mom ˈsaid, "You bought the wrong ˈsoap!"

I love to play in ˈsand. I play in ˈsand whenever I can. I hope we go ˈsomewhere where I can play in ˈsand in the ˈsummer. ˈSun and ˈsand and cold water to ˈswim in. There can't be anything better. ˈSometime maybe you can go with me. Then we can build in the ˈsand. Bring a bucket. We can dump ˈsand with it. Then we can ˈswim in the water to get rid of the ˈsand on our feet. If you don't get the ˈsand off your body it will go all over the ˈseat of the car. Then dad will yell, "I told you to get that ˈsand off your feet before you get in the car!" He will yell, but really he will be happy that we had a good day in the ˈsand and in the ˈsun.

"ˈSo long!" ˈsaid ˈSophie, "ˈSee you tomorrow!" ˈSophie ran home. I wanted to go to her apartment with her to eat a ˈsnack with her mom and her dog, ˈSappy, but I had to walk my ˈsibling to painting ˈschool. ˈSappy might be a ˈsmall and ˈsilly dog. ˈSappy might be a ˈspoiled and ˈsad dog. ˈSappy might be a dog that nobody can ˈstand. But ˈSophie ˈsaid her mom ˈsaid that I could have her!!! And my mom and dad ˈsaid I could have her too! And on Friday I will get her!!! ˈSo I don't care how ˈsmall, ˈsilly, ˈspoiled, ˈsad and unwanted ˈSappy may be. I don't care if nobody can ˈstand her. I love her and on Friday ˈSappy will be mine!

Habituating Tongue Position with /t/

The process of producing spontaneous speech is automatic and the normal speaker does so with perfect articulation. The impaired speaker also speaks automatically, but he does so with speech movement patterns that are incorrect. Final success in treating the frontal or lateral lisp involves bringing that which is unconscious and automatic to full consciousness control during the automatic process of conversation. In other words, we work in slow, careful steps at first. Gradually we speed things up to match the characteristics of spontaneous speech that must be placed under automatic control. We are trying to build correct habits that dominate during conversation. Natural sequences using the /ts/ cluster are the easiest way to accomplish this as described below.

Rate Is Key
A rapid sequence is about as close to conversation as we can get. This is because a sequence can be produced with great speed over time. Start slow and increase speed as the client demonstrates control over tongue position. The idea is that we are not teaching correct phoneme production. Instead, *we are teaching the client how to move the jaw, lips and tongue in to and out of correct position during the rapid sequential movement tasks of conversation.* This way we practice the required oral-motor pattern many times in a row, drilling it in order to habituate it. The client starts slowly to control the oral movements perfectly. But perfect motor patterns at this point do not necessarily mean that the target phonemes will be produced perfectly. The targets may be produced with a little sloppy acoustic quality. But the key movement patterns (keeping the tongue inside the mouth and maintaining midline airflow) will be achieved.

Counting Sequences
Counting sequences can simulate the rate of speech found in conversation. The client will be learning to keep his tongue behind his teeth while engaged in a tightly controlled yet ballistic speech movement event. For example, ask the client to count from 70 to 79 using /ts/ at the beginning of each number. The client will say, "ᵗseventy, ᵗseventy-one, ᵗseventy-two, ᵗseventy-three" and so forth. Other number sequences with "ᵗseventy" can be used as well:

Count from 70 to 79	Count from 170 to 179	Count from 270 to 279
Count from 370 to 379	Count from 470 to 479	Count from 570 to 579
Count from 670 to 679	Count from 770 to 779	Count from 870 to 879
Count from 970 to 979		

Rote Speech Events
An utterance that is rote is one that can be rattled off fairly easily for the client. For example, the client can recite his address if he knows it by heart. Work with the client to discover all the words that contain /s/ in these sequences. For example, the client's address might be "1347 Sand Lake Boulevard, Silver Lake, Oregon." The client can substitute ts/s in the words *seven*, *Sand* and *Silver*. He can practice saying this many times in a row, increasing speed over time. This is a fantastic way to habituate tongue position on /s/. He also can recite just his town name several times in a row: "Silver Lake, Silver Lake, Silver Lake …" He also could practice many other words or phrases this way: his telephone number, the alphabet (especially, ABCDEFG and PQRST), the name of his school, a memorized short prayer or a grocery list.

Picture Naming
Habituating a ts/s substitution produced in the initial position of words also can be accomplished by engaging in quick picture-naming tasks. For example, place five cards face-up on the table in a row. Use single-syllable words like *sun, soap, sink* and *Sam*. Ask the client to name the pictures from left-to-right rapidly. Rehearse them several times until the client can name them as rapidly as if he were speaking a sentence spontaneously.

Grammatical Forms

Use grammatical forms to build sequences or phrases that can be recited fast. For example, name a row of pictures and use an article before each name. Have the client say: *a school, a sink, a star, a soap*, and so forth. Or use a pronoun as in *my school, my sink, my star, my soap*. Or use a full sentence as in *I see a school, I see a sink, I see a star*. Produce these with a repeating intonation pattern and rhythm, and work as fast as the client can without error.

Memory Games

One of my favorite ways to increase control over spontaneous productions of speech is to make the speech task simple but to increase the likelihood that the client will forget what he is trying to accomplish. For example, play a memory game where you name a word, then the client must name your word and a new word. Then you name those two words and add another, and so it goes. Use words that all have the same structure. For example, list words that start with /s/. See how many words you and the client can remember in sequence. Use words that reflect the speech pattern being targeted. Pretend this task is difficult for you, make mistakes and struggle a little so that the field is even. A dialogue might look like this:

> THERAPIST: ᵗsoap
>
> CLIENT: ᵗsoap, ᵗsink
>
> THERAPIST: ᵗsoap, ᵗsink, ᵗsoup
>
> CLIENT: ᵗsoap, ᵗsink, ᵗsoup… uh… ᵗsand!
>
> THERAPIST: Oh, I hope I can do this… ᵗsoap… ᵗsink… ᵗsoup… ᵗsand, and… Ummm… ᵗseven!!
>
> CLIENT: ᵗsoap, ᵗsink, ᵗsoup, ᵗsand… What was that word? Oh… I can't…, ᵗSeven! And, um… Let's see… ᵗStar!
>
> THERAPIST: Oh man, I don't think I can do it. ᵗsoap, ᵗsink, ᵗsoup, ᵗsand… um… ᵗSponge? ᵗStar?
>
> CLIENT: Ah-ha! I won. You blew it!

A memory game like this forces the client to keep his mind on productions while he is also using his mind to be creative. His mind is trying to remember the words already named in the list. And his mind is searching for a new word to add to the list. This process works to train the mind to hold the speech pattern while it is preoccupied with the task. The more fun and wild this game becomes, the more control the client will acquire.

The Final Step

The final step of the Long T Method and the Cornerstone Approach is to eliminate the /t/. Some clients will begin to eliminate it on their own. Their rote sequences will become so fast that the /t/ will drop out all by itself. Others will have to be shown how to do this as follows:

1. Separate the /t/ from the rest of the word with a silent pause as the tongue lowers. For example, practice a word like ᵗ*soap* with the /t/. Then tell the client to position the tongue for /t/, but not to say anything. Tell him to lower the tip away from the alveolus before saying anything. Tell him to exhale after the tip is lowered. Once the client gets the idea, practice many words this way.
2. If the client needs more help, have him say /ts/ and then hold the /s/ for several seconds. He will say, "Tsssssss." Then tell him to hold that position and inhale and exhale through the opening without moving his tongue out of position. The client will say, "/ts/… /s/… /s/…." with inhalation and exhalation as if he was panting through the position. As he exhales he will be producing /s/.

Success

The Long T Method and the Cornerstone Approach will be all the therapy that many clients need. These two methods together completely train the oral mechanism to produce /s/ correctly. As stated earlier, /s/ is selected because of its importance in the English language. Many clients begin to generalize the knowledge they are learning about /s/ to the other sibilants, and they begin to make changes in them along with the /s/. Clients who generalize easily can work on /z/, /ʃ/, /ʒ/, /tʃ/ and /dʒ/ right away, and their work on these sounds even can overlap the work they do on /s/. Other clients will need to work one phoneme at a time.

Chapter 7 Summary
The Cornerstone Approach

- The Cornerstone Approach is a process of locking in on one perfect sound the client can make, and then gradually helping him use it in increasingly more complex oral-motor patterns.

- The Cornerstone Sound is the first correct motor pattern the client can produce. The best cornerstone sound for the frontal and lateral lisp is the cluster /ts/.

- With the cornerstone /ts/ sound in place, we move on to Cornerstone Syllables by rehearsing /ts/ after a vowel in a VCC syllable shape. We expand to Cornerstone Words like *eats, its, eights, oats* and *outs*. Then we move one to phrases, sentences, paragraphs and conversation with the cornerstone words.

- Next we move into words that are constructed with the CVCC or CCVCC pattern, for example, *bats* or *brats*. We practice them in phrases, sentences, paragraphs and conversation.

- Next we expand into words in which /ts/ occurs in the middle of a word, for example, *Betsy*. We use these in phrases, sentences, paragraphs and conversation.

- Next we rehearse phrases and sentences in which /ts/ occurs across words, for example, *cat soup*. We practice these as phrases and sentences.

- Many clients cannot produce /s/ without /t/ for a long time. So we begin practicing words with a ts/s substitution in the initial position of words. We practice these in phrases, sentences and conversation.

- We begin to rehearse rote speech constructions like counting from 70-79. We work on speed and habituation.

- The final step of the Cornerstone Approach is to eliminate the /t/. Many clients do this on their own with no specific instruction.

- The Long T Method and the Cornerstone Approach will be all that many clients need to fix their frontal or lateral lisp.

Chapter 8

Remediation Specific to the Frontal Lisp

Techniques specific to the frontal lisp range from the simple to the complex, and from the superficial to the invasive. Complex and invasive techniques may be necessary, but that is not where we begin. We begin with the simple and the superficial, and we progress to the complex and invasive as necessary. This is because many of these clients can learn the skills they need with the easiest and the most superficial of methods, including the Long T Method and the Cornerstone Approach described in the last chapters. The Long T Method and the Cornerstone Approach are highly effective for many clients with a frontal lisp. They can function as a direct route for remediation. This chapter helps us put those techniques into a broader context for the remediation process specific to the frontal lisp. It describes more traditional articulation therapy techniques for the frontal lisp, as well as more direct oral-motor techniques for frontal lisps that prove more difficult.

Goal and Objectives of Therapy

The ultimate *goal* of therapy for the frontal lisp is to establish correct articulation of the misarticulated phonemes in all speaking situations. The *objectives* designed to reach this goal are highly individualistic and depend upon the work needed to achieve that goal. The *techniques* of this chapter support the objectives and build skill toward the ultimate goal.

Onset of Treatment for the Frontal Lisp

How old must a client be before he can benefit from treatment for a frontal lisp? This is the question asked most often by therapists seeking information about this problem. Traditionally, a client with a frontal lisp who demonstrated no other speech or language delay or disorder was enrolled in articulation therapy by age eight or nine years of age. The basis of this decision was a developmental one. Since most children outgrow a frontal lisp by eight or nine years of age, it makes sense to wait to enroll them until after that age. That way, the children who will naturally outgrow the problem – those who ultimately would never have needed therapy in the first place – will have outgrown the problem. By waiting until this age, speech-language pathologists are not wasting their time providing therapy services to children who do not really need them.

This traditional view of therapy was formed by speech therapists who worked in the public schools in the 1950's and 1960's. The youngest children they served were six years of age and were enrolled in regular education. The great majority of these children were very likely to outgrow the frontal lisp problem. It made sense to wait back then.

This traditional view was formed when children with very severe speech and language impairment related to cognitive or neurological impairment were not enrolled in public school. Therefore, children with frontal lisp who also had other forms of severe expressive speech disorder were not considered when decisions about enrollment were being formed. But today we do see children with interdental tongue placement that is part of pervasive motor-based speech disorders in school and in private practice. Thus we must, in this book, discuss how to handle the frontal lisp when it occurs alone and when it is a part of a much broader expressive speech disorder.

Today we see children with a frontal lisp at younger ages because parents often are willing to take them for private speech services. Some of these children are enrolled in weekly therapy if it is clear that they can benefit from early treatment. Others are seen for a few sessions to boost their skills, and then they are monitored over time to make sure they outgrow the problem. Monitoring can be done once every three-to-six months. This allows the speech-language pathologist an opportunity to watch how the child's speech develops and to determine if and when treatment should begin. Children who do not show positive change over time and those who have not changed by eight years of age are enrolled.

The Traditional Progression

Traditional articulation therapy taught us to work in the following sequence when training a client to produce new sounds: isolation, syllable, word, phrase, sentence, paragraph and conversation. While I don't think anyone works in such a rigid fashion any more, it is very helpful to THINK along these lines while structuring the long haul of therapy. I have found that once a client can produce a phoneme in isolation, it makes sense to use it in each of these levels right away. In other words, if he can say /s/ in isolation, then have him use it right away in a syllable, word, phrase, sentence, paragraph and conversation. That way we are working toward conversational speech right from the onset of treatment. Each session pushes the client as far as he can successfully advance toward this ultimate point.

Most therapists establish a phoneme in isolation and then stop only briefly on syllables before moving on to words. But some of the early phonetics and the phonological literature points to the notion that the syllable, and not the phoneme, is the basic unit of speech. Therefore, I like to move through these levels by structuring the program around specific syllables like /sa/, /so/ or /see/. Clients with no oral motor dysfunction related to their frontal lisp can gain skill quickly here because they have very few problems generalizing their phoneme productions to multiple syllabic environments.

Select practice material that is void of other error phonemes if possible. For example, in addressing /sa/, work in the following order:

- Isolation: /s/
- Syllable: /sa/
- Word: "sock"
- Phrase: "my red sock"
- Sentence: "My red sock fell down."

- Paragraph: "My red sock fell down and I couldn't find it. I think it fell behind the bed. I told my mom that I needed a new red sock. My mom thought I could find the red sock if I really tried."
- Conversation: Talk about socks. Make the client say this topic word with correct articulatory placement. Ignore the errors he makes on other words with this key sound. Tell the client that you do not care how he produces any other word. Tell him, however, that you will be listening very carefully for the /s/ in the word "sock." Use a simple device – such as a clicker – to mark correct productions. Gradually decrease the use of the clicker as the client gains control of his own productions.

Practice like this prevents a client from being stuck rehearsing words lists for months on end with no carryover to more sophisticated speech events. Working through all levels throughout the course of treatment brings in the metaphonological work necessary to engage cognitive processes.

One Phoneme at a Time for the Frontal Lisp

Traditional articulation therapy also taught us to approach the remediation of articulation errors one phoneme at a time. This can be an excellent way to approach the remediation of the frontal lisp with an easy client. Remember, the easiest of our clients have a habitual frontal lisp pattern with no underlying oral-motor or auditory processing deficit. Directing therapy toward the phonemes themselves right from the beginning is an excellent approach for them. When working one phoneme at a time we need to choose a phoneme with which to begin, and we need to order the introduction of the other phonemes in logical ways.

First Level

The phoneme with which most therapists begin the remediation process is S. Certainly S is chosen because it is the most frequently occurring phoneme of the English language. When a client has a frontal lisp, S is the error phoneme that stands out. In fact, most parents who call me to make an initial evaluation appointment and who do not know the term "frontal lisp" usually say that their child "says 'S' wrong." This is true even if their child misarticulates all six sibilant phonemes.

As such, /s/ almost always is the phoneme first on the list of remediation targets. This makes sense when one realizes that if correct /s/ is spoken, the overall positive impact on speech will be tremendous. Changing /s/ first is logical based upon frequency of occurrence. Since /s/ is usually targeted first, we shall base our entire discussion of the frontal lisp on it. All the activities and exercises presented in the balance of this chapter assume that the client is being stimulated for /s/ unless otherwise specified.

Second Level

Selecting letter Z as a second target also is something that most therapists do. This is because letter Z is produced essentially exactly like /s/ except for the addition of voice. It is very easy to move on to /z/ once /s/ is established. However, there are very few important and regularly spoken words that contain letter Z. How often does a child need to say *zoo, zebra, zero, Zorro, buzzard, gizzard, bizarre, buzz, fuzz* or *pizzazz*? The infrequent use of letter Z as a phoneme in words makes it seem as if the phoneme is of little importance.

However, as we have discussed in our previous chapter, letter S often is pronounced with voicing so that it is produced as /z/. Consider the words *is, was, has, his, hers, ours* and *theirs*. Letter S also is pronounced as a voiced /s/, a devoiced /z/, or /z/ itself when it is used as a morpheme adjacent to vowels, diphthongs and voiced consonants. Voicing is added due to the co-articulatory effect. Consider the way we pronounce S in the following:

1. Main Verb to be: *dad's below deck, Bob's there too*
2. Auxiliary Verb to be: *he's running, the dog's barking*
3. Plural: *two cabs are on the way, four bugs were caught*
4. Possessive: *the boy's arm, the man's boat*
5. Third Person Verb Marker: *he plays ball, she runs easily*

Third Level
Beyond /s/ and /z/, most therapists seem to target phonemes /ʃ/, /ʒ/, /tʃ/ and /dʒ/ in no specific order. Therapists probe their client's abilities to determine if they have a particular readiness for any of these four phonemes. And they move on to any for which the client shows readiness.

Readiness
Speaking of readiness, a client's readiness to pronounce any one of the six sibilant phonemes affected by the frontal lisp often is a therapist's main criteria for initial phoneme selection. As such, /s/ may not be the first target. Any phoneme that proves ready for change is selected. I have begun work on the frontal lisp with /ʃ/ and /tʃ/ quite often to good success. The key is to determine what phoneme can change the most easily and with the least amount of effort. We are probing for stimulability. These decisions sometimes are made during the initial diagnostic appointment, but they usually are ongoing throughout the course of treatment.

Overlap and Mass Phoneme Training for the Frontal Lisp

The traditional approach of addressing one phoneme at a time allows one to concentrate deeply on a single phoneme, and to see it through to its conclusion. Then you move on to another phoneme. Sounds nice. But in reality, therapy would take years that way. There must be ways to shorten the process.

One way to shorten the process is to overlap our work on one phoneme with another. So as our work on /s/ evolves, we introduce /z/, and as work on /z/ evolves, we introduce /ʃ/, and so forth. After a few weeks or months all phonemes are being addressed within most sessions. Clients with normal oral motor function can handle this method as can those with at least normal intelligence.

Another way to shorten our time in treatment is to address all six phonemes *en masse*. Begin with all six phonemes from the onset of treatment. Clients who like to multi-task enjoy this type of approach. But the multiple phoneme approach can be confusing to young clients and to those older clients who get lost and confused in multi-tasking. Mass training also can be a disaster if oral motor control or auditory discrimination problems are significant. Select clients carefully for this approach.

Generalization from the Single Phoneme

Rarely does one work on one phoneme without that work causing positive development on other phonemes. For example, facilitating correct oral position on /s/ usually translates directly to correct production on /z/. We call this *generalization*. Generalization is one reason clients continue to make progress in speech therapy during breaks from treatment. And generalization is the reason that one rarely has to address the interdental tongue position problem on every phoneme in error when a frontal lisp is the problem. Fixing the pattern on one phoneme often generalizes to correct positioning on the others. Each subsequent phoneme learned in treatment is acquired more quickly. As such, a client may spend several weeks, even months, working directly on his first target sound. Then he may be able to go directly to work on all the other sibilants within just a few sessions. This often happens when the client realizes that the tongue-inside-the-mouth pattern applies broadly to all sibilants

Simple Instructions for the Frontal Lisp

The most straightforward technique for the client with a frontal lisp is to tell him to keep his tongue inside his mouth while speaking. This may sound obvious, but this simple instruction can be overlooked. Consider the following story of Mary. Mary did not have a frontal lisp, but her situation reveals the importance of direct instruction.

Mary

Mary was a geriatric resident of a nursing home and a regular patient at an urban hospital. Her problem was that her mouth was always open. The open mouth was bothering the staff and other residents. No one knew what to do for Mary to help her keep the mouth closed. The problem was evaluated by a variety of physicians and therapists. No one knew what was wrong with Mary or what to do about the problem. Then she visited the speech-language pathologist who told her, "Keep your mouth closed. No one wants to see it open all the time." Mary nodded in assent and closed her mouth.

This story represents a simple yet critical need in therapy: Tell clients what you want. Structure your statements at a language level the client can grasp. Remember that information is power. A client with well-developed jaw, lip and tongue control can make his oral mechanism respond to a specific rule about tongue movements for speech. The rule is: "Never let your tongue come out from between your teeth."

A client who can understand and try this rule can move right into words, phrases, sentences and conversation within the very first session. His speech may sound sloppy, stiff or stilted, and he may have to slow his rate of speech way down to keep the tongue in. But his attempts will bring him immediate success in the major speech pattern he needs to conquer. If the client can understand the rule and accomplish this most basic skill, he can begin practicing this at home with word, phrase or sentence lists, and even in some conversational situations.

There is of course an exception to this rule, and that is the tongue-tip is allowed to protrude when articulating /θ/ and /ð/. Therefore, after the client understands the basic rule about keeping the tongue in at all times, teach him the exception to this rule: "Except for Th." Keep your practice lists void of words that contain /θ/ while the client is learning /s/ unless you are using it as a contrasting phoneme.

The Oldest Technique for the Frontal Lisp

Perhaps the oldest technique employed for teaching correct tongue position for the sibilants when a client has a frontal lisp is to begin with /s/ and to instruct him, "Bite, smile and blow." This is a great technique because it trains the three most basic oral motor needs for the frontal lisp: (1) stabilize the jaw to create the dental barrier, (2) get the lips out of the way and retract the tongue, and (3) exhale through the teeth to create stridency.

1. *Bite:* Ask the client to bite down at the molars. (Make sure the client is not biting down at the incisors.) This stabilizes the jaw in an elevated position. The jaw position actually is too high for the final position needed for sibilant production, and the central incisors are not properly positioned, but the position works to stabilize the jaw in a gross way to begin the process. This high jaw position will create an anterior dental barrier for nearly correct airflow cutting. And perhaps most importantly, with the dental barrier in place, the tongue cannot slip between the anterior teeth. Over time, the tight clenched position can be loosened for a more natural dental position. Ultimately the jaw must position itself so that the mouth is in a slightly graded open position, and this initial direction to "bite" will head him in this direction.
2. *Smile:* Ask the client to smile broadly (retract the lips). This gets the lips out of the way and influences tongue grooving positively. Smiling broadly helps the tongue retract further back into the mouth, to spread laterally, and to increase muscular tension slightly. Smiling broadly is a great first step to include in treatment but it will have to be reduced over time.
3. *Blow:* "Blow" means "exhale" in this exercise. Ask the client to exhale as he bites and smiles. This creates voiceless frication to emerge from between the teeth. A gross sibilant sound that is midline should result. Do not tell the client to say /s/ or any other sibilant sound. That will cause him to shift from the gross yet beautiful position you have just created into the inappropriate interdental position he usually uses. Keep him focused on the jaw and lip positions explained above. (Reminder: "Blow" does not mean *to blow* as in the sense of blowing out a candle; it means to exhale.)

This tried and true old-fashioned technique works wonders with the "easy" client who has a frontal lisp and no other oral-motor problems. A high-functioning client will have the oral-motor skills to comply with each of these three directions. He will be able to bite with the molars and hold the position while spreading the lips. And he will be able to maintain both these positions while exhaling air. His tongue naturally will form into a groove behind the teeth because that is the way it already functions.

A client with a frontal lisp who has never produced a correct sibilant phoneme behind the front teeth will do so automatically when he follows these three simple directions. The phoneme will sound slightly distorted however and will have to be shaped with auditory discrimination training over time. At the earliest stages of therapy, however, the gross sound should be accepted as long as it is produced with the tongue behind the teeth and as long as the airflow emerges at midline. Acoustic quality is sacrificed for oral position at first. Over time the acoustic quality will be shaped.

It should be noted here that this straightforward technique can force a lateral lisp to occur on occasion if bringing the tongue in behind the teeth this quickly causes the client to alter his tongue stability. You do not want this to occur. Remember, the frontal lisp is an easier pattern to remediate. Slow down your therapy by switching to another technique and do everything possible to avoid this result.

Adjust Tongue Position Behind the Teeth
When asked to bite and blow, many clients with a frontal lisp shove the tip of the tongue forward and bang it against the backside of the upper incisors. This does not allow enough air to come through the teeth, and it often causes a thumping or occluding sound that has to be eliminated. Ask the client to pull the tongue back so more air will get through. Those with normal oral-motor skill will be able to do so while maintaining a central groove. Teach the client to listen carefully to the acoustic result. Tell him we do not want to hear that thumping sound.

The Long T

The Long T Method and the Cornerstone Approach can work well for the frontal lisp. It was described fully in the chapter six. The steps are summarized here:

1. Say /t/ and then "blow more air through the T" in order to produce a "Long T." By blowing more air through /t/, the client will produce a /t/ with strong aspiration. We write this as /tᶜ/. The excess air is not an /s/. It is simply aspiration.
2. Shape /tᶜ/ into /ts/ by helping the client to make the excess air "tinier" or by telling him to "squeeze the air." Modeling the sound will be critical here so the client will know what to do. And helping him listen carefully and use his powers of auditory discrimination will be the key to helping him shape the aspiration into /s/. The result will be a slightly distorted /ts/ blend.
3. Throughout, do not ask the client to produce /ts/ because he will slip into his frontal lisp pattern. In fact, tell him NOT to produce /s/.
4. A good /ts/ will result if the client focuses on the oral position for /t/. Make sure he does not lose control of tongue position for /t/. Make him keep the tongue in position behind the teeth for both the /t/ and the extra air. Allow for the /s/-part to be slightly distorted. In other words, focus on keeping the tongue behind the teeth and do not worry if the strident phoneme does not sound perfect at this point.
5. If the client cannot attain a sound close to /ts/ in this process, it is recommended to keep the air channel wide to allow more air to escape. It is more important to

rehearse sloppy sounds with a wide channel of air formed behind the teeth than it is to make any sound with the tongue protruding. Over time the sibilant sound will become more /s/-like.

6. If the client cannot narrow the channel to get an /s/-like sound, try switching to /ʃ/ It is a wider sound to begin with and thus may come more naturally to the client. He actually will be saying /tʃ/ if the tongue makes enough noise coming down from the palate.
7. Some clients make a sound that is more like /tʃ/ here. If so, go with it.

Tucking /θ/ Behind the Teeth

Perhaps the simplest way to get the tongue back behind the teeth for production of /s/ is to produce /θ/ and then to slide the tongue-tip back behind the teeth while still exhaling (figure 48). This gently slips the tongue tip behind the teeth. Most clients will produce a sloppy /s/ with a wide airs stream. But a client with exceptionally good oral motor skills will maintain midline air stream and will produce a decent /s/ right away. Occasionally this method will force a lateral lisp to occur as the client pulls the tongue back behind the teeth. Abandon the method if this is your result.

The Alternating /s/-and-/θ/ Slide

A great way to wake up the tip of the tongue and to get the tip behind the teeth is to have the client say, "th-s-th-s-th-s-th-s…" back and forth in one continuous air stream. This practice stimulates the tip of the tongue through tactile means as it rubs forward and back against the upper central incisors. A client with good oral-motor abilities will be able to do this action easily, and it will help him become aware of his tongue tip position. His /s/ will not be great, but his tongue should form a nice groove behind the teeth because it grooves naturally. Practice this sequence even if the /s/ sound that results is slightly distorted as long

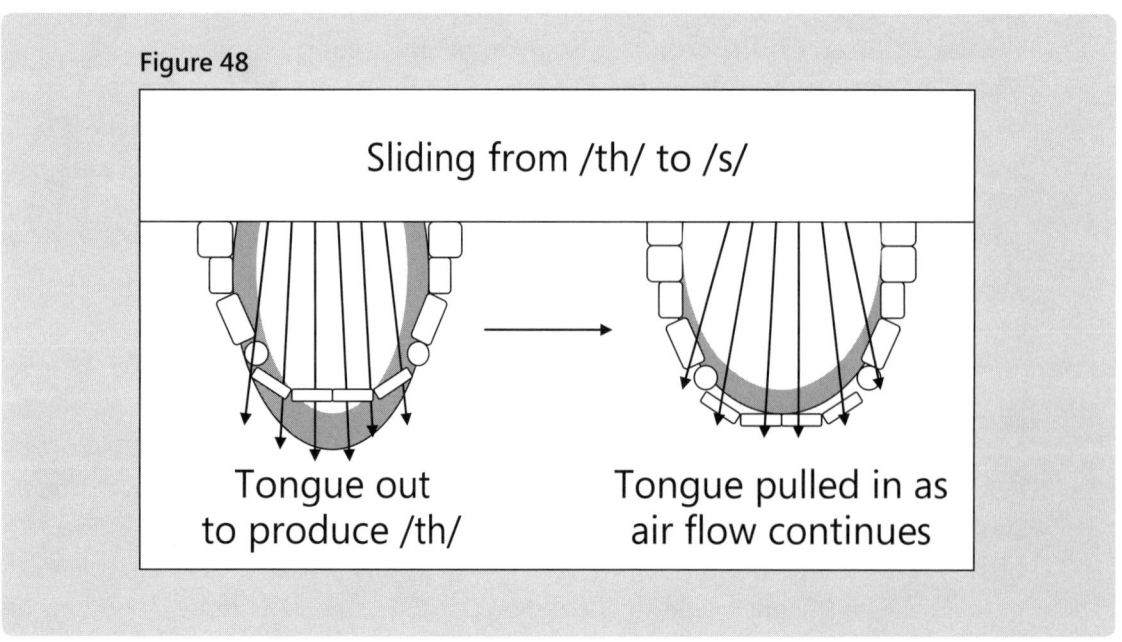

Figure 48

Sliding from /th/ to /s/

Tongue out to produce /th/ → Tongue pulled in as air flow continues as the air channel is midline. But do not practice it if the technique forces a lateral lisp when the tongue slips behind the teeth.

Creating Space for the Air Stream

Sometimes we literally have to teach clients how to make enough space for air to travel through after they learn to move the tongue back behind the central incisors. This is because they jam the tip of the tongue against the back of the incisors in order to recreate the feel of tip protrusion. We can tell the client not to push his tongue forward, and most clients at this level of treatment can comply. But if the client has trouble, there are at least two other easy ways to teach them to back the tip away to create more airspace.

- *Dental Floss:* Tie a wad of knots at the end of a piece of dental floss. Then draw the floss between the upper central incisors so that the knots sit behind them at the alveolar ridge (figure 49). Ask the client to rub the tip of the tongue against the knot to feel its position. Then ask him to push air out the mouth right at that spot. Tell him to make air flow around the knot on its way out. The dental floss knots work quite well for this task because the knots are so small that they can help the tongue create a tiny airspace.
- *Tool with Ball on the End:* Shop around at a "party store" and look for a swizzle stick or a cake-decorating tool that has a small ball on the end. The ball should be no bigger than 1/4-inch in diameter, and it should be permanently fastened to the stick. You don't want the ball to fall off and be swallowed by the client. Modern swizzle sticks and cake decorating tools are made of a single piece of plastic and serve this requirement. Place the tool in the mouth so that the ball sits behind the upper central incisors. Ask the client to feel for the ball with the tip of his tongue. Then ask him to blow air at it so that the air is forced around it in order to escape the mouth.

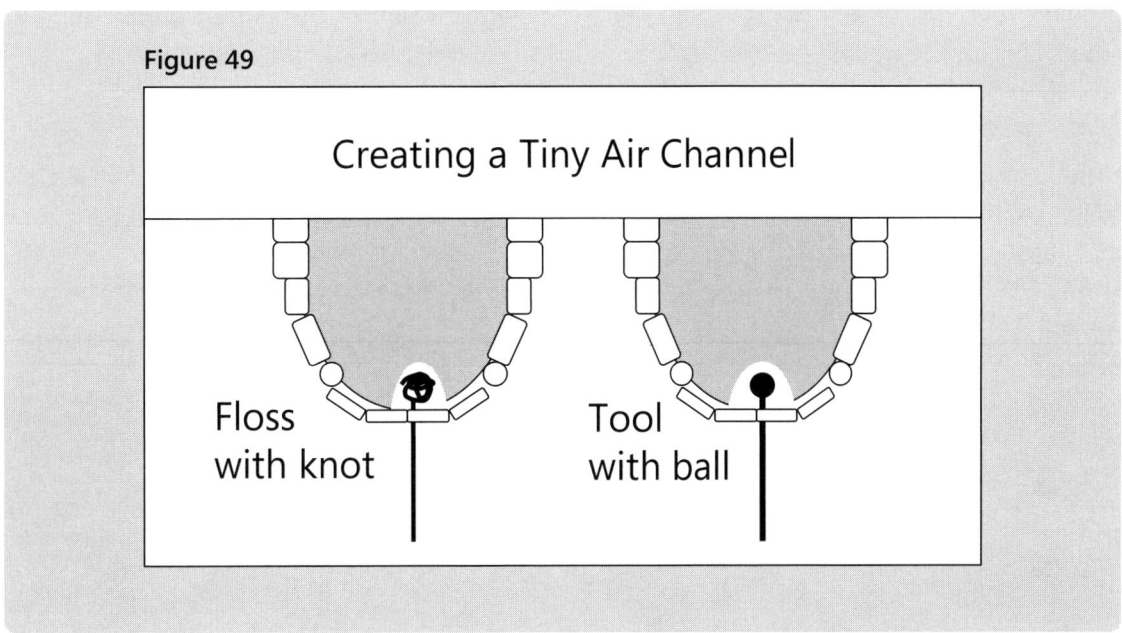

Figure 49

Creating a Tiny Air Channel

Floss with knot

Tool with ball

The ball on a stick works well to create a large central groove for air behind the teeth. However, there are two drawbacks. First, the ball is quite large and therefore will create too big of an air channel. The acoustic result is a sibilant sound with much distortion. Second, the stick forces the jaw to lower too far. It puts the jaw out of range for good sibilant production. This creates even further sound distortion. With these faults, however, the ball on a stick can be a great tool to introduce ideas about appropriate airflow.

Compare /s/ and /θ/ in Isolation

A client with a frontal lisp and good oral motor control should be able to produce a decent /s/ in isolation within the first few minutes, or at least within the first few sessions of therapy. Once /s/ emerges we can begin to contrast its acoustic quality and its feel of production with /θ/. We do this with the phonemes in isolation. Allow the client ample opportunity to hear and see you make these sounds. Then let him hear and feel himself make the sounds. Use a mirror for visual feedback, and use slight amplification to help the phonemes stand out. Experiment by saying one sound and then the other, back and forth. Talk about how the two sounds are similar and how they are different.

Minimal Pair Training for the Frontal Lisp

Another technique that can be very beneficial to the client with a frontal lisp is to differentiate between real words that are different only by a single phoneme. This has been called *minimal pair training* in the phonological literature. Comparing and contrasting /s/ with /θ/ in words is an excellent way to begin to train the ear to hear the differences that are marked by place shifts as they effect the meanings of words. This begins to address metaphonological skills. Word meaning differences bring a new awareness about the reason for doing this work. Minimal pair rehearsal also it is an excellent way to train the mouth, especially the tongue, to feel the subtle differences in place that differentiate /s/ from /θ/.

Model these words yourself for auditory discrimination training, and have the client produce them for placement training. Help the client recognize the importance of tongue placement on the meaning of words. The following word pairs can be used:

Minimal Pairs: /s/ and /θ/, Initial Position

sink	think
sank	thank
sought	thought
sick	thick
some	thumb
cymbal	thimble
saw	thaw
seem	theme
sigh	thigh
sing	thing

Minimal Pairs: /s/ and /θ/, Final Position

bass	bath
face	faith
miss	myth
mass	math
moss	moth
mouse	mouth
pass	path
Ross	Roth

Sentences with /s/ and /θ/ Minimal Pairs

I think about the sink.
I sank and said, "Thank you!"
I thought and sought and caught a frog.
It was thick and I got sick.
He had some gum on his thumb.
He played a cymbal with a thimble.
I saw it thaw.
Make a seam and write a theme.
That thing could sing!
The bass took a bath.
I had to face my faith.
Don't miss the myth.
I can't do math in mass.
The moth landed on the moss.
The mouse had a big mouth.
I can pass on the path.
Roth and Ross are already here.

Triune Practice

Triune practice is defined here as the rehearsal of three phonemes for the purpose of discovering the importance of place differences between them. In the case of the frontal lisp, the sets of three phonemes to be practiced include the voiceless set /θ/-/f/-/s/, and the voiced set /ð/-/v/-/z/. This rehearsal is a fantastic way to train the client to recognize the place relationships between each member of the sets. He discovers that /θ/, /f/ and /s/ are almost exactly the same except for their subtle differences in place of articulation. And he discovers the same for the set comprised of /ð/, /v/ and /z/. We begin rehearsing the three phonemes of each set in isolation. Then we move on to syllables and then to words. A few word sets constructed with /θ/, /f/ and /s/ can be used.

Words

Thor	Four	Sore
Think	Fink	Sink

Thin	Fin	Sin
Thad	Fad	Sad
Thigh	Fi*	Sigh
Thought	Fought	Sought

* As in the story line, "Fee-Fi-Fo-Fum. I smell an Englishman."

Sentences

Thor was sore from falling at four.
I think Mr. Sink is a fink.
It is a sin that the fin is so thin.
Thad is sad about the fad.
The giant slapped his thigh and then did sigh, "Fee-fi-fo-fum."
I thought, he sought, and we fought.

Front-to-Back Phoneme Practice

We also can contrast and rehearse all the voiceless and voiced hissing phonemes in isolation in the following sequences:

- Voiceless: /θ/ – /f/ – /s/ – /tʃ/ – /ʃ/
- Voiced: /ð/ - /v/ - /z/ - /dʒ/ - /ʒ/

When rehearsed in sequence, each of these sets provides direct instruction on the relationship between place of articulation and phoneme produced. The first phoneme in each set is perceived as the most anterior, and the final phoneme in each sequence is perceived as the most posterior.

Teenage and adult clients who are interested in language and speech find this work especially interesting for most have never thought about these similarities before. Rehearsing these sequences in this order teaches the client to pay very careful attention to the place of articulation and the acoustic result of each sound within the sequence. This is a powerful way to teach him the importance of precise articulation gained through specific place of production.

We can use a few word sets that represent all the voiceless and voiced sounds within the sets. The words can be compared for their acoustic and tactile similarities and differences.

Words

Th-word	**F-word**	**S-word**	**Ch-word**	**Sh-word**
Thor	four	sore	chore	shore
thin	fin	sin	chin	shin
thad	fad	sad	Chad	shad
thigh	fi	sigh	chai (tea)	shy

Sentences

1. Thor was sore he had to do his shore chore at four.
2. His shin, fin and chin were as thin as sin.

3. Chad and Thad ate shad, a sad fad.
4. Don't be shy about your thigh as you sigh and drink chai tea.

Discover the Tongue Tip

Many children need a little help to understand what the "tongue tip" is before they can begin to control it. The following simple ideas are designed to accomplish greater understanding of the tongue tip. Clients with excellent oral motor skills will be able to do most if not all of these right away. These ideas are to bring greater awareness of the tongue tip.

1. *Mirror:* Look in a mirror at the entire tongue; locate the tip
2. *Picture:* Draw a picture of the tongue and mark the tip
3. *Words:* talk about the tongue tip, name it, discuss it
4. *Texture:* Rub the tip with a rough surface: finger tip, toothbrush bristles, Nuk tip, toothette sponge
5. *Teeth:* Rub the tip up against the under surfaces of the upper central incisors
6. *Teeth:* Rub the tip around the mouth to discover all the teeth
7. *Tapping:* Tap the tip with the finger tip
8. *Raspberries:* Produce a lingua-labial raspberry to feel the excessive vibration of the tip against the lips
9. *Trill:* Trill the tip of the tongue against the aveolar ridge
10. *Lick:* Lick cold foods with the tip of the tongue: icecream, ice, ice pops. Make sure the client is using the tip and not the blade
11. *Poke:* Poke the tip of the tongue into a small round hole on a baby chew toy
12. *Click:* Click the tongue. Make sure the tip is the last part to flop down to the floor of the mouth.
13. *Pinch:* Gently pinch the tip of the tongue with the child's own fingertips
14. *Produce /t/:* Have the client say /t/ several times in a row (this assumes that he produces it with active elevation of the tongue tip)

Discover the Mouth

Some clients with a frontal lisp may need preliminary work to discover their mouth before they can benefit from the ideas above. Younger clients and those with cognitive, sensorimotor or oral-tactile sensitivity deficiencies are examples of clients in this group. These clients may need several weeks or months coming to greater awareness of their entire mouth before they can focus on the mobility of the tongue tip or the stability of the back lateral margins. The reader is referred to a good introductory class or book on oral-motor therapy. The following simple ideas will get you started.

1. *Snacking Activities:* Have the client eat a snack. Help him discover everything about the process: biting, chewing, transferring, forming a bolus, suctioning, swallowing, evacuating.
2. *Complete Evacuation:* Teach the client to move the tongue and lips enough, and to suction strong enough to completely evacuate the mouth of food after a final swallow.

3. *Mirror Activities:* Have the client discover his mouth at the mirror. View and label the all the parts. Put gloss on the lips and lotion on the face. Discuss the movements each part can make.
4. *Mouth Noises and Speech Sounds:* Have the client make a wide variety of mouth noises and speech sounds. Click the tongue, pop the lips, and produce a variety of raspberries. Practice all the vowels, stops, glides and nasals, and talk about how they are made.
5. *Blow Toys:* Have the client play with a variety of blow toys and talk about how the jaw, lips and tongue are used to sound them. Use whistles, horns, kazoos and so forth.
6. *Vocabulary of the Mouth:* Talk about the mouth, label its parts, discuss what each part can do.

Jaw Stabilization Techniques

As discussed in chapter four, the frontal lisp is more than a problem of tongue position. It also is a problem of jaw stability. Therefore, treatment of the frontal lisp also must include activities to stabilize the jaw for many clients. Once again we must stress that oral motor techniques like those that follow are not always necessary for every client. But they are necessary for a good number of these clients, and they are necessary always when oral motor skills are delayed or impaired.

We began to discuss jaw stabilization above when we instructed our clients to "Bite, smile and blow" earlier in this chapter. But some clients are unable to comply with a verbal instruction only. This group includes those who cannot follow the direction, those whose oral muscle tone is very low, those whose oral tactile sensitivity is very low, those with postural instability, and those too young or too distracted to carry out the direction. Therefore we need to incorporate more direct oral-motor activity to get the jaw to stabilize.

Biting Tools

A jaw stabilizer (a biting tool) helps clients understand the action of biting down at the molars. A biting tool is any long thin item on which is it safe for a client to bite. Biting on a tool brings *external stability* to the jaw. It keeps the jaw in a good position so that tongue work can be most effective.

- *Tools:* Biting tools can be wide or thin. Examples include straws, coffee stirrers, toothettes, and swizzle sticks. Wider tools take the jaw out of neutral and make the tongue stretch far to reach its destination against the palate (figure 50). Narrow tools pull the jaw up higher and therefore put the tongue in closer approximation to the palate (figure 51). The width of the flat side of a coffee stirrer brings the jaw up even higher and into neutral for speech. A straw works well if the client bites down and crushes it (figure 52). Using the narrowest biting tool places the jaw in a much better position than that achieved by biting molar-to-molar as described in "Bite, smile and blow" above.
- *Placement:* The client is given the item and told to bite down upon it with the molars on one side. The tool should be placed along the line of the teeth (figure 53

Figure 50

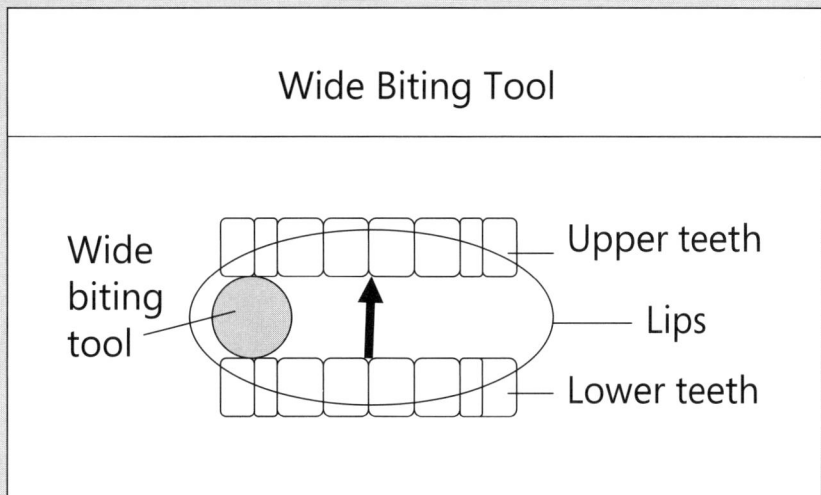

Figure 51

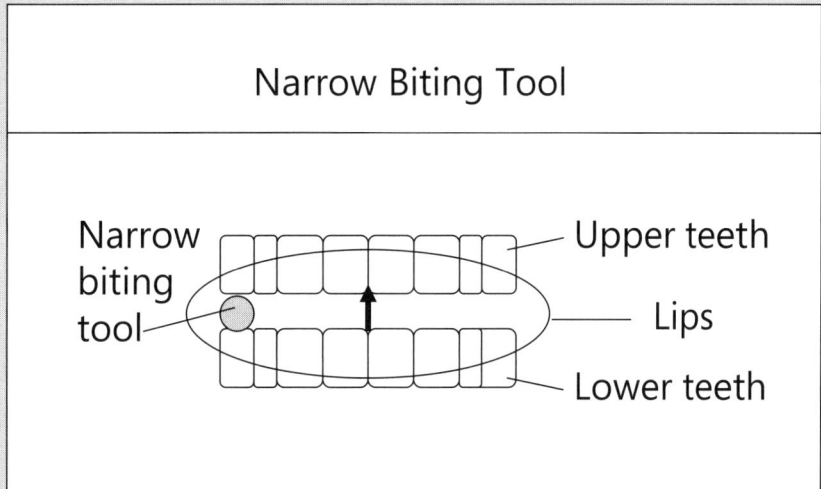

Figure 52

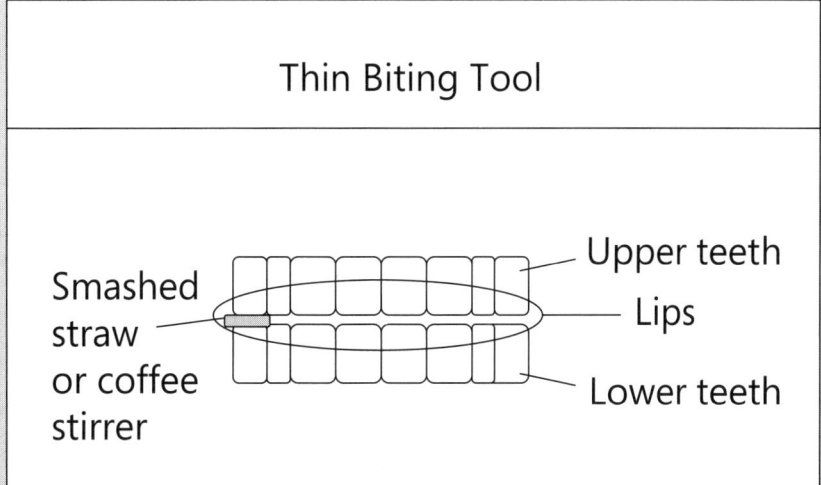

on page 113). Most clients need assistance in placing the jaw stabilizer in the right position. Give it a slight tug to make sure the client is biting down on it with his molars. (Please note that clients with cross bite often cannot hold a jaw stabilizer in place because of misalignment at the molars.)

- *Procedure:* With the tool in place, ask the client to produce /ts/. A good sound with the teeth in the right position should result. If the client pushes his tongue too far forward, he may lower the jaw to do so and the biting tool will fall out as a result. This is an excellent way to teach the client about holding a stabile jaw position. If he holds it stationary, the tool will stay in place. If he allows his jaw to lower, the tool will wiggle or fall out. And as long as he keeps the jaw elevated to hold the tool in place, his tongue should be forced to stay inside the mouth behind the teeth.

Resistance Training

Resistance training also can be used to facilitate improved masseter strength and jaw stability. The basic idea is to have the client bite down on a biting tool, and then to tug gently but firmly on it, pulling outward away from the mouth (figure 54). This gentle tugging stimulates the client to bite harder. If his molars are well aligned and he bites hard enough on the item, it will stay in the mouth between the teeth. If he does not bite hard enough, the item will slip out as you tug. This is a fantastic way to help a young client learn to bite harder. Simply tell him, "Don't let me pull it out!" He will be motivated to bite harder in order to prevent you from removing the item from between his teeth. Biting harder stimulates better co-contraction of the muscle of clenching. Please note here that we are not talking about a tremendous amount of force. Tug as if you were yanking on someone's hair to get their attention, not to hurt their head.

Resistance also can be accomplished by putting gentle but firm upward pressure against the jaw as the client opens the mouth (figure 55). I usually do this once on my frontal lispers and then show them how to do it to themselves. The client can resist his own jaw movements by leaning with his chin against the palm of his hand. (*Warning:* BE SAFE! Do not put so much pressure on the jaw that the temporomandibular joint is placed at risk. Use firm but gentle downward pressure, and stop immediately if the client complains of even the slightest pain.)

Tighten the Masseters

Clients can be taught to tighten up their bite by learning to clench the masseters voluntarily. The masseter muscles are the large muscles on the outside of the jaw, the ones that sling down around the corner of the jaw (figure 56 on page 114). These muscles bulge outward when we clench our teeth. Please understand that we are not talking about popping the jaw out of socket. We are talking about biting down firmly so that the masseters tighten up to their maximum extent.

It is strongly suggested that therapists try this themselves before they ask clients to do this technique. Place your fingertips on your masseters. Palpate at that point. Now clench your jaw and press into the masseters gently but firmly so that you can feel the clenching of the muscles themselves. I call this "popping" for the kids. It actually is just the feel of the

Figure 53

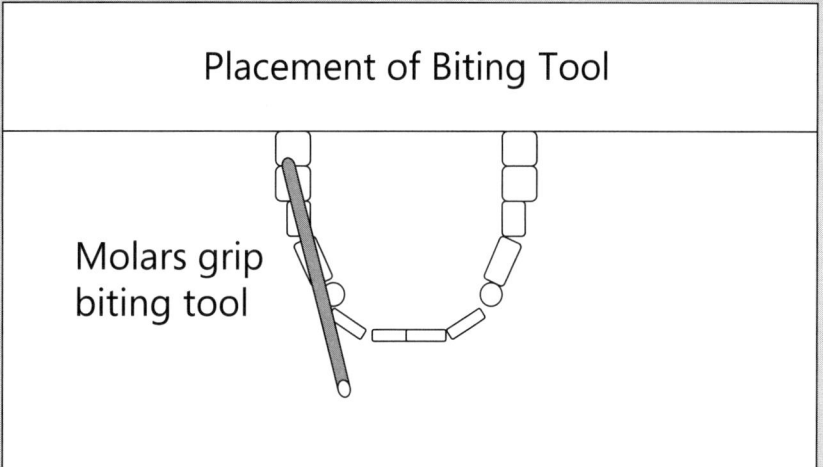

Placement of Biting Tool

Molars grip biting tool

Figure 54

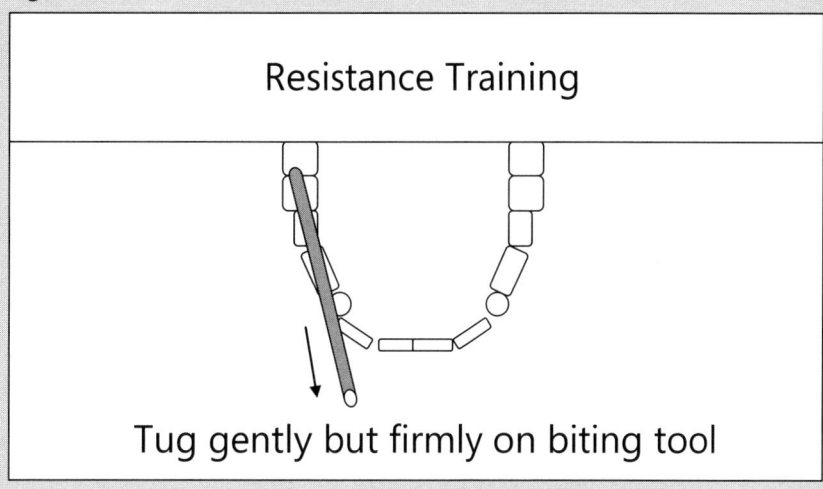

Resistance Training

Tug gently but firmly on biting tool

Figure 55

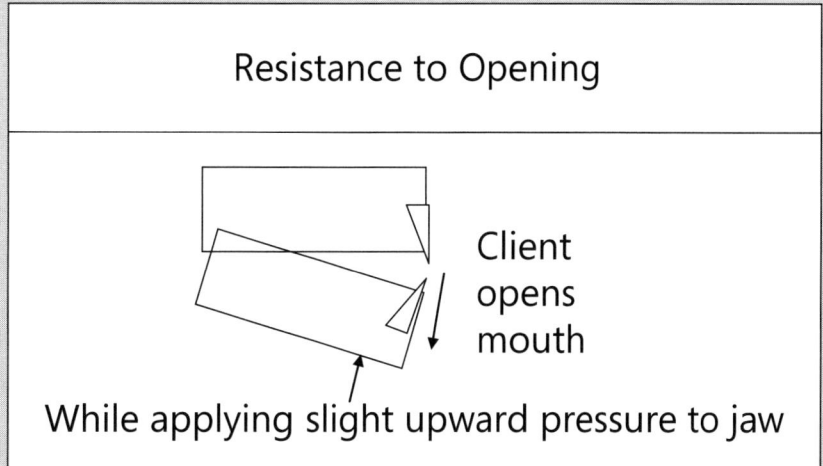

Resistance to Opening

Client opens mouth

While applying slight upward pressure to jaw

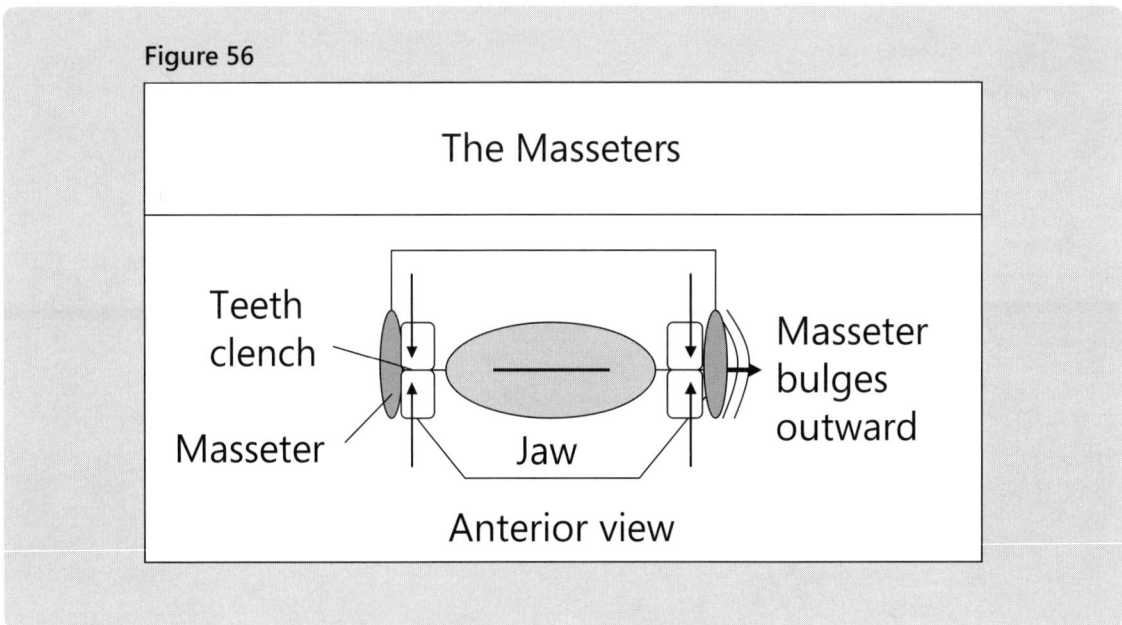

Figure 56

masseters hardening and thickening as the muscle fibers shorten in upon themselves. Repeat several times so that you are sure of the sensation. This will be easier to feel on yourself or another adult than it will be on a child's small and relatively weaker muscles. Practice ahead of time to make sure you know what you are feeling.

Teach the client to tighten the masseters as a way to help him learn how to draw the jaw upward firmly. The client can do it with or without a biting tool, but the biting tool helps make the activity easier to understand and it places the jaw in an excellent position. With a few practices children with average intelligence and a frontal lisp can perform this action as long as they do not have significant oral motor problems. "Popping the masseters" can be practiced a few times over a few sessions until he gets the idea of holding his jaw more upward and with more stability. (Please note that children with very low tone will take longer to learn this technique, and children with cognitive impairment may be unable to learn it at all.)

Feeding Techniques
Facilitating mature bite and chew patterns will help strengthen the masseters and subsequently facilitate jaw stabilization.

Bite: Teach the client to bite into foods of increasingly firm textures. For example, many of these clients cannot take a good strong bite into pizza. Teach them to "bite hard" or "make a strong bite." Use bagels, pizza or soft pretzels.

Chew: Also teach the client to use a mature chewing pattern instead of the immature munch pattern most of them use. The immature munching pattern emphasizes the downward movements of the jaw. It is a weak chewing pattern that persists while oral strength is low. The mature chewing pattern, on the other hand, emphasizes the upward movement of the jaw. It is a strong pattern that requires greater masseter strength, and it emerges as oral strength improves. This kind of therapy usually means working through the food texture groups and training the client to "chew hard" or "work really hard to mash up all the pieces." Teach him to really squeeze the masseters as he chews. Use gum also.

Establishing Back Lateral Tongue Stability

As discussed in chapter four, the frontal lisp is the result of both jaw and tongue instability. In this section we shall describe how to facilitate improved tongue stability in order to keep the tongue inside the mouth and behind the teeth.

To review, tongue stability occurs at its back lateral margins. Tongue stability is accomplished by maintaining close approximation of the tongue's back lateral margins (the stabilizing zones) to the molars and palate. The tongue's stabilizing zones remain in relative contact with the palate and molars located directly above them during almost all aspects of speech production. The sibilants are produced by moving the lateral margins of the tongue toward and away from the palate while maintaining back lateral stability at the stabilizing zones.

We can help our clients keep the tongue inside the mouth by developing this back lateral stability. We do this by helping him become aware of learning to control the stabilizing zones during all levels of speech production, from isolated sound to conversation. We can help our clients develop back lateral tongue stability in several ways.

Draw a Picture
Introduce the idea of back lateral tongue stability by drawing a picture of the tongue. Indicate the back lateral margins by shading them in (figure 57).

Stroke the Zones
Improved awareness of the back lateral margins can be gained by providing tactile stimulation to the areas. Use an item with a rough texture to stroke the back lateral margins in an anterior-to-posterior direction (figure 58). Use the bristles of a toothbrush, the sponge of a toothette or the bumps of a Nuk Toothbrush.

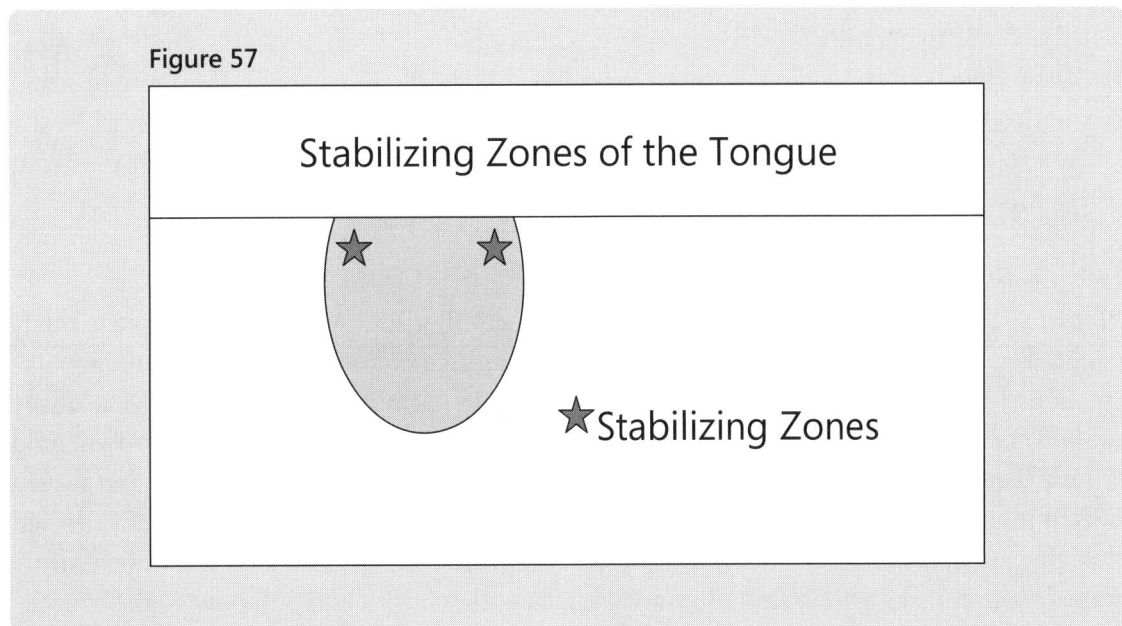

Figure 57

Smile

A client who habitually holds the jaw low and the tongue low and forward needs a program to encourage jaw elevation and posterior pulling of the entire tongue. Smiling broadly is a simple way to facilitate this (figure 59). Smiling broadly is an exercise the client with a frontal lisp can do daily to strengthen posterior movement of the tongue. Ask your client to smile broadly five times each time he brushes his teeth. With each smile, tell him to hold the smile for a count of five. Make sure he is smiling with his teeth articulating in the back at the molars. Telling the client to "bite" and then "make a big smile" can help. Biting first forces the tongue to pull inside the mouth. Activities to increase biting strength will help this process.

> *Try this yourself:* Place your jaw low and your tongue low and forward, and simply feel the position. Now smile broadly, spreading your lips as wide as you can to both sides. What happens to your jaw and tongue? You should feel that your jaw elevates and your tongue automatically pulls back inside your mouth, spreads laterally and elevates its lateral margins. Many clients will respond this way.

Bite Gently into the Zones

Ask the client to bite down onto the back lateral margins with the molars on both sides simultaneously. Most clients will be able to do this easily. Ask the client to bite gently but firmly several times to bring his awareness to those areas.

Establish the Butterfly Position

Once a client can bite down on the back lateral margins (see above), begin to teach him to stabilize his tongue there. Do so by asking the client to push upwards with the parts of the tongue on which the molars are biting. You are asking the client to perform two steps in sequence: to bite down on the back lateral margins and to push up against the molars with them. This action creates what I have called the "Butterfly Position" (figure 60).

The Butterfly Position is an exaggerated form of the basic tongue stabilization position. It allows a client to feel tongue stability in a gross and rudimentary form. This basic position is practiced a few times to solidify it as a motor position. The Butterfly Position pulls the entire tongue into the mouth. In this position the tongue tip cannot protrude out the front of the mouth.

Hold the Butterfly Position

Holding the Butterfly Position can be the key to elimination of the frontal lisp for many clients because it keeps the tongue from protruding. A professional speech-language pathologist once told me that she learned about tongue mobility and stability at one of my oral motor workshops and until then she had not known how to change her own mild frontal lisp pattern. After learning about the Butterfly Position, she went home and forced herself to put her tongue into that position and use it all the time as she spoke. She reported that that was all she had to do and her lisp disappeared in short order. Holding the Butterfly Position takes a great deal of awareness, strength, control and will power. The speech-language pathologist who used the technique was highly aware of her situation and highly

Chapter 8 — Remediation Specific to the Frontal Lisp   117

Figure 58

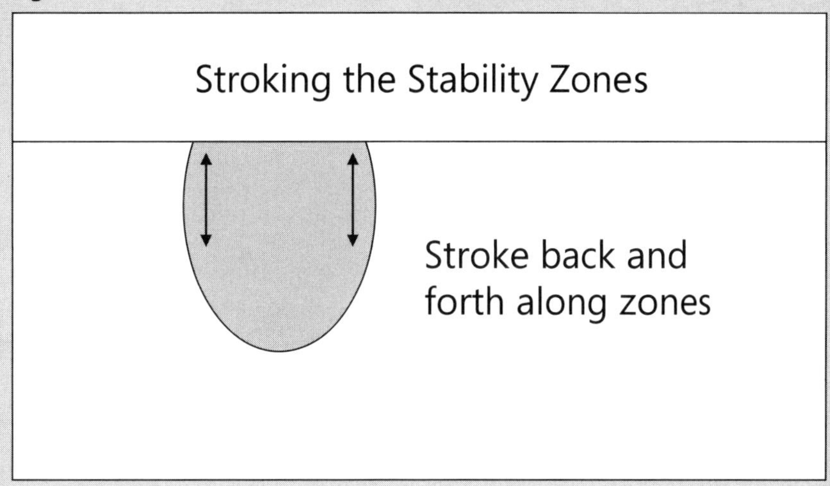

Stroking the Stability Zones

Stroke back and forth along zones

Figure 59

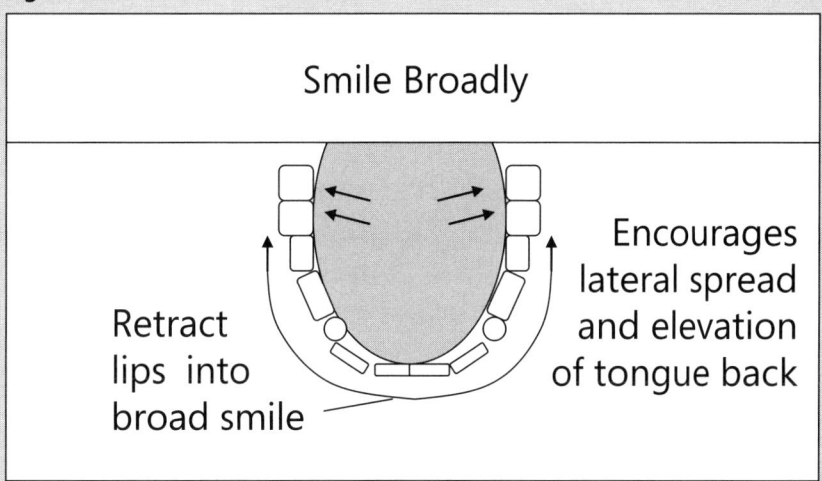

Smile Broadly

Retract lips into broad smile

Encourages lateral spread and elevation of tongue back

Figure 60

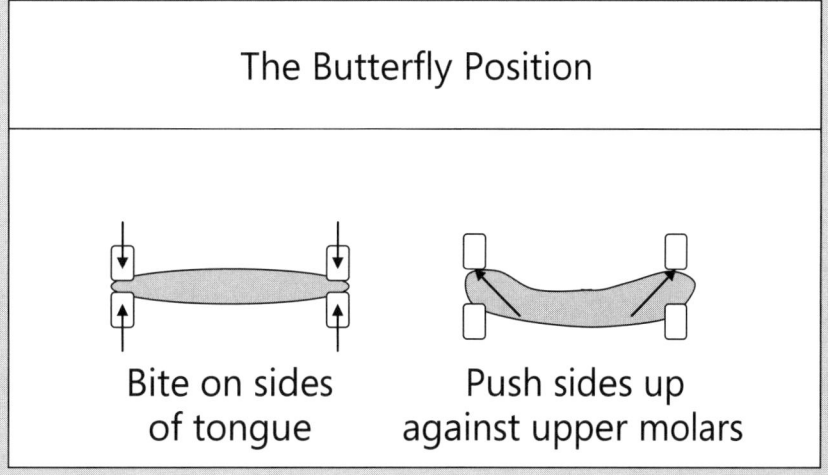

The Butterfly Position

Bite on sides of tongue

Push sides up against upper molars

motivated to make this change. Thus she was able to implement the technique and use it right away, during speech, oral rest and feeding activity.

Most clients, especially younger ones, are not able to take full control of the Butterfly Position like this right away. We must build their strength, stamina, awareness and control of it gradually. We can do so in the following sequence. Ask the client to hold the Butterfly Position:

1. Intermittently throughout the session
2. While speaking a word
3. While speaking a phrase
4. While speaking a sentence
5. While reading a paragraph
6. While engaging in conversation

Clients with relatively good oral motor control can advance their skills in this way within a few sessions. Therapy is designed to increase the difficulty of the butterfly task by increasing the length of time the client can hold the position while speaking. The progression is the same as that proposed in the traditional progression described in the beginning of this chapter except that our objective is different. In this current case we are building strength and endurance for the position.

Holding the Butterfly Position establishes back lateral tongue stability. This is the *static* or relatively unmoving part of speech the client must learn. Then, speaking while holding the Butterfly Position teaches the *ballistic* or moving part of speech sound production. Training static and ballistic movements independently and then together reflects the standard way many ballet, gymnastics, skating and other highly stylized movement patterns are learned. The position is learned, exercised, strengthened and controlled, and then it is put into a movement pattern.

Don't worry if your client's speech becomes distorted because he is beginning to hold the Butterfly Position while reading or speaking. Remember, you are training him to use a new motor pattern. It will be used grossly or sloppily at first. But his movements will become more refined with time and his speech will clear up.

Spread the Back of the Tongue
Some clients are unable to spread the back of the tongue well enough to bite down on both back lateral margins simultaneously for the Butterfly Position. This is fairly common in some forms of oral-motor delay and oral-tactile defensive behavior. When this occurs we employ techniques to spread or widen the back.

The least invasive method we can use is to ask the client to use the back sides of his tongue to feel his molars on either side. Ask him to try to stretch his tongue toward the molars on each side. Many clients are able to do this right away. However, a few clients will need a more powerful stimulus. The most powerful is to stimulate the gag reflex (figure 61). The gag response will cause an automatic widening of the entire tongue as it flattens and flares in response to touch stimulation. Stimulating the gag is not a pleasant technique to use in treatment, however. But it can be quite effective when used selectively with some clients.

Another method to help with lateral spread at the back lateral margins is to push medially into the tongue from the side. Ask the client to push against the stimulus (figure 62).

Elevate the Back Lateral Margins

Some clients are unable to figure out how to push the back lateral margins of the tongue up in order to achieve the Butterfly Position. A method must be employed to stimulate this upward movement. A proprioceptive technique using resistance will work best. Press gently but firmly downward (caudally) into the back lateral margins. Use a firm and textured item such as a Nuk toothbrush. Ask the client to push upward at the points where he feels your object (figure 63 on next page).

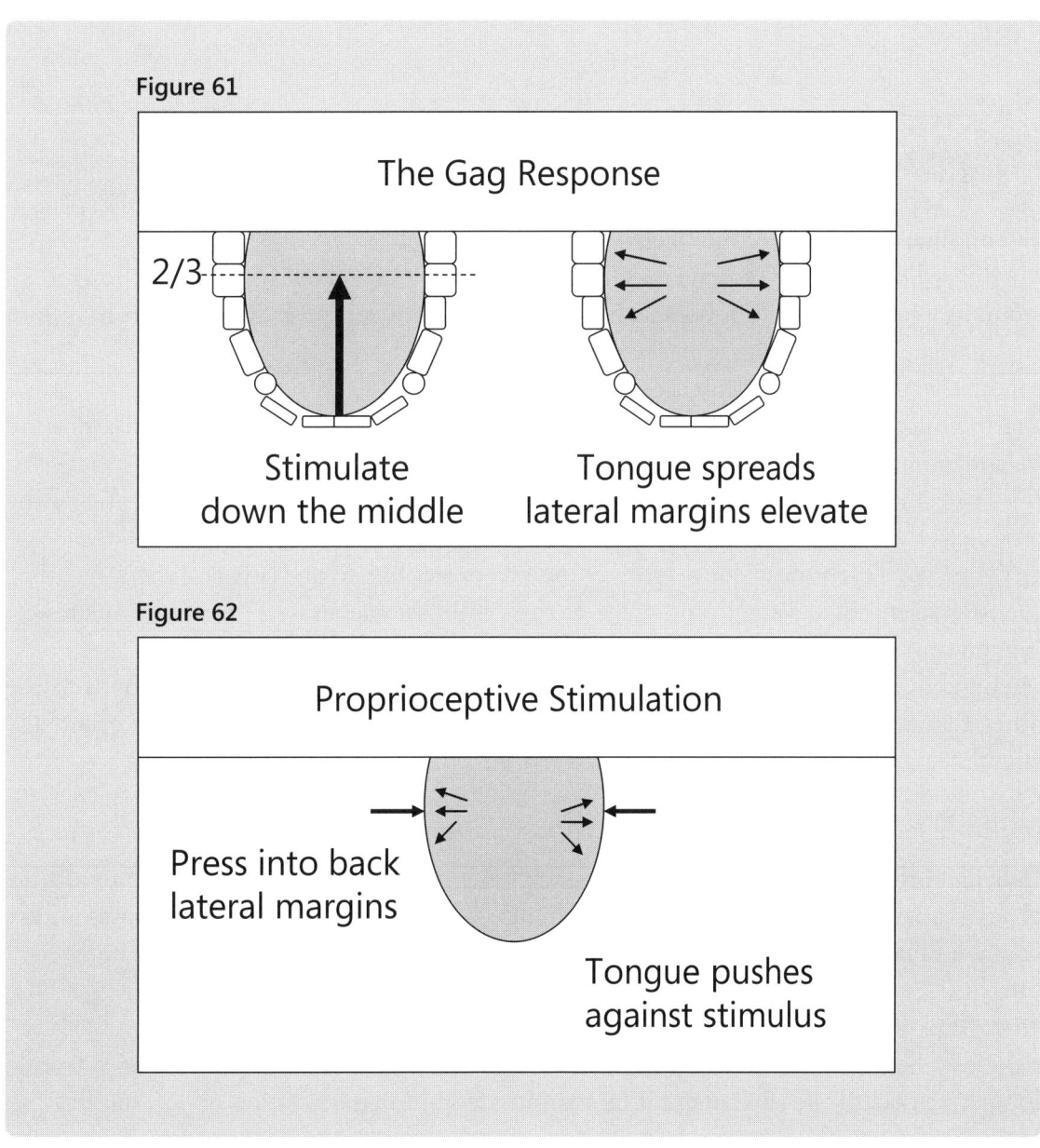

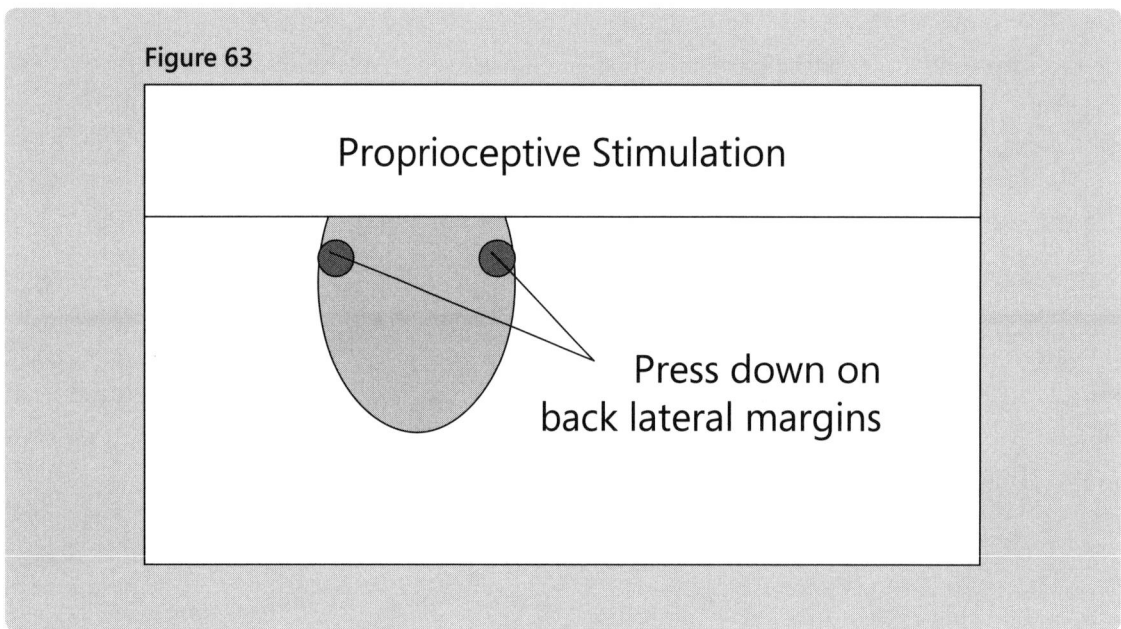

Figure 63

Proprioceptive Stimulation

Press down on back lateral margins

Feeding Techniques

Feeding techniques can be employed to increase strength and control of lateral elevation and midline depression of the tongue.

<u>Bolus Formation:</u> Use dry crackers to teach your client how to move his tongue all around to gather food for a bolus. Have him watch in a mirror as he eats, and have him view a bolus you form with a mashed cracker. Motivate him to get his food to form into a cohesive wad. Bolus formation is only possible when the tip and sides of the tongue elevate and the middle depresses. The client's motivation to form a bolus stimulates him to move his tongue in increasingly mature patterns in order to achieve it.

<u>Tip Elevation:</u> Use the eating of a dry snack to teach your client to use the tip of the tongue to sweep the entire mouth to gather moist bits of food for a second swallow.

<u>Transfer:</u> Teach the client to transfer food from midline to one side and then the other. Transfer strengthens lateral movement of the whole tongue and eventually stimulates elevation of the tongue's lateral margins.

<u>Lateralization:</u> Teach the client to lateralize food from one side of the mouth to the other. Lateralization also strengthens lateral movement of the whole tongue and eventually stimulates elevation of the tongue's lateral margins.

Multiple Paths of Training for the Frontal Lisp

Individual therapy sessions can contain many techniques and can be focused on multiple objectives when we work on the frontal lisp. Let's consider one therapy session as an example for clarity.

Sam

Sam is a client of mine who is eight years of age and in the third grade. He has a frontal lisp pattern on all the sibilants, and he has interdental tongue position on /t/, /d/ and /n/.

The fourth lingua-alveolar, /l/, has not emerged and is substituted with /w/, as is /r/. Sam demonstrates oral-motor immaturity in speech and feeding, but he has no other identified cognitive or neuromuscular problems.

Sam's work is designed to mature his oral movement patterns while stimulating him to listen to, think about and produce his target phonemes. He cannot produce his target phonemes with perfect articulation at this time because his oral motor patterns are immature. But the work we are doing on jaw strength and stability eventually will match the skill he needs to stabilize his jaw in a partially-graded open position for his targets. This session was typical and took about 30-minutes. It included the following:

1. *Chit-Chat:* I always begin with a minute or two of chit-chat during which I can quickly evaluate how the client's speech has progressed since our last session (2 minutes).
2. *Production of /t/, /d/, and /n/ with Correct Placement:* We reviewed our lists of /t/, /d/ and /n/ words placed in his speech binder during prior weeks. These were simple one-syllable words with initial targets. Sam was required to produce them with the jaw clenched and the tongue behind the teeth. He repeated each word until it was correct and I drew stars next to each word as it was produced correctly. We talked about how great he was doing on this work. I reminded him that the words sound "funny" for now but that he was doing exactly as I required. I told him I was proud that he was following my instructions, and that the more carefully he followed them, the sooner he would be done with this work (4 minutes).
3. *Auditory Discrimination Training:* I produced words with initial /s/ or /θ/ and Sam's job was to point to the correct word written on a page in his binder. I used minimal pairs such as *thin* and *sin* (2 minutes).
4. *Production of /s/ in Isolation:* Sam practiced the Long T and was learning to shape it into /s/. He was placing tiny dog stickers on a picture of a large doghouse he drew himself. He got one tiny dog sticker for every correct production. He practiced this off-and-on throughout the entire session. At the end there were about 30 dogs in, on and around his doghouse (on-and-off throughout session; maybe 2 minutes altogether).
5. *Increasing Jaw Strength:* Sam learned to "Pop his Masseters." He also ate four gummy bears while feeling his masseter muscles contract. We talked about how strong his jaw was getting (3 minutes).
6. *Jaw Stability in Speech:* Sam and I took turns reading riddles out of a *Highlights* magazine. We read with clenched jaws in order to stabilize the jaw in gross fashion and to prevent the tongue from slipping forward. We had a good laugh and talked about how some people speak this way when they are mad. He spoke freely about a particular teacher he had who "always talks that way." This became the main activity of the session because he was doing much better on it that day than he had the week before, and because we were having such a good time (8 minutes).
7. *Increasing Back Lateral Tongue Stability:* Sam learned to bite down on the back lateral margins of the tongue. We discussed how he is to do this at home every day after brushing his teeth. His mother was part of this discussion at the end (4 minutes).

8. *Cognitive Stimulation:* We made a list of words that contain /s/. These were words of high value and importance in his life. The list included the names of his friends (*Chri_s_topher* and *Ca_s_ey*), the name of his dog (*Bo_s_co*), the nick-name used by his family for his sister (*_S_issy*), and the name of his town (*_S_nohomish*.) We put these into his speech binder and practiced these with a clenched jaw. He was instructed to practice saying these words every day with a clenched jaw. We also wrote them on an index card that he was going to tape on his dresser next to his bed. He was to practice these names one time each in bed at night before going to sleep. This activity also was done at the end with his mother in the room. She helped think of the names (2 minutes).
9. *Planning:* I talked with Sam and his mother about the other phonemes he would need to work on, including /l/ and /r/. I modeled correct production of the phonemes. We talked about his progress so far, and we talked about how long therapy might take (3 minutes).

Severe Cases

In the most severe cases, a frontal lisp occurs in the middle of a severe expressive speech disorder related to apraxia, dysarthria and/or severe cognitive impairment. In these cases the frontal lisp is viewed as one tiny part of the neuromuscular, sensorimotor integrative or intellectual problem, and thus considered quite insignificant in comparison to the client's other speech, language and communication needs. The frontal lisp itself may never become a focus of treatment for these clients.

In cases of severe receptive and expressive speech and language disorder, speech treatment is geared toward maturing the oral-motor system, stimulating auditory awareness and processing, and facilitating a wide variety of expressive speech needs including syllables, prosodic features, nasality, consonants and vowels. The oral-motor work will be designed to lead toward maturation of the skills that underlie mature production of the sibilants. This will include: jaw mobility and stability, tongue mobility and stability, differentiation of oral movement, and oral-tactile awareness and discrimination. Therapy also will include facilitation of basic cognitive processing, auditory awareness and discrimination, and general communication skills.

The sibilants themselves may or may not emerge in a client with a severe expressive speech disorder. Progress will depend upon a number of factors including cognitive level, neuromuscular status and number of words spoken by the child. If the sibilants do emerge, the phonemes may be produced with a frontal or a lateral lisp. In either case the lisp itself probably will be left uncorrected.

Pulling It All Together for the Frontal Lisp

The general plan for the frontal lisp is one of working from least invasive to more invasive. Again we always do as little as possible at all times. That means we start with the simplest, easiest, most superficial and least invasive techniques. Over time we include techniques that are increasingly more complex and invasive. We advance through therapy as its results dictate. The plan is can be summarized in four basic stages.

Least Invasive

Approach the frontal lisp first from a traditional articulation perspective. This means to get the client to say his targets from simple models. Model the correct way to say the target and see if he can follow your lead. This is simple but it is the essence of traditional articulation therapy. Many clients can make the appropriate changes this way. It is straightforward teaching through visual and auditory means. There is no need to get more invasive with technique if simple models work for your client. This method works for some but not all clients. If they all were this easy, this therapy would be very easy. In fact, if all of our clients responded to this simple method, a technician, not a therapist, could do this work.

More Invasive

At first we get a little more complex by going beyond the simple model. We can do so by employing the Long T Method. Remember, /t/ is a movement springboard for /s/. We use /t/ to help the client understand and begin to control tongue position, i.e., to keep it inside the mouth and behind the central incisors. With /ts/ we are beginning to alter how he controls oral movements, and we are doing so in the way that toddlers naturally do so.

Even More Invasive

The next level of treatment is to introduce toys and tools to help with oral positioning. For example, we have advocated the use of a Biting Tool in working with a frontal lisp. The biting tool is used to help stabilize the jaw in a finely graded open position. A biting tool such as a straw or coffee stirrer helps a client learn to put his jaw into correct position for sibilant production. A biting tool might be thought of as an aid or a crutch. We introduce these types of aids only when we need to. And we fade them out as soon as the client has learned the lesson he needs from them.

Most Invasive

The most invasive work we can do in articulation therapy is to introduce tactile and proprioceptive techniques for the purpose of maturing the oral motor system for correct speech sound production.

For example we advocated the use of chewing gum to strengthen the masseters for jaw stability because jaw stability is needed to facilitate appropriate tongue position. The purpose of such procedures is to aid in the maturation of oral movements. *But oral-motor work by itself to mature oral movement patterns by themselves will not improve speech*. It will only support and give better foundation for and allow success in the speech work you are doing.

In other words, do not replace articulation therapy with oral-motor therapy. For example, do not replace your work on the sibilants with work on chewing because learning to chew better will not help your client's speech. Instead, use oral-motor therapy techniques as a means to support and help develop the speech targets you have in mind. We use oral-motor techniques *within* a program of articulation therapy. Better oral control is not your end product: better speech is.

Chapter 8 Summary
Remediation Specific to the Frontal Lisp

- The ultimate *goal* of therapy for the frontal lisp is to establish correct articulation of the misarticulated phonemes in all speaking situations.

- Traditionally, a client with a frontal lisp who demonstrated no other speech or language delay or disorder was enrolled in articulation therapy by age eight or nine years of age. Today we can see children with a frontal lisp at younger ages because parents often are willing to take them for private speech services.

- Traditional articulation therapy taught us to work in the following sequence when training a client to produce new sounds: isolation, syllable, word, phrase, sentence, paragraph and conversation.

- A client's readiness to pronounce any one of the six sibilant phonemes affected by the frontal lisp often is a therapist's main criteria for initial phoneme selection.

- Work on one phoneme causes positive development on other phonemes.

- The most straightforward technique for the client with a frontal lisp is to tell him to keep his tongue inside his mouth while speaking.

- Perhaps the oldest technique is to instruct the client to "Bite, smile and blow." This old-fashioned technique works wonders with the "easy" client who has no oral-motor problems.

- The Long T can work well for the frontal lisp. It works only when clients can produce /t/ with correct tongue position behind the teeth.

- A simple technique to learn correct tongue position is to produce /θ/ and then to slide the tongue-tip back behind the teeth while still exhaling.

- Wake up the tip of the tongue by having the client say, "th-s-th-s-th-s-th-s..." back and forth in one continuous air stream.

- Sometimes we have to teach clients how to make enough air space.

- Use minimal pairs to benefit the client with a frontal lisp. Begin with /s/ and /θ/ contrasts.

- Individual therapy sessions can be focused on multiple objectives when we work on the frontal lisp.

- Many children need a little help to understand what the "tongue tip" is before they can begin to control it.

- Some clients with a frontal lisp need preliminary work to discover their mouth.

- Treatment of the frontal lisp also must include jaw stabilization activities for many clients.

- We can help our clients keep the tongue inside the mouth by developing back lateral stability in many ways including the "Butterfly Position."

- The frontal lisp itself may never become a part of treatment in the most severe cases of expressive speech and language disorder.

- The general plan for the frontal lisp is one of working from least invasive to most invasive.

Chapter 9

Remediation Specific to the Lateral Lisp

The lateral lisp can be one of the most difficult errors to fix. This is despite the fact that it has traditionally been categorized as a "mild" articulation error. The reference to the mildness of this error seems to be related to the fact that only a few phonemes are affected by it. But there usually is nothing "mild" about the lateral lisp. It is one error that many therapists dread.

There are three main reasons that therapists have difficulty "fixing" a lateral lisp. First, it is imperative that one understands the oral movements and positions necessary for correct production of the sibilants as outlined in chapters two and three. Second, it is critical that one understands the oral movements and positions of the error at hand. These were described in chapter five. Third, it is absolutely critical that one reinforces only those productions that are really correct.

Readers who have skipped ahead to this chapter in order to find a quick fix to their problematic lateral lisp need to go back and carefully read chapters two, three and five. If you have studied those chapters and/or you feel you understand the oral positions and movements related to correct and incorrect airflow, then please feel free to continue here. If not, may I strongly urge you to go back to the beginning of this book and start there.

Goal and Objectives of Therapy

The primary *goal* of therapy for the lateral lisp is to establish correct articulation of the misarticulated phonemes in all speaking situations. Our first and primary *objective* is to establish midline air stream. With a midline air stream established, we move on to other objectives as necessary for the individual client. The *techniques* of this chapter support the objectives and build skill toward the final goal. Establishing midline air stream is the most important and fundamental objective of therapy for the lateral lisp. No matter what else we do, we must establish midline air stream. All the techniques of this chapter are designed to move the client in this direction.

Onset of Treatment for the Lateral Lisp

How old must a client be before he can benefit from treatment for a lateral lisp? Treatment techniques can be effective with children as young as two years of age. However, when the lateral lisp is the only error pattern, most therapy in the public schools and privately is withheld until the client is eight or nine years of age, or even older. Unlike the frontal lisp, however, waiting to treat a lateral lisp is not done to see if the client will outgrow the problem.

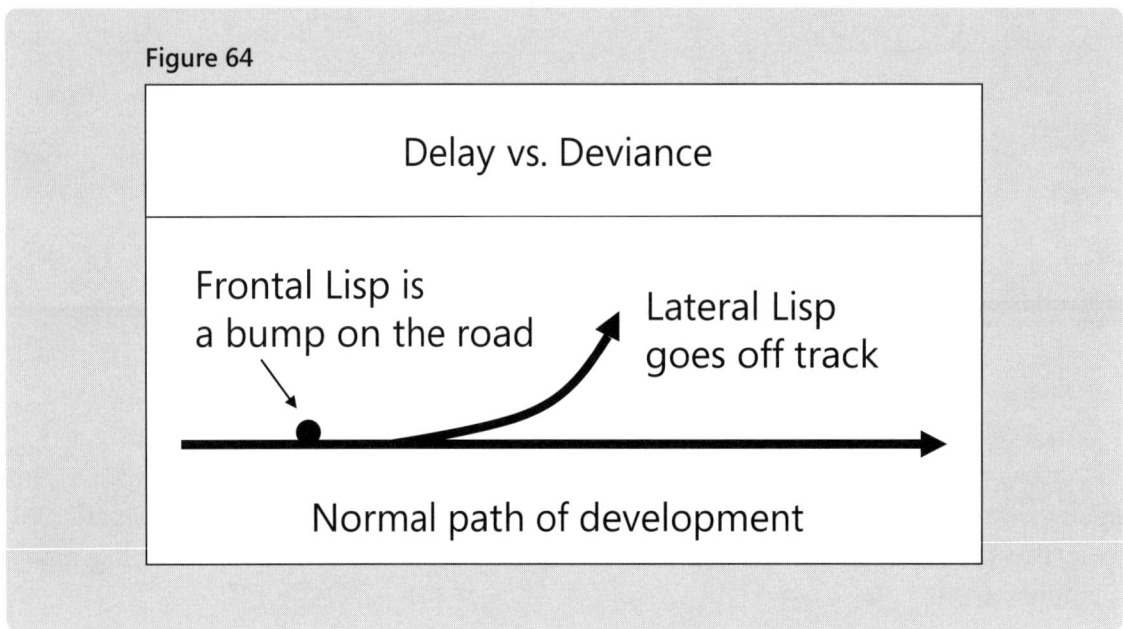

Figure 64

He won't outgrow it. The wait is to assure that the client can understand the problem and its solution. We wait so the client can comprehend what we are trying to change.

Delay vs. Deviance

The lateral lisp is a *deviant* as opposed to a *delayed* oral-motor pattern. A deviant oral-motor pattern is one that has taken a child off the normal path of development. A deviant oral-motor pattern leads him in another direction, an inappropriate direction (figure 64). A child cannot outgrow a lateral lisp because his speech development is no longer on the normal developmental path. Like heading south when he should be heading north, the client will never get where he needs to go as long as he is heading in the wrong direction. A deviant oral movement pattern that is habituated will not change without instruction designed to get the client back on the right path. As such, a client will keep a lateral lisp pattern until he figures out how to get on the right path. Some people figure this out by themselves. Most need help and that's what speech therapy for this error is all about.

Organization of Therapy

Like our chapter on the frontal lisp, the treatment techniques of this chapter are arranged from simple to complex. The easiest techniques are tried first to see if they will be effective for the client. More invasive and complex techniques are withheld until the client proves that he needs them. As in our work with the frontal lisp, therapy is designed to use as few techniques as possible within each session. We shall discuss techniques that can be used with children of all ages, including those as young as two years of age.

Client Awareness

Developing a midline air stream begins with client awareness of the problem he has with his air stream. He must be told that his air stream is moving through his mouth in the

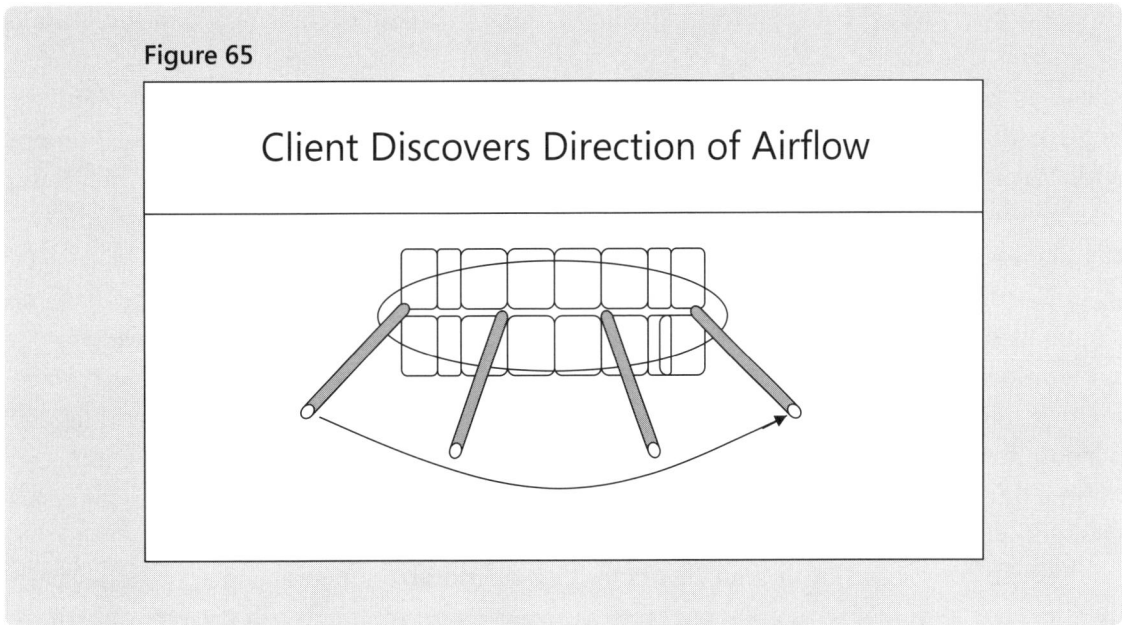

Figure 65

Client Discovers Direction of Airflow

wrong direction. He must understand that his air stream is escaping laterally, and that medial air stream is what is required. The easiest way to teach him this idea is to use a straw. We discussed using a straw as a diagnostic tool in chapter five. Here we are talking about using it as a therapeutic activity. This can be done during the evaluation session or during the first session of therapy.

Give the client the straw and ask him to place one end at his incisors. Ask him to say /s/ and to sustain it while sweeping the straw from the incisors to the molars on one side. Repeat from midline to the other side. Tell the client to listen carefully in order to discover where his air is coming out. Have him slowly sweep the straw back-and-forth like this until he can figure out where his air is escaping (figure 65). Work the straw for him if the client has difficulty.

The client should discover that his air stream for /s/ is escaping from between the teeth on one side or the other, or both. Point out what is unique about his air stream, and then tell him how the rest of us produce /s/. I usually tell my clients, "The correct way to make 'S' is to make the air come right out the middle." It is always amazing to me to realize that the client and his parents have no idea what is wrong with the sound, but most do not. They may know the sound is in error, but they usually have no idea why or how. Discovering that they are making the air stream come out the wrong direction is an eye-opening experience for them. I have seen clients change their sibilants immediately upon hearing this information.

Repeat this process for the other phonemes in error so the client sees the pattern. Use this activity to introduce your objective of therapy: to produce a midline air stream. This activity can be repeated as often as necessary. It's an excellent way to remind the client why he is coming to speech.

Return to the Normal Path

A good old-fashioned traditional technique to remediate a lateral lisp is to teach the client to substitute a frontal lisp for his lateral one. This technique has been around for a long time. I am unsure where the idea first came from, but many therapists across the United States and Canada have used it and have attested to its effectiveness.

Why teach a client to use one error instead of another? The answer is simple. Remember that the frontal lisp is an error that occurs on the normal path of speech development while the lateral lisp is not. When we train a client to substitute a frontal lisp for his lateral one, we are leading his oral movement patterns back onto the path of normal development. It's a way to turn the situation around in a natural way.

Although this method is an excellent one, it has one very important drawback: some clients won't do it. It has been my experience that the average child of four or five years of age or older already has an internal sense that a frontal lisp is an immature speech movement pattern. They say it is "baby talk." Therefore some children won't use a frontal lisp on purpose if they are determined not to present themselves as babies anymore. A client also may be unwilling to try a frontal-for-lateral lisp approach if he is shy or ashamed about his speech.

We can coax some but not all clients to try the frontal-for-lateral lisp approach. Luckily, there is a simple way to go about this with those who refuse. Teach them to substitute sibilant phonemes with /θ/ and /ð/. There is no important difference between a frontal lisp and /θ/ or /ð/. Therefore, teaching a client to make these substitutions on purpose essentially is the same as training him to use a frontal lisp instead of his lateral one. This method will work only with those clients who produce both /θ/ and /ð/ correctly. Use words lists with initial target sibilants. Substitute /θ/ for the voiceless sibilants and /ð/ for the voiced ones. Write the words out correctly and then again using "th" in place of the target. Practice this skill in word, phrases, sentences and conversation. Most children find this practice interesting and amusing. In fact some find it hilarious. It motivates them to pursue this idea with many different types of words. Children often go along with this idea if they can see the words written and if they perceive this as a reading or spelling task. This prevents them from thinking about this as talking like a baby. The goal of this work is to habituate a gross midline air stream during sibilant productions. This is essentially what many toddlers do during the period when they are acquiring the sibilants.

Target Word	Practice Form	Target Word	Practice Form
Sand	Thand	Soap	Thoap
Seven	Theven	Shoe	Thoe
Shop	Thop	Shovel	Thovel
Chop	Thop	Chew	Thew
China	Thina	Zoo	Thoo
Zebra	Thebra	Zero	Thero
Jump	Thump	Jam	Tham
Jar	Thar		

Phrases with th/s, t/sh, t/ch
Sand – the thand in my boot
Seven – theven and then eight
Shop – thop around town

Soap – the thoap on a rope
Shoe – the thoe rack
Shovel – thovel the driveway

Chop – thop the wood
China – the good thina

Chew – thew gum

Phrases with ð/z and ð/J
Zoo – the thoo in Tampa
Zero – thero credibility
Jam – tham and bread

Zebra – the thebra and her baby
Jump – thump down
Jar – a full thar

Sentences with θ/s, θ/sh and θ/ch
Sand – The thand paper didn't work.
Seven – I want theven of them.
Shop – Come thop with me.
Chop – I will thop wood for the fire.
China – I went to Thina in 1999.

Soap – My thoap ran out.
Shoe – Her thoe didn't fit.
Shovel – Thovel the walk tomorrow.
Chew – Don't thew gum at school.

Sentences with ð/z and ð/J
Zoo – The thoo won't open until May.
Zebra –-The thebra can eat hay all day.
Zero – We made it to thero hour.
Jumped – He thumped down from the table.
Jam – Put peanut butter and tham on my bread.
Jar –The thar is only half full.

Paragraph with θ/s – soap, some, suds, so
Take the thoap to the laundry room and do a load for me. I will dry the load thome time later in the day. That thoap will work well. Don't you think tho?

Paragraph with θ/sh – shoe, shod, should, shine
My thoe is muddy. I had it re-thod yesterday. I thould have had them thine it too.

Paragraph with θ/ch – chew, cherry, chop
Thew the therry well. Or thop it up, and then eat it.

Paragraph with ð/z – zebra, zoo, Zanzibar
A new thebra will come to the thoo tomorrow. It will be a female and we hope it will have a baby while here. The thebra will come from near Thanthibar.

Paragraph with ð/J – jump, Josh, Jimmy, Jake, janitor
Thump down, Thosh. Thimmy will have a turn after you, and then Thake. After all three of you thump, a thanitor will clean up the room.

Conversation
Conversation constructed around any of the words presented in this section will do for practicing the substitution of /θ/ and /ð/ for all words with initial sibilants. Ignore any other sibilants that come up in other positions of words.

Substituting Everything

A way to stretch your clients skills into experiencing a frontal lisp pattern is to have conversations in which every word is produced with an initial /θ/ or /ð/. For example, the question, "See what I mean?" would be produced, "Thee that thigh thean?" This is a super-experience of the frontal lisp. It is overkill. But it can be an effective way to help a client begin to habituate a midline air stream. Remember, a midline air stream – not perfect phoneme production – is your initial objective.

Blowing Over the Tongue

Another simple way to teach a client to attain midline air stream is to have him blow over the dorsum of his tongue while it is protruding, and then to pull it back in while continuing to blow. Tell him to pay attention to the air as he blows lightly over the top surface of his tongue. Then ask him pull his tongue inside and see if he can keep the air blowing lightly over the surface (figure 66). Many clients will slip right into their lateral lisp pattern when they bring the tongue inside behind the teeth. But you may have success with a few clients so the technique is worth trying. Tell your client not to try to say any particular phoneme, just to keep blowing gently as his tongue pulls in. Ask the client to make the tongue move forward and back against the upper incisors as he continues to blow over the dorsum of the tongue.

If the client can keep his tongue in a fairly neutral position as he slips it back inside behind the teeth, he will be producing a very gross midline sibilant sound. Do not worry about sloppiness of the sound, and do not worry if it does not sound like any particular phoneme. It shouldn't. In fact, sloppiness can be good because it indicates that he is keeping his tongue out of the lateral lisp position he usually uses. Keep it loose and sloppy to reinforce the midline direction of air. If done well, this gross midline sound can be practiced every day at home. Use it only if the client can produce the sound at midline as he retracts the tongue behind the teeth.

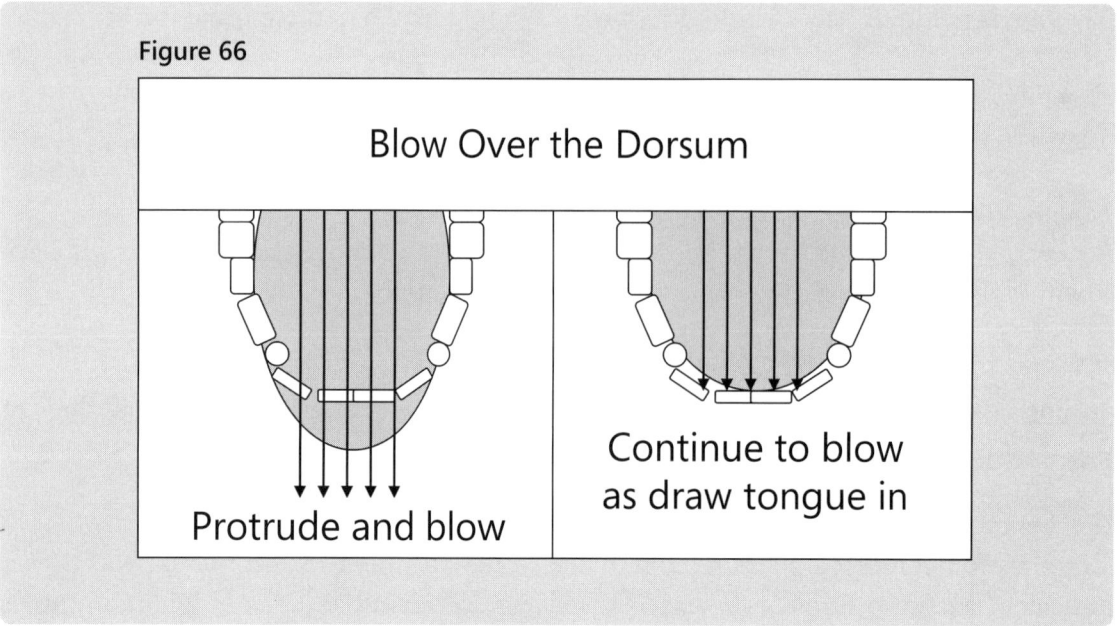

Figure 66

Blow Over the Dorsum

Protrude and blow

Continue to blow as draw tongue in

Long T Method

As discussed in chapter six, the Long T method can work quite well for the lateral lisp. Remember, the Long T is a /t/ produced with excessive air. We write it as /tᶜ/. It is a highly aspirated /t/. If the client can position his tongue correctly for /t/, it will be situated inside the mouth exactly as it should be for /s/. Thus if a client can produce /t/ with correct tongue position, we can use this to train him to produce /s/ in correct position. To use /t/ to teach correct oral position for /s/, we instruct the client in the following sequence:

1. Say /t/ and then "blow more air through the T" in order to produce a "Long T." By blowing more air through /t/, the client will produce a /t/ with strong aspiration. We write this as /tᶜ/. The excess air is not an /s/. It is simply aspiration.
2. Shape /tᶜ/ into /ts/ by helping the client to make the excess air "tinier" or by telling him to "squeeze the air." He can do this if he keeps the jaw high. Essentially have him keep his jaw higher. Modeling the sound will be critical here so the client will know what to do. And helping him listen carefully and use his powers of auditory discrimination will be the key to helping him shape the aspiration into /s/. The result will be a slightly distorted /ts/ blend.
3. Throughout, do not ask the client to produce /ts/ because he will slip into his lateral lisp pattern. In fact, tell him NOT to produce /ts/.
4. A good /ts/ will result if the client focuses on the oral position for /t/. Make sure he does not lose control of tongue position for /t/. Make him keep the tongue in position behind the teeth for both the /t/ and the extra air. Allow for the /s/-part to be slightly distorted. In other words, focus on keeping the tongue behind the teeth and do not worry if the strident phoneme does not sound perfect at this point.
5. If the client cannot attain a sound close to /ts/ in this process, it is recommended to keep the air channel wide to allow more air to escape. It is more important to rehearse sloppy sounds with a wide channel of air formed at midline than it is to make any sound with lateral air escape. Over time the sibilant sound will become more /s/-like.
6. If the client cannot narrow the channel to get an /s/-like sound, try switching to /ʃ/ It is a wider sound to begin with and thus may come more naturally to the client. He actually will be saying /tʃ/ if the tongue makes enough noise coming down from the palate.
7. Some clients make a sound that is more like /tʃ/ here. If so, go with it.

The /ts/ Progression

If your client with a lateral lisp can produce /ts/ or /tʃ/ correctly using the Long T method, then he will be ready to progress through the Cornerstone Approach as discussed in chapter seven. The cornerstone approach will work as effectively for a client with a lateral lisp as it does for a client with a frontal lisp. Use the /ts/ words, phrases, sentences, paragraph and conversational offerings of that chapter. We will not reprint that material again here. Please return to chapter seven for these lists. Make sure your client is producing /ts/ correctly throughout. Do not use the /ts/ material if your client cannot produce a midline /ts/ with it.

When Do We Add More Direct Oral-Motor Work with a Lateral Lisp?

Most clients with a lateral lisp can begin to produce a gross midline sound by working with the /ts/ cluster of the Long T method described above if the techniques is approached carefully. If your client can accomplish this feat, then you can be fairly assured that the client's lateral lisp was the result of simple habit. Simple habit means that at some point in his development he learned to produce sibilants with lateral airflow. Although this learned behavior was habituated, there was nothing actually wrong with the client's oral-motor development that caused it in the first place. A client who has a lateral lisp that is the result of simple habit will be able to learn the Long T method quite easily because his oral-motor abilities have been in tact from the start.

However, some clients have a lateral lisp that is the direct result of oral-motor problems. Clients who lisp because of a shifting jaw will need direct oral-motor technique to stabilize the jaw at midline. Also, clients whose tongue movements are developing along an aberrant path need more specific work to facilitate correct tongue movement patterns. The techniques that follow in the rest of this chapter are designed to do just that. They are designed to transform incorrect tongue movement patterns into correct one that will support the correct production of sibilants.

Developing a Midline Depression

Some clients with lateral lisps have overused the midline of the tongue so much that the midline depression that should be a part of normal tongue movement is absent. Instead, the middle bulges out. This is easily identified when the client extends the tongue forward and out the mouth. The middle portion of the tongue will elevate higher than the sides (figure 67). This tongue is over dependent upon the midline to move itself. The sides are lax and low, and they are not activating much or at all as the tongue moves. For many of these clients, this is the actual reason they ended up with a lateral lisp in the first place. If the middle is overactive, and the tongue continually initiates its movement with the middle, a bilateral lisp will be the result in speech.

Facilitating lateral extension and elevation of the sides of the tongue while facilitating midline depression can be accomplished in several ways. Primary are methods to stimulate the tongue bowl response and to normalize oral-tactile sensitivity.

Tongue Bowl Response
The best technique to develop midline depression is to stimulate the Tongue Bowl Response (TBR) (figure 68). It is summarized as follows:

- *Stimulation:* Stroke the tongue along its midline from the tip to a point halfway toward the back (Use a toothbrush or toothette)
- *Response:* The tongue should flatten, flair, elevate its tip and lateral margins, and depress in the middle.

Most clients with a lateral lisp can learn to stimulate this response themselves within a few trials. Then it can be assigned as homework. Ask the client to stimulate the tongue bowl

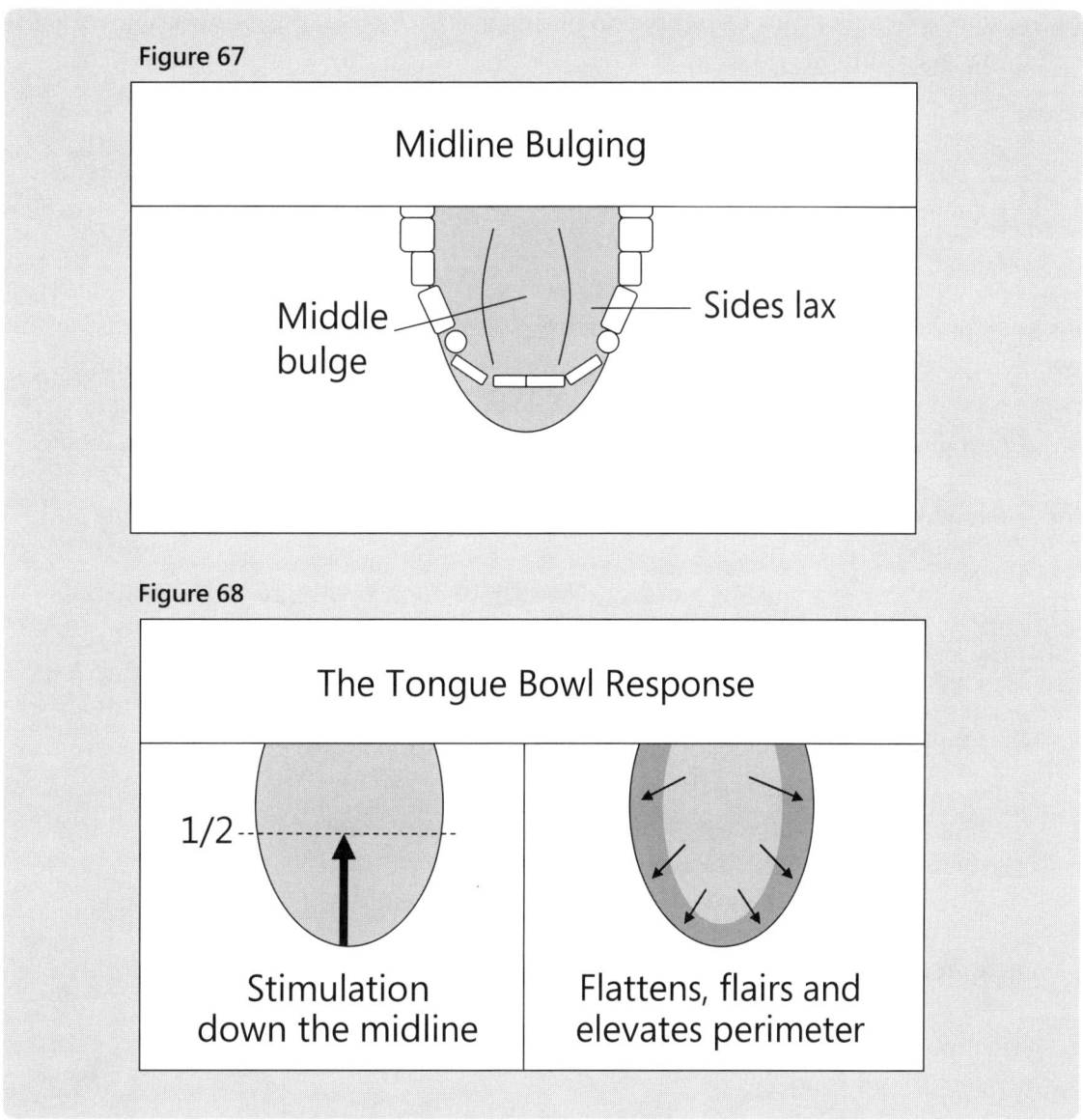

Figure 67
Midline Bulging
Middle bulge — Sides lax

Figure 68
The Tongue Bowl Response
1/2
Stimulation down the midline
Flattens, flairs and elevates perimeter

response three times after each brushing of his teeth. The client will learn to pull the middle section of his tongue down voluntarily. He then can use this skill to hold the middle section down while blowing air over the dorsum as described above.

Feeding Method
Feeding techniques also can be used to facilitate tongue bowling during spoon feeding. Use a spoon to present purees in the same way that you use the toothbrush or toothette above. Present the spoon to the tip and blade of the tongue and wait for the tongue bowl response to occur (figure 69). Placing the spoon too far back may trigger a tongue retraction response that will cause the middle of the tongue to bulge upward. You do not want this. You want to present the spoon in such a way that a bowl or cup-shape is stimulated.

Some therapists us a spoon to press directly downward on the middle of the tongue to create a bowl shape. I do not find this effective because downward pressure on the center of the tongue actually stimulates upward pushing of the center. Push down and wait. The client may relax into the position.

Normalizing Sensitivity

Clients with oral-tactile hypersensitivity gag easily. They also tend to hold the tongue in a high guard position with the middle elevated. This is a habituation of the tongue retraction response, and it is there because the client is in a perpetual state of guard against the gag. He is unconsciously trying to prevent his gag. A client with a lateral lisp who uses this error because he habitually holds his tongue in a *high guard position* needs therapy to reduce his overall oral sensitivity. Techniques revolve around exploring in the mouth while learning to suppress the gag. Active suppression is possible by most clients. I usually tell them, "Hold it… Don't choke…" Work from the tip of the tongue to the middle. Suggestions include:

- Explore the mouth with a mirror, talk about and label all the parts, become more familiar with the mouth
- Talk about gagging – what it is, why we have it, its use as a normal oral function
- Talk about how one can learn to stop gagging by using simple techniques
- Suck on ice chips, ice cubes or popsicles for a few minutes before or during activities to reposition the tongue
- Hold an object (finger, toothette, tongue depressor) on the tongue tip for five seconds while suppressing the gag
- Hold an object (finger, toothette, tongue depressor) on the middle of the tongue for five seconds while suppressing the gag
- Place a vibrator on the lips, tip of the tongue or middle of the tongue while suppressing the gag
- Stroke the tongue from tip to middle along midline while suppressing the gag

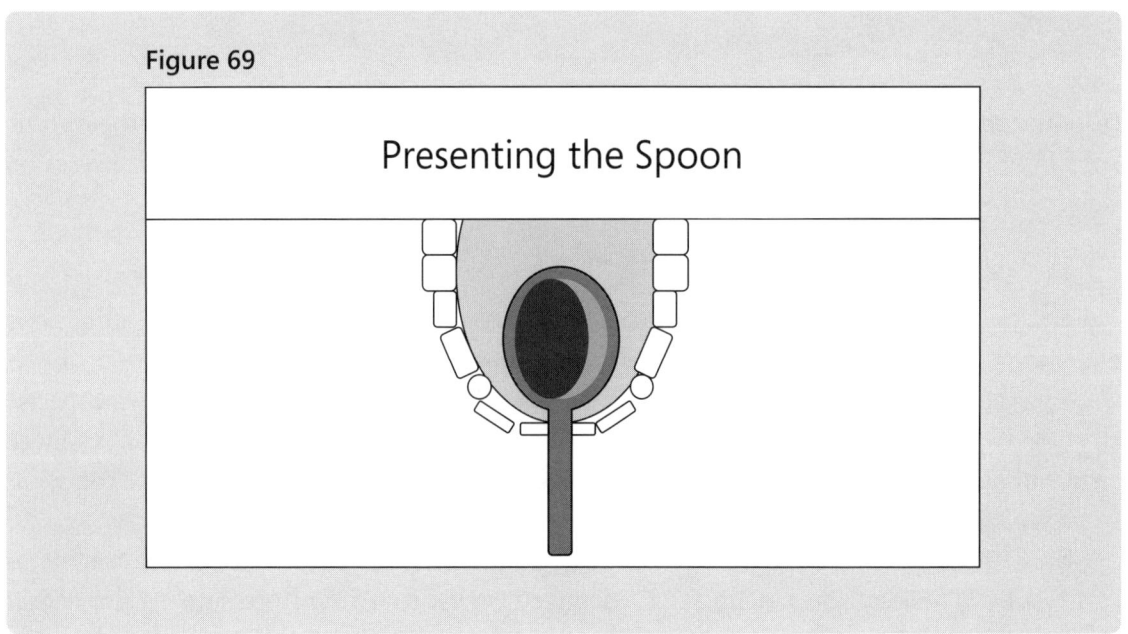

Figure 69

Presenting the Spoon

Developing Tongue Stability and Lateral Elevation

Developing back lateral tongue stability is a major component of eliminating a lateral lisp when oral-motor skills are impaired. Lateral elevation and stability is the very skill lacking in a motor-based lateral lisp. It goes hand-in-hand with lack of midline depression. Techniques to train back lateral stability and the stabilizing zones were discussed in chapter eight. Readers are referred back to that chapter for specifics on the methods listed here:

- Drawing a picture of the zones to increase conceptual awareness
- Stroking the zones to increase tactile awareness (figure 70).
- Biting down on the zones to help locate the exact position of elevation (figure 71 on next page).
- Establishing the butterfly position to get the zones high on both sides simultaneously
- Holding the butterfly position to increase strength and endurance for the position
- Spreading the back of the tongue laterally while smiling broadly
- Pressing down on the zones to stimulate muscle activity there
- Using feeding techniques: cleaning, transfer, lateralization, bolus formation

Dealing with Tongue Retraction

Tongue retraction is a posterior movement of the whole tongue that causes the entire tongue to be drawn into the rear of the mouth (figure 72 on next page). The tongue takes on high elevation there. It is as if the tongue pulls up and back into a ball-shape in the oropharynx. I have termed it the Tongue Retraction Response (TRR). I have also called it a "pre-gag" movement because it tends to occur right before a gag is elicited when the tongue is stroked down the midline. The sides and tip are lax. The middle is bulging. The TRR functions to prevent a foreign object from traveling posterior into the oropharynx and stimulating a gag (Tongue Gag Response – TGR).

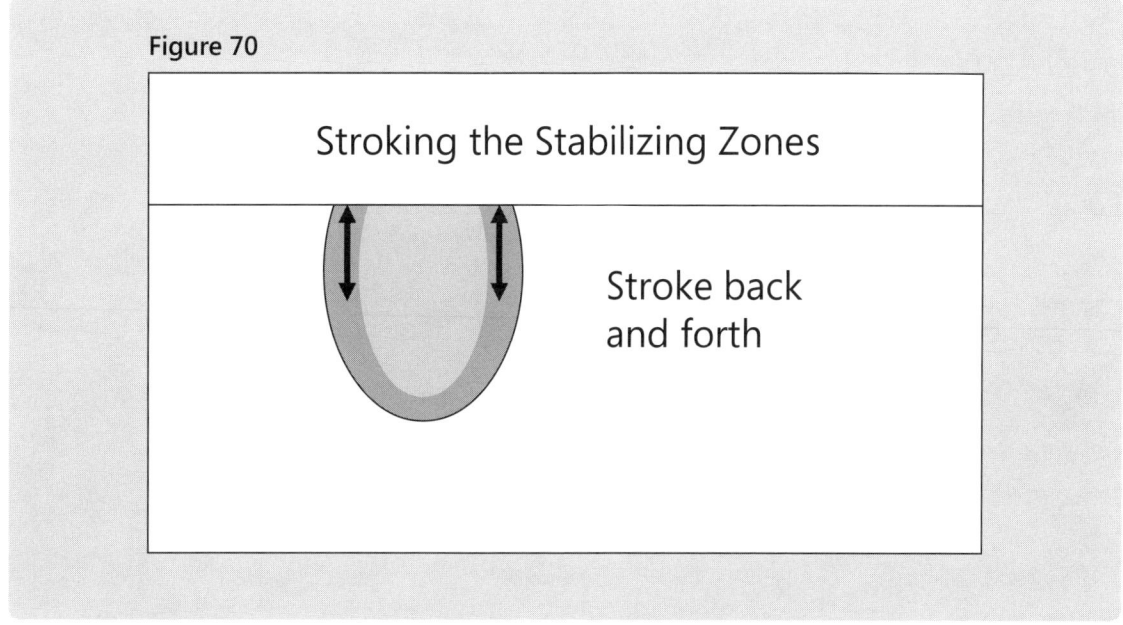

Figure 70

Stroking the Stabilizing Zones

Stroke back and forth

Figure 71

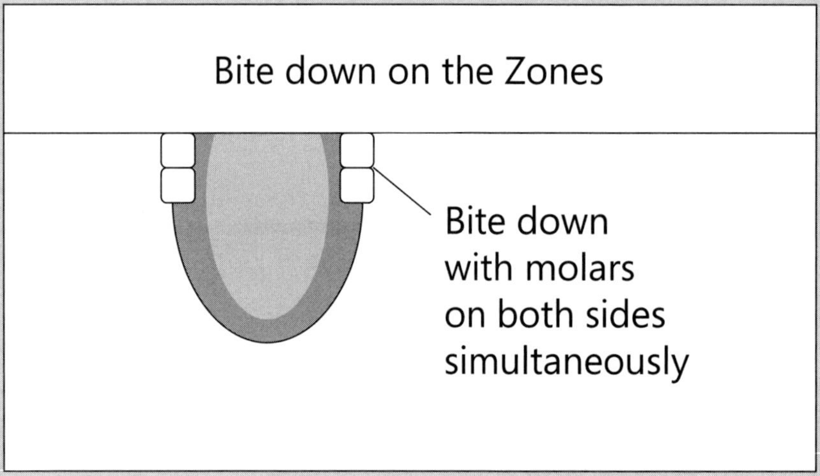

Bite down on the Zones

Bite down with molars on both sides simultaneously

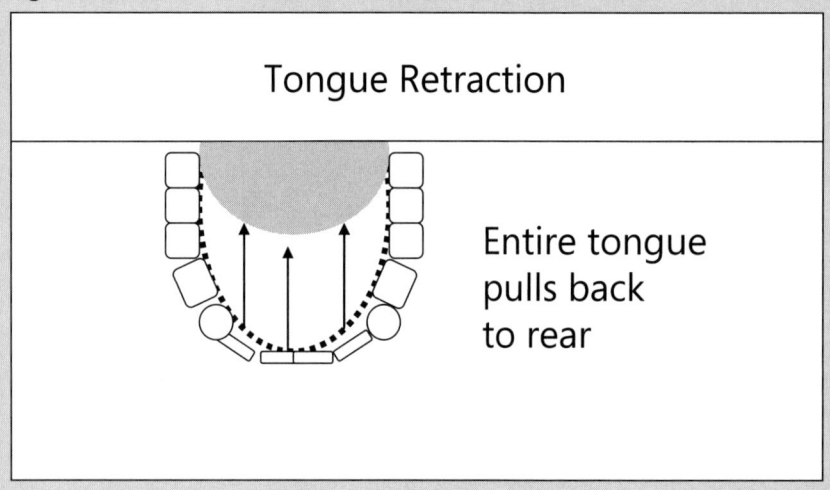

Figure 72

Tongue Retraction

Entire tongue pulls back to rear

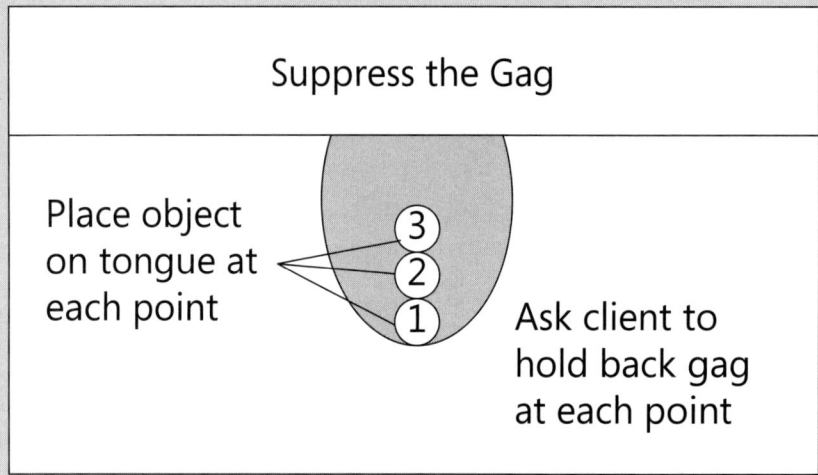

Figure 73

Suppress the Gag

Place object on tongue at each point

Ask client to hold back gag at each point

The TRR is stimulated naturally in the posterior half of the tongue. In cases of oral-tactile hypersensitivity, the TRR is stimulated in the anterior half of the mouth. The TRR is prevalent in clients with spasticity. It represents a tongue that is tight and pulling back and medially. The tongue takes on a boxy appearance.

A hyperactive TRR can be the very cause of a lateral lisp, and hyperactive tongue retraction interferes with our efforts to create a flat tongue with a midline groove. The TRR reduces as oral-tactile sensitivity normalizes. General techniques to normalize oral-tactile hypersensitivity are in order. These include:

- Use cold stimulus to elevate the threshold of sensitivity: suck on ice chips, eat ice cream
- Teach the client to suppress the TRR: hold a stimulus on the tongue front and tell the client "Don't move." Teach him to breath through his tendency to pull back. Then move your stimulus back slightly. Ask the client to continue to breathe through the sensation and suppress his gag. Repeat until you move the gag to the rear where it is supposed to be (figure 73).

Jaw Stabilization

The lateral lisp that is the result of simple jaw lateralization to the right or left simply needs jaw stabilization. Use a narrow biting tool (chapter 8) to discover the problem and stabilize the jaw at midline during speech activities. Fade use of the tool over time.

Pulling It All Together for the Lateral Lisp

The general plan for the lateral lisp is one of working from least invasive to more invasive. Just like working with the frontal lisp, we always do as little as possible all the time. That means we start with the simplest, easiest, most superficial and least invasive techniques first. Over time we include techniques that are increasingly more complex and invasive. We advance through therapy as its results dictate. The plan is can be summarized in four basic stages.

Least Invasive

Approach the lateral lisp first from a traditional articulation perspective. This means to get the client to say his targets from simple visual and auditory models. Model the correct way to say the target and see if he can follow your lead. This is simple but it is the essence of traditional articulation therapy. Many clients can make the appropriate changes this way. It is straightforward teaching. There is no need to get more invasive with technique if simple models work for your client. This method works for some but not all clients. If they all were this easy, this therapy would be very easy. In fact, if all of our clients responded to this simple method, a technician, not a therapist, could do this work.

More Invasive

At first we get a little more complex by going beyond the simple model. We can do so by employing the Long T Method. Remember, /t/ is a movement springboard for /s/. We use /t/ to help the client understand and begin to control the escape of air at midline. With /ts/

we are beginning to alter how he controls oral movements, and we are doing so in the way that toddlers naturally do so.

Even More Invasive
The next level of treatment is to introduce toys and tools to help with oral positioning. For example, we have advocated the use of a Biting Tool to help stabilize the jaw in a finely graded open position. A biting tool such as a straw or coffee stirrer helps the client learn to put his jaw into correct position for sibilant production. A biting tool might be thought of as an aid or a crutch. We introduce these types of aids only when we need to. And we fade them out as soon as the client has learned the lesson he needs from them.

Most Invasive
The most invasive work we can do in articulation therapy is to introduce tactile and proprioceptive techniques for the purpose of stimulating or inhibiting oral movement for correct speech sound production. For example, we advocated the use of methods to suppress the tongue retraction response. We use this method to stimulate more appropriate and more advanced tongue movements, specifically, tongue bowling. The purpose of the procedure is to aid in the maturation of tongue movements. *But this oral-motor work by itself will not make his lateral lisp go away.* It will only support and give a better foundation to the speech work you are doing. In other words, do not replace articulation therapy with oral-motor therapy. Do not begin to stimulate oral movement and forget to work on the sibilants. Instead, use oral-motor techniques *within* your program of articulation therapy. Better oral control is not your end product. Better speech is.

Chapter 9 Summary
Remediation Specific to the Lateral Lisp

- The lateral lisp can be one of the most difficult errors to fix.

- The primary *goal* of therapy for the lateral lisp is to establish correct articulation of the misarticulated phonemes in all speaking situations.

- Our first and primary *objective* is to establish midline air stream.

- Treatment techniques can be effective with children as young as two years of age. However most therapy in the public schools and privately is withheld until the client is eight or nine years of age, or even older.

- Developing a midline air stream begins with client awareness of the problem with his air stream. We use straws to begin this process.

- A traditional technique that has been around for a long time is to teach the client to substitute a frontal lisp for his lateral one. This puts his error back on the natural path.

- Another simple way to teach a midline air stream is to blow over the dorsum of the tongue while it is protruding from the mouth.

- The Long T helps a client begin to control midline air stream. It will work if the client produces /t/ with correct tongue position.

- Some clients with lateral lisps have overused the midline of the tongue so much that the midline depression that should be a part of normal tongue movement is absent. They must learn to pull the midline down.

- Developing back lateral tongue stability often is a major component of eliminating a lateral lisp.

- Hyperactive tongue retraction is sometimes seen in clients with a lateral lisp. A hyperactive TRR can be the very cause of the lateral lisp.

- The general plan for the lateral lisp is one of working from least invasive to most invasive.

Chapter 10

Auditory Training Through the Program

Auditory training is the process of teaching a client how to listen carefully to speech at gradually more refined levels. There are two purposes of auditory training for either the frontal or lateral lisp: (1) to discriminate between each of the six sibilant phonemes and (2) to discriminate between correct and incorrect productions of each individual phoneme. Before we discuss specific methods of this training, let's review several basic concepts.

First, the best articulation therapy integrates oral-motor and auditory training techniques from the onset of treatment. The oral positions that differentiate each of the six individual sibilant phonemes vary in quite subtle ways. In fact, it is nearly impossible for the average child to understand and feel the difference between the tongue positions for each sibilant at the onset of therapy. We cannot teach a client to produce the sibilants differentially through descriptions of oral position alone. The only way to assure that a client will learn the rest of these sibilant phonemes is to train him to use his listening skills.

Second, our job is to help our clients divide their large set of acceptable productions into two smaller sets: one for correct and one for incorrect productions of their own making. We do this by training the client to listen to his own productions as he is in the middle of changing his oral position. In other words, a client has to listen to the changes in acoustic quality of his own sounds as he experiments with his jaw, lip and tongue positions. I call this *auditory tuning*. Like dialing in a radio station, a client has to learn to make subtle changes in oral position and listen to the result. He dials his oral mechanism back and forth in very subtle ways in order to tune his speech. This means that he has to have refined control of oral movement.

Third, oral-motor work and auditory work cannot be treated as if they were diametrically opposed. In fact, the exact opposite is true. Like two shoe laces working together to make a bow, oral-motor work and auditory work are intricately connected all throughout therapy. The decision about how to integrate auditory and oral-motor work is a personal one made by the therapist in light of her style of teaching, the client's learning style, and the skills that the client already has achieved in treatment. Auditory and oral-motor work can be integrated at every moment for close interrelationship between the two. Or distance can be created between the two by devoting one session to auditory work and another to oral-motor work. Therapists must use trial and error to determine the direction of each session.

Forth, as a client gains skill in creating a correct channel, he gradually tunes his production to achieve acoustic perfection. The reader will recall that throughout our chapters on the Long T Method and the Cornerstone Approach, we emphasized that a client could rehearse with a fairly sloppy sound. What we shall say in this chapter does not negate that idea. A sloppy sound is allowed for a while as the client is learning to shape his mouth into correct position to achieve a midline air stream behind the teeth. Once he has begun to habituate that production, he can begin to tune. Do you understand this? In other words, the precise acoustic quality of his sounds is compromised as the client is learning to make a grossly correct midline acoustic channel behind the teeth.

It may seem odd to allow a sloppy sound for a while. The idea goes contrary to a more traditional approach in which a client is required to produce a perfect sound first. But we are viewing this from an oral-motor perspective. In an oral-motor view, all movements begin gross and are refined over time. Typically developing young children learn to produce strident phonemes with a sloppiness that is considered normal at first. We simply are allowing this sloppiness by our clients for a short while as they learn correct oral position. Once the gross position is established, we tighten up the productions. Simply stated, *auditory tuning is employed after grossly correct oral movements are established.*

Finally, let us say a word about ethical treatment in regard to auditory training. The key to helping a client learn to discriminate the sibilant phonemes lies in a therapist's ability to model them correctly. It is my opinion that a therapist who cannot produce these phonemes correctly is ethically bound to refer these clients to another therapist who can. This is because the therapist's model is the very heart of treatment. Modeling phonemes is done to demonstrate the correct way to produce them. Modeling each one correctly, clearly and with distinction develops the client's auditory discrimination skills and points him toward his goal.

Gross Auditory Attention

Our work to encourage auditory discrimination often begins in a gross manner. Gross auditory attention refers to a client's ability to actively listen to sound and speech. This may seem like an obvious fact unworthy of discussion, but auditory attention is a critical factor of treatment for the frontal and lateral lisps. Many of our clients enter treatment with limitations in their ability simply to quiet themselves and listen to speech. Clients who are unable to actively listen to phonemes will benefit little from treatment to remediate a frontal or lateral lisp. This group includes clients who are too young or cognitively too low functioning to pay careful attention to phonemes. This group also includes certain clients with attention deficit disorder whose general attention problems may interfere with their ability to develop a refined level of auditory attention, discrimination and memory. Clients who will not benefit from this therapy also may include those with significant hearing loss and those with global communication problems like that seen in autism.

Gross auditory attention to spoken language is developed in many ways during childhood. This skill can be encouraged at home and at school by:

- Listening to verbal reading
- Listening to music, both children's songs and "adult" music
- Singing songs
- Making up rhymes
- Telling jokes, making puns

- Whispering to one another
- Purposefully naming items incorrectly for the humor of it
- Memorizing rhymes, verses, prayers
- Dampening auditory stimuli by covering the ears
- Listening through earphones
- Playing listening games with bells, whistles, horns, etc.

These activities are designed to help kids tune out extraneous auditory stimuli (the *ground*) and to pay attention to a salient auditory stimulus (the *figure*). Most clients with an isolated frontal or lateral lisp will breeze through these activities. On the other hand, a client's inability to attend to or process auditory input in these simple ways signals that the client probably is not ready for direct treatment of the lisps.

Refined Auditory Attention

I use the term "refined auditory attention" to refer to a client's ability to notice and draw his attention to the individual phonemes of treatment. This skill is initiated early and developed throughout an entire articulation therapy program. It is a process of encouraging the client to listen actively to the phonemes of their program. We focus our clients' attention to phonemes by instructing them with words that reflect their receptive language level. This is classic articulation therapy at its best. We can say, for example:

- Listen.
- Listen to me.
- Listen to this word.
- Listen to this sound.
- Listen to the way I say this.
- I am going to say something. I want you to listen to me.
- Did you hear what I said?
- Are you ready? Here we go. Time to listen.
- Get your ears ready.
- Put on your big elephant ears so you can hear me really good.
- I am going to say the sound of "S." It is a funny sound. I want you to hear what it sounds like. Listen carefully.
- Okay. Pay attention. I am going to say it…
- Are you ready? Are your ears ready?
- You know what "S" sounds like, don't you? I will say it, and I want you to listen. Ready? Listen really hard, and then we will talk about it.

Then we give our client feedback about his listening activity:

- Perfect! You were listening hard.
- Excellent. I could tell you were listening to the sound I said.
- You heard it!

- It was hard, but you were listening.
- Thank you. Now listen to this …
- Hey! I don't think you were listening.
- Oops. You forgot to listen.
- You didn't hear that, did you? I think you were listening to that phone ringing. Is that right? Okay. Let's try again. Listen vary carefully.

Identifying Presence or Absence of Sound

A classic way to draw a client's attention to the phonemes of treatment is to train him to identify the presence or absence of the target phoneme in a word. This is a process consisting of saying words that contain the target and others that do not. The client's job is to identify the words that contain the target. It is a simple task that most clients find interesting for a few moments. Then it becomes tedious and boring to them. Activities need to be spiced up to keep clients actively engaged. For example, stack blocks.

Stacking Blocks Activity: The therapist says one word at a time. Some of the words contain the target phoneme and others do not. The client's job is to stack a block each time he hears the target in a word. Continue the process until the stack of blocks topples over. The anticipation of the crash keeps the client going through many words. The thrill of the crash rewards them for listening. The fun of the whole thing makes him want to do it again.

Most clients of normal intelligence who are of kindergarten age or older can succeed in these types of activities. Interestingly, I find that the activity itself does more for me than it does for the client. It helps me differentiate between those clients who can listen at this level and those who cannot. Children who can't identify target sounds in words need more training in the gross process of listening to speech. Those who can identify presence or absence of sounds in words will be ready to move on to more advanced auditory discrimination work. The task also can be done with phrases, sentences or paragraphs.

Identifying Word Position

Another classic way to train the ear to listen to target sounds is to require the client to identify the position in the word in which the target appears. Most therapists use a simple framework for this: beginning, middle and end. The question to be answered is, "Where is our sound in this word: at the beginning of the word, in the middle or at the end?" This activity is appropriate for clients who can read at a first grade level or better. This is another simple way to focus the ear on the underlying skills of articulation therapy.

Auditory Thinking

I use a term I call "auditory thinking." Auditory thinking is the active process of thinking about a target phoneme. Just like he might think about a ball game or a new pair of shoes, a client must be able to think about his target phonemes. An easy way to activate this type of thinking is to ask, "Do you know any words that have our sound?" The client must generate a small list of words that contain the target. We can model this type of thinking by saying, "Let's see, I know one. What about ___? That has our sound, doesn't it?" Help your client begin to generate these words by focusing his mind in certain categories. Have him think about the names of objects in the room, family members, friends, pets, movie titles, school subjects, numbers, colors, computer games, and so forth.

For example, one nine-year-old boy with a lateral lisp was enrolled in a soccer program the summer he came to therapy. We spent several weeks talking about the vocabulary of the game for part of each session. We took our time identifying key words. Each was recorded and analyzed for phoneme content. We talked all about the phonemes as:

- We drew a simple picture of a soccer field with its lines and goals.
- We drew little O's and X's representing each position on the field and we named the positions.
- We named all the equipment used in the game.
- He told me the rules as he understood them. I wrote them down in short versions and we highlighted the target sounds.
- He wore his uniform to therapy one day and brought in a ball. We reviewed all the pertinent labels.
- We looked up the team website that had been created by one of the dads. He named all the players and coaches in the team photo.

Auditory thinking gets a client's mind focused on target phonemes as they are represented in the things he thinks about. This helps make the work much more practical and personalized than a random list of words that are unattached to the client and his life. It also helps the client begin to realize how important these sounds are to his everyday experiences. The soccer activities drew this otherwise reticent boy into verbal discussion with me. He loved having someone listen to him talk in detail about a subject dear to his heart.

Same or Different Auditory Discrimination

Same or different auditory discrimination refers to a client's ability to determine if two sounds are the same or different. For the lisps, a client must be able to hear and recognize the auditory differences between each of the six sibilant phonemes. Games and activities are designed to make clients tell if models spoken by the therapist are the same or different. For example, a therapist might say twenty pairs, "/s/-/s/, /ʃ/-/s/, /ʃ/-/ʃ/" and so forth. The client's task is to listen to the pairs of sounds, to clap if they are the same and to shake his head if they are different. Again, an activity like this can be very boring to a client so the activity must be jazzed up. For example, use tiny dog stickers. After a correct response, the client receives a sticker to place in a picture of a doghouse. A simple reward system like this can keep a client's mind on the task at hand.

Discriminating Minimal Pair Words

Another way to train a client to listen carefully to the phonemes of a frontal or lateral lisp program is to use minimal pairs. Minimal pairs are sets of words that are different by only one phoneme. The therapist says two words that are the same or different, and the client indicates that. For example, the therapist says, "Sheet. Sheet. Same or different?" The client's response should be, "Same." The following minimal pair words can be used. Use the same intonation pattern on each word so they are nearly identical except for the target phonemes. These word sets also are excellent ones to practice once the phonemes emerge.

/s/ and /ʃ/ Initial Position

Sack	Shack	Sake	Shake
Sam	Sham	Same	Shame
Sane	Shayne	Seat	Sheet
Seen	Sheen	Seep	Sheep
Sin	Shin	Sip	Ship

/s/ and /ʃ/ Final Position

Class	Clash	Crass	Crash
Gas	Gash	Gus	Gush
Lease	Leash	Mess	Mesh
Russ	Rush	Swiss	Swish

/s/ and /tʃ/ Initial Position

Sap	Chap	Sat	Chat
Seat	Cheat	Sick	Chick
Sink	Chink	Sip	Chip
Soak	Choke	Sore	Chore
Sue	Chew	Sum	Chum

/s/ and /tʃ/ Final Position

Bass	Batch	Cass	Catch
Ess	Etch	Fess	Fetch
Hiss	Hitch	Lease	Leach
Mass	Match	Miss	Mitch
Pass	Patch	Peace	Peach

/ʃ/ and /tʃ/ Initial Position

Shayne	Chain	Sheet	Cheat
She's	Cheese	Ship	Chip
Shoe	Chew	Shoes	Choose
Shop	Chop	Shore	Chore

/ʃ/ and /tʃ/ Final Position

Bash	Batch	Cash	Catch
Crush	Crutch	Dish	Ditch
Hash	Hatch	Lash	Latch
Leash	Leach	Mash	Match
Wash	Watch	Wish	Witch

Chapter 10 — Auditory Training Through the Program

/s/ and /z/ Initial Position

Sag	Zag	Sap	Zap
Seal	Zeal	See	Zee
Seek	Zeek	Seuss	Zeus
Sink	Zinc	Sip	Zip
So	Zoe	Sue	Zoo

/s/ and /z/ Final Position

Bus	Buzz	Dose	Doze
Fleece	Fleas	Fuss	Fuzz
Gross	Grows	Hiss	His
Lice	Lies	Loss	Laws
Mace	Maize	Niece	Knees

/ʃ/ and /z/ Initial Position

Shar	Czar	Shag	Zag
Shayne	Zane	She	Zee
She'll	Zeal	Sheik	Zeek
Ship	Zip	Shoe	Zoo
Shone	Zone	Show	Zoe

/ʃ/ and /z/ Final Position

Ash	As	Fish	Fizz
Hash	Has	Rash	Raz
Welsh	Wells	Wish	Wiz

/tʃ/ and /z/ Initial Position

Chain	Zane	Chaney	Zany
Chap	Zap	Char	Czar
Chest	Zest	Chew	Zoo
Chink	Zinc	Chip	Zip
Chit	Zit	Choose	Zoos

/tʃ/ and /z/ Final Position

Beach	Bees	Breach	Breeze
Dutch	Does	Each	Ease
Fetch	Fez	Hatch	Has
Hitch	His	Itch	Is

/dʒ/ and /z/ Initial Position

Gee	Zee	Gyp	Zip
Jack	Zak	Jane	Zane
Jar	Czar	Jest	Zest
Jew	Zoo	Joe	Zoe
Juice	Zeus	Jute	Zoot

/dʒ/ and /z/ Final Position

Budge	Buzz	Cage	Kay's
Fudge	Fuzz	Huge	Hue's
Rage	Raze	Wage	Ways

/dʒ/ and /s/ Initial Position

Gel	Sell	Jack	Sack
Jam	Sam	Jane	Sane
Jaw	Saw	Jay	Say
Joe	Sew	Job	Sob
Joke	Soak	June	Soon

/dʒ/ and /s/ Final Position

Age	Ace	Badge	Bass
Budge	Bus	Cage	Case
Fudge	Fuss	Ledge	Less
Midge	Miss	Page	Pace
Rage	Race	Wedge	Wes

/s/ and /ʒ/ Final Position

Base	Beige

/dʒ/ and /ʃ/ Initial Position

Gee	She	Gel	Shell
Gene	Sheen	Gin	Shin
Jack	Shack	Jade	Shade
Jam	Sham	Jane	Shayne
Jaw	Shaw	Jeer	Sheer
Jeff	Chef	Joe	Show
Jot	Shot	Jut	Shut

/dʒ/ and /ʃ/ Final Position

Badge	Bash	Fledge	Flesh
Sludge	Slush		

/tʃ/ and /dʒ/ Initial Position

Chin	Gin	Chip	Gyp
Chain	Jane	Char	Jar
Chas	Jazz	Cheer	Jeer
Chill	Jill	Choke	Joke
Chug	Jug	Chunk	Junk

/tʃ/ *and* /dʒ/ *Final Position*

Age	H	Badge	Batch
Edge	Etch	Midge	Mitch
Ridge	Rich		

Verbalizing the Similarities and Differences

All six sibilant phonemes have acoustic similarities and differences, and most therapists develop a vocabulary to specify these characteristics. We use words and phrases of comparison that help clients understand what to listen to in order to develop distinction between the sibilants. Let's use /s/ and /ʃ/ as an example. We can describe how /s/ and /ʃ/ sound the same:

- Both sounds use air
- Both sounds have a hissing element
- Both sounds are "slushie"
- They sound almost the same
- Both sounds come out the front of the mouth
- Both sounds come out the middle of the mouth
- The teeth make both sounds
- Air hits the teeth to make both sounds

We also can use words and phrases to describe how /s/ and /ʃ/ sound different:

- They sound different
- They sound almost the same, but different
- /s/ sounds tight while /ʃ/ sounds loose
- /s/ sounds high while /ʃ/ sounds low
- /s/ sounds narrow while /ʃ/ sounds broad
- /s/ sounds small while /ʃ/ sounds big
- /s/ sounds restricted (up tight) while /ʃ/ sounds wild

Along with describing the similarities and differences in the way target phonemes sound, we also develop a vocabulary to describe the way they *feel*. These descriptions are nearly identical to those given above. For example, /s/ feels narrow while /ʃ/ feels broad. Building a conceptual framework for the similarities and differences in the way phonemes sound and feel is essential to articulation therapy for the frontal and lateral lisps.

Correct or Incorrect Auditory Discrimination

The ultimate act of auditory discrimination comes when a client can discriminate between correct and incorrect productions of each target phoneme. This develops in two stages: (1) discrimination of the therapist's models and (2) discrimination of the client's own productions. Usually the first of these skills is easy and the second is hard. The goal of correct and incorrect auditory discrimination training is to help the client restrict the range of phonemes he finds acceptable. At first he accepts his own incorrect productions as within the acceptable range of allophonic variations of the target. Over time he learns to restrict his range of acceptable productions. He gains this skill as we help him listen very carefully.

Mirror Images

Many therapists find it very helpful to model the client's frontal or lateral lisp so that he can see what it looks like and hear what it sounds like when produced by another person. It is so exciting to see a client's eyes light up when he realizes how bad his speech looks and sounds when imitated by someone else. The best way to do this is, of course, to imitate the client's incorrect production exactly. It may seem cruel to inexperienced therapists to think about modeling a client's incorrect productions. But it is not cruel when done discriminately. One never imitates a client's error in order to tease or belittle him. But one can do it to jolt him into awareness of the error. I have seen clients fix their errors practically overnight after I have introduced this powerful method. Save this technique for after you already have established good rapport with the client. Don't be afraid of it, but use it wisely.

Amplification

A slight amount of amplification can help our clients learn to listen better during any of the activities described above. Amplification is especially important in the training of the sibilants because of their quiet nature. We can use a wide variety of toys and tools to amplify the sibilants:

- Tubes – speak into a flexible tube that reaches from a client's mouth to his ear
- Plastic elbow joints – speak into a curved plastic pipe that directs sound from a client's mouth to his ear
- Small echo chambers – speak into boxes, bowls, pots or cups
- Large echo chambers – speak in stairwells, closets or very large boxes
- Electronic amplifiers – speak into an auditory trainer, phonic ear or tape recorder

Chapter 10 Summary
Auditory Training Through the Program

- The only way to assure that our clients will learn each sibilant phoneme is to train them through the auditory channel.

- Therapists produce target phonemes correctly in order to model the client's goal of treatment.

- Like dialing in a radio station, a client must learn to make subtle changes in oral position and listen to the result in order to learn each sibilant phoneme.

- Gross auditory attention refers to a client's ability to actively listen to sound and speech, to tune out the ground and attend to the figure.

- Refined auditory attention refers to a client's ability to notice and draw his attention to the individual phonemes of treatment.

- Draw a client's attention to the phonemes of treatment by training him to identify the presence or absence of the target phoneme in a word.

- Train the client to listen to target sounds by requiring him to identify the position in the word in which the target appears.

- Auditory thinking is the active process of thinking about a target phoneme in words common to a client's life experiences and interests.

- Same or different auditory discrimination refers to a client's ability to determine if two sounds are the same or different.

- Train a client to listen carefully to the phonemes of his program by using minimal pairs that contain the targets.

- The ultimate act of auditory discrimination comes when a client can discriminate between correct and incorrect productions of the target phonemes.

- The ultimate aim of auditory training is to help a client divide his large set of allophones into two smaller sets: one for correct and one for incorrect productions of his own making.

- A slight amount of amplification can help a client learn to listen to specific phonemes for any of the activities described above.

- Like two laces working together to make a bow, oral-motor work and auditory work are intimately connected all throughout therapy.

- A powerful method of auditory training is to mirror the client's error back to him. Use this method wisely and discriminantly.

Chapter 11

Onward to the Other Sibilants

The Long T Method described a simple process for achieving midline stridency behind the teeth for a production of /ts/. The Cornerstone Approach taught us how to take that single production all the way into conversational speech and how to change /ts/ into /s/ at all levels of speech production. A client who is successful with those methods will be able to move from /ts/ and /s/ to the rest of the sibilants. That is, the client will begin work on /ʃ/, /tʃ/, /z/, /ʒ/ and /dʒ/. That is the work presented in this chapter. This therapy requires that our clients learn to make a wider groove for the palatal sibilants, to occlude sound for /tʃ/, and to add voicing for the voiced cognates. We train the client to listen to the specific features of each individual sound to alter voice and oral position.

The order in which we present each of these phonemes will vary from one client to the next. Throughout this therapy, encourage the client to separate the sibilant sound from the rest of the word to help him achieve correct oral movement and position. For example, have him practice "sheep" as "sh-eep." Don't worry if this slows him down. He needs to work slowly in order to maintain control over the sounds. Start slow and work with greater speed over time.

TEACH INITIAL /ʃ/

Use the ear to tune the client's production from /s/ to /ʃ/. This requires widening the groove and rounding the lips. Simply have him produce /s/, then round his lips while prolonging it. This will get him started, and he may slip naturally into /ʃ/. If he doesn't, use the Butterfly Position to widen the back of the tongue. These will be easy tasks for the client with good oral control. Practice /ʃ/ before and after every vowel, then proceed to the following.

Simple CV Words with Initial /ʃ/

She	Shoe	Shaw	Shay	Show

CVC Words with Initial /ʃ/

Shade	Shake	Shame	Shape	Shack
Sham	Shave	Sheen	Sheep	Sheer
Sheet	Shin	Shine	Shire	Ship
Shock	Shop	Shot	Shun	Shut

Phrases with Initial /ʃ/ Words

One shoe	Shade tree	Shake a leg
The shame of it	Shape up	Shave and shower
Crummy old shack	A big sham	Good sheen
Ten sheep	Sheer coat of paint	Bed sheet
Rain or shine	The Shire	Shin bone
Ship shape	A shock	Shop around the clock
Shot dead	Shut down	

Sentences with Initial /ʃ/ Words

We ate under a shade tree.
Shape up or ship out.
He built a crummy old shack.
You got a nice sheen on the car.
Put on one sheer coat of paint.
The game will go on rain or shine.
I hit my shin bone!
The end of the movie shocked me.
Shut down the power.
We will shop around the clock until we find the perfect gift.

He yelled, "Hurry up! Shake a leg!"
Bob shaved and showered before he left.
It was a big sham but he didn't fool us.
We counted ten sheep.
Get the bed sheet if you don't mind.
The Hobbit lived in the Shire.
Make it ship shape.
He might be shot dead already.
The shame of it came when he forgot the work.

Paragraphs with Initial /ʃ/ Words

On Friday we went to our family reunion. Mom said, "Rain or shine, we are going to that picnic!" Before we left, dad had to shave and shower. Mom yelled, "Hurry up! Shake a leg!" When we got to the park we ate under a shade tree. The shame of it came when we forgot our food. Luckily, everybody there brought a ton of food. I loved the apple pie!

The captain cried, "Shape up or ship out!" I got frightened. Did he really mean that I had to shape up or leave? What would he do without me? I thought it could be a big sham. But I know my dad. He can really get mad about keeping my room clean. I want to be captain of my own home one day. Then the captain will not bug me any more.

I read about a poor old man who lived in a crummy old shack. He had one new shoe and one old shoe. He had no sheet on the bed. He had no food but a bit of bread. It shocked me to learn how the poor live.

TEACH FINAL /ʃ/

Simple Words with Final /ʃ/

Ash	Bash	Hash	Mash	Flesh
Mesh	Dish	Fish	Wish	Hush
Lush	Mush	Push	Rush	

Phrases with Final /ʃ/ Words

Ash in the fire	Bash it	Mashed potato
Flesh wound	Mesh together	A new dish
Fish in water	Wishing well	Hush up
Lush pillow	Mush melon	Push together
Rush around		

Sentences with Final /ʃ/ Words

There will be <u>ash</u> under the fire.
<u>Bash</u> the nail right on the head.
<u>Mesh</u> them together, if you will.
He put the little <u>fish</u> back in the water.
<u>Hush</u> up now! The baby went to bed.
Mom ate the <u>mush</u> melon.
You don't have to <u>rush</u> around to get there on time.

I love <u>mash</u> potato pie.
He got a broken arm and a <u>flesh</u> wound.
Mom made a new <u>dish</u> for dinner.
I threw my quarter into the <u>wishing</u> well.
I want a <u>lush</u> pillow on my bed.
Will you <u>push</u> everything together?

Paragraphs with Final /ʃ/ Words

I love to go to my cabin. We make a fire and get <u>ash</u>. Then we put the <u>ash</u> in the garden. We grow watermelon and <u>mush</u> melon. We go <u>fishing</u>, too. We eat the big <u>fish</u> but throw the little <u>fish</u> back in the water to let them grow more. One time a <u>fishhook</u> caught my arm and I got a <u>flesh</u> wound.

Mom put a <u>plush</u> new pillow on my bed. I love it! Mom told me, "<u>Hush</u> up now and go to bed." I told her, "Okay! I can't wait to put my head on that <u>plush</u> pillow! Goodnight!"

"<u>Bash</u> the nail right on the head." Dad helped me make a project over the weekend. We made a <u>wishing</u> well for the back yard. We took our time and did not <u>rush</u> around to do it. Dad told me, "Don't <u>rush</u> or you might <u>bash</u> your thumb!" But I didn't pay attention and did <u>bash</u> my thumb. When we <u>finished</u>, I threw a penny into the <u>wishing</u> well. I <u>wished</u> my thumb didn't hurt!

TEACH INITIAL /tʃ/

Use the ear to tune to the sound of /tʃ/. When differentiating it from /ts/, ask the client to widen the groove with the Butterfly Position, and to round the lips. To differentiate it from /ʃ/, tell him to stop the sound with tip elevation before releasing the stridency. Practice /tʃ/ before and after every vowel, then proceed to the following.

Simple words with Initial /tʃ/

Chad	Chain	Chap	Chat	Cheat
Cheep	Chew	Chill	Chin	Chip

Phrases with Initial /tʃ/

Chad Moore	A good chap	Chat with me
A pull chain	Don't cheat	A cheep trick
Chew on it	Go chill	Chin up
Potato chip		

Sentences with Initial /tʃ/
Chad Moore will be my new friend.
A good chap came along.
Chat with me about your trip.
Pull the chain carefully and don't yank it.
Don't cheat on your paper.
That might be a cheep trick.
Go chill out before you call her.
Keep your chin up when you tell the truth.
The potato chip fell under the table and the dog ate it.
Chew on it for a while before you make up your mind.

Paragraphs with Initial /tʃ/ *words*
The chain fell off my bike. It broke when I tried to put it back on. I think it might be a cheep chain. It chipped and broke far too quickly.

My old Great Grandma inquired, "Will you chat with me for a while?" And I replied, "Do you want to chew the fat after I put another blanket on you?" Grandma had a chill. We chatted for an hour, and then Great Grandma took a nap.

Charlie taught me how to be a good chap. We caught Charlie cheating in our game. I got a chill when one guy told Charlie off. But Charlie didn't get mad. He kept a chin up when he made up for his cheating.

TEACH FINAL /tʃ/

Words with final /tʃ/

Ouch	Bunch	Butch	Couch	Crutch
Lunch	Much	Munch	Punch	Touch

Phrases with final /tʃ/ *words*

Ouch!	Couch potato	My friend Butch
A crutch	Too much	Don't touch
Lunch at noon	A bunch of money	Munch a bunch
Hard punch		

Sentences with final /tʃ/ words

He said, "Ouch!"	Don't be a couch potato.
Butch wanted to be an outlaw.	I need a crutch for my knee.
I feel much better.	Don't touch the wet paint.
Lunch will be at noon today.	I found a bunch of water on the floor.
He wanted to munch a bunch of lunch.	We will have punch at the party.

Paragraphs with final /tʃ/ words

"Ouch!" said mom, "That hurt!" Mom knelt on a pin in the couch. In fact, there were a bunch of them that had fallen out of the thread box. "It didn't hurt too much," Mom told me later.

Butch wanted to be an outlaw. He robbed a bunch of money before lunch, after lunch, and all the time. My mom told me not to be like Butch. Mom told me that if I were like Butch I would be too much trouble.

If you punch me, I will be mad! Don't touch me, or I will get angry. If you knock me down, I might break my leg, and then I would need a crutch to walk. Be careful!

TEACH FINAL /z/ WITH /dz/

We can work with /z/ in the same way we worked with /s/ by teaching the client to use a Long D. Have the client put his tongue into position for /d/. Tell him to hold his tongue into position for /d/ and then to lower the tip only ever so slightly while making voice through it. A /dz/ production should result although the strident element may be weak. Tell the client NOT to make a /z/ because to do so probably will result in his usual error. Practice this new somewhat weak /dz/ before and after every vowel, then proceed to words which have /dz/ in the final position. Words that end in /dz/ are produced by most of us with a devoiced /z/ or even an /s/. But for this practice we shall make sure that the client makes a /z/. Over time we can explain the difference to him and help him soften the voicing element.

Simple Words with Final /dz/

Ads	Beds	Bids	Buds	Dads
Duds	Eds	Fads	Kids	Lads
Lids	Pads	Pods	Reds	Rods

Simple Phrases with Final /dz/

Ads in the paper	Make the beds	Many bids
Flower buds	Dad's here	Colorful duds
Ed's car	Fads fade	For the kids
Bright lads	Pot lids	Pads of paper
Pea pods	Made of reds	Hot rods

Sentences with Final /dz/
We put <u>ads</u> in the paper today.
Make the <u>beds</u> before you leave.
Many <u>bids</u> came in for that painting.
The flower <u>buds</u> will open by the end of the week.
<u>Dad's</u> here and ready to take you to the park.
Tamara can wear colorful <u>duds</u>!
<u>Ed's</u> car fell apart and he will get a new one.
<u>Fads</u> fade away right away.
Grandpa put up a playground for the <u>kids</u>.
Bright <u>lads</u> can enter the top college.
Pot <u>lids</u> have to fit properly.
Put the <u>pads</u> of paper in the drawer.
Help me open the pea <u>pods</u> for dinner.
The clothing line will be void of <u>reds</u>.
I love hot <u>rods</u>!

Paragraphs with Final /dz/
We read all the <u>ads</u> in the paper to help look for <u>dad's</u> new car. I could not believe how many car <u>ads</u> there were. And did you know that people put <u>ads</u> in the paper for everything you can think of? There were dog <u>ads</u>, cat <u>ads</u> and furniture <u>ads</u>. But by far, there were more car <u>ads</u> than any other.

<u>Fads</u> come and go, according to Mr. Black. "<u>Lad's</u>," he commented, "Don't get hooked on <u>fads</u>. They are a poor way to manage your money." I think he could be right. Have you found that clothing <u>fads</u> are different every year?

The little <u>kids</u> put the <u>pads</u> of paper under the <u>beds</u>. We could not find them. We looked everywhere. Little <u>kids</u>! When we finally looked under the <u>beds</u>, we found pot <u>lids</u>, clothing <u>rods</u> and pea <u>pods</u> too! Do you believe it?

TEACH INITIAL /^{d}z/

We also can use the Long D in the initial position of words by practicing non-standard forms.

Simple Words with Initial dz/z Substitutions

Word	**Pronunciation**	**Word**	**Pronunciation**
Zany	^{d}Zany	Zebra	^{d}Zeber
Zeke	^{d}Zeke	Zing	^{d}Zing
Zip	^{d}Zip	Zipper	^{d}Zipper
Zone	^{d}Zone	Zoo	^{d}Zoo
Zoom	^{d}Zoom	Zoro	^{d}Zoro

Phrases with Initial dz/z Words

Many ᵈzany people	The ᵈzebra	That boy ᵈZeke
ᵈZing-a-ling!	ᵈZip up	My ᵈzipper
In the ᵈzone	Our ᵈzoo	ᵈZoom down
ᵈZoro jumped		

Sentences with Initial dz/z Words

Many ᵈzany people eat weird food.   The ᵈzebra ate all the hay.
ᵈZeke went to play on the climber.   "ᵈZing!" went my heart.
ᵈZip up your coat, Danny.   My ᵈzipper broke
Our ᵈzoo got a new elephant.   ᵈZoom down to the market for me.
He went in the ᵈzone marked, "Keep Out!"   ᵈZoro jumped down from the roof.

Paragraphs with Initial dz/z Words

Our ᵈzoo will get a new elephant from ᵈZanᵈzibar. He will be big and fat. He will be put into a different part of the ᵈzoo than the ᵈzebra even though the ᵈzebra came from ᵈZanᵈzibar too.

The ᵈzany people went home already. Man! They were weird! One of the ᵈzany people did a cartwheel right in the middle of the living room. Another ate under the table. I think they were trying to get me to think about why I don't want to be ᵈzany too.

ᵈZoro jumped down from the roof. "ᵈZip up your coat, Danny! Come on!" he yelled at me. "But my ᵈzipper broke," I called back. ᵈZoro helped me ᵈzip it up. It might have been a heroic deed, but I don't think it qualified.

TEACH FINAL /z/

Once a client can produce /ᵈz/ in the initial position, it usually is easy to teach him how to get rid of the little /ᵈ/. Have him listen carefully as he produces the sound without touching the tip to the alveolus. Help him learn how to put his tongue into position for /d/, then to lower it before beginning to voice.

Words with Final /z/ Words

Bays	Boys	Bees	Buys	Cries
Days	Dies	Fries	Knees	Lies
Maize	Pays	Pies	Praise	Please
Rise	Tease	Ways		

Phrases with Final /z/ Words

Three bays	Bees in their hive	Boys and men
Great buys	Cries for help	Days of fun and fortune
Many Dyes	French fries	Bended knees
Lies to me	Eat the maize	Pays a lot

Pies and cake	Please come	Praise for you
Don't tease	Sun rise	Ways to go

Sentences with Final /z/ Words

We went to three different <u>bays</u>.
Both <u>boys</u> and men will love this car.
We heard her <u>cries</u> for help.
Many <u>dyes</u> were included in the work.
He knelt down on bended <u>knees</u>.
We will eat the <u>maize</u> at the picnic.
The <u>pies</u> and cake are for after dinner.
Sun <u>rise</u> will be at five.
Good job! I have nothing but <u>praise</u> for you!

The <u>bees</u> are in their hive.
Great <u>buys</u> are found in that town.
It was the <u>days</u> of fun and fortune.
French <u>fries</u> are great!
He <u>lies</u> to me every time.
The owner <u>pays</u> a lot for good work.
<u>Please</u> come to by birthday party.
Don't <u>tease</u> your brother.
There are many <u>ways</u> we can go.

Paragraphs with Final /z/ Words

We found great <u>buys</u> in town and on the way home I had a burger and <u>fries</u>. The <u>boys</u> had <u>fries</u>, too. And they were great <u>fries</u> too. It <u>pays</u> to <u>praise</u> the cook.

Do you know anything about the <u>ways</u> of <u>bees</u>? <u>Bees</u> live in a hive where they work all day long. They <u>rise</u> early during warm <u>days</u>. They gather pollen and make honey. <u>Please</u> don't <u>tease</u> <u>bees</u>. They will get you for that!

We went to the fair today, and we ate a lot of food. I went on my <u>knees</u> when I tried the <u>pies</u>. They were great! And the corn, the <u>maize</u>! It was yummy! I am not telling <u>lies</u>.

TEACH MEDIAL /ʒ/

We work with /ʒ/ the same way we work with /ʃ/ except we add voice. Or, from /z/, we make a wider groove with the Butterfly Position and round the lips. Use the ear to tune the sound. /ʒ/ does not occur in the initial position of words, so we begin medially.

Words with Medial /ʒ/

Delusion	Fusion	Leisure	Occasion	Persia
Provision	Treasure	Television	Version	Vision

Phrases with Medial /ʒ/

A delusion	New fusion	With leisure
On occasion	In Persia	A provision we need
A television set	Gold treasure	Correct version
Good vision		

Sentences with Medial /ʒ/

It all could be a <u>delusion</u>.
We want to offer the new <u>fusion</u> food.
I will do it at my <u>leisure</u>.

On <u>occasion</u> we go out for dinner.
He lived in <u>Persia</u> for a while.
We bought every <u>provision</u> we needed.
Our <u>television</u> broke and we got a new one.
I want to go to <u>Treasure</u> Island.
I have to read the new <u>version</u> of the epic tale.
I have good <u>vision</u> both near and far.

Paragraphs with Medial /ʒ/
Don't live under the <u>delusion</u> that I like new <u>fusion</u> in food. I prefer to eat a meal from my mom who, on <u>occasion</u>, will cook for me. I go to her home and eat in <u>leisure</u>. I do like new <u>fusion</u> clothing, however. And I particularly like to wear clothing from <u>Persia</u>.

"Look at the <u>treasure</u>!" cried the head of the digging team. "The finding of <u>treasure</u> like that will fund our entire trip. It will be the <u>provision</u> we need to completely map the area. That will create a new <u>version</u> of the village and people who lived here at one time."

I got an old tiny <u>television</u> from my uncle. He cannot rely on <u>vision</u> anymore and did not need it. He got a bigger one he can view better.

TEACH FINAL /ʒ/
Words with Final /ʒ/

Beige	Camouflage	Corsage	Entourage	Garage
Massage	Mirage	Prestige	Sabotage	

Phrases with Final /ʒ/

Beige and brown	Camouflage it	A pretty pink corsage
The entourage	Two-car garage	Massage oil
A mirage	The prestige	A sabotage

Sentences with Final /ʒ/
<u>Beige</u> and brown will dominate the room.
We need to <u>camouflage</u> the car.
The <u>corsage</u> will be pink and white.
Her <u>entourage</u> came here today to get the room ready.
Park the car in the <u>garage</u> and bring down the door.
<u>Massage</u> my feet, okay?
The <u>mirage</u> made the water appear near by.
The <u>prestige</u> of our work may be great.
Don't <u>sabotage</u> my plan by telling him.

Paragraphs with Final /ʒ/
<u>Beige</u> might be my favorite color. I like it on my wall and in my <u>corsage</u>. Do you think my date will buy me a <u>beige</u> <u>corsage</u>? Probably not. It will probably be pink like the rest of my prom <u>camouflage</u>.

Massage oil can help a massage become warm and calming. Have you ever had a real massage? They are wonderful if you are too tight on your arm or leg.

A mirage can really fool you! When you look out on hot ground, a mirage can make you think that a lake of water might be right in front of you. Then when you get there, you find out that the water went bye-bye. It had to be only a mirage.

TEACH INITIAL /dʒ/

Words with Initial /dʒ/

| Jab | Jack | Jam | Jaw | Job |
| Joe | Jog | Joy | Jug | June |

Phrases with Initial /dʒ/

Jab him	Jack and Jill	Jam and bread
Jaw bone	On the job	Joe and Bob
Jog along	Joy to the world	A jug of water
June or July		

Sentences with Initial /dʒ/

Don't jab him in the rib to wake him up!
Jack and Jill went up the hill.
I like to eat peanut butter and jam on bread.
I broke my jaw bone.
He will go on the job on Monday.
Joe ran to the market for me.
Run or jog along after we get home.
I feel joy in my heart today.
The jug of water might be in the back of the camper.
June will be the hot month again.

Paragraphs with Initial /dʒ/

Jab Jack in the rib to wake him up. He and Joe and I are going to look for a job today. We want to find a job we all can do together, one near our home. We don't care about how hard it might be. We just want a job!

Do you like jam and peanut butter on your bread? I do. I like blue berry jam and cranberry jam. My mom can make blueberry jam. We make it in July.

We had a June bug on the patio. I jogged around it to avoid jumping on it. I thought, "Oh, joy, the June bug colony came back again another year. I put one in a jug.

TEACH FINAL /dʒ/

Words with Final /dʒ/

| Age | Badge | Cage | Edge | Gage |
| Huge | Ledge | Lodge | Rage | Ridge |

Phrases with Final /dʒ/

At any <u>age</u>   <u>Badge</u> of honor   A <u>cage</u> for the bird
On the <u>edge</u> of time   Gas <u>gage</u>   One <u>huge</u> error
On the <u>ledge</u>   The old <u>lodge</u>   Rant and <u>rage</u>
Rugged <u>ridge</u>

Sentences with Final /dʒ/

You can go there at any <u>age</u>.
He won the top <u>badge</u> of honor.
The <u>birdcage</u> needed a cleaning.
My home will be built on the <u>edge</u> of town.
The gas <u>gage</u> read, "Empty."
I made a <u>huge</u> cake for her birthday.
The book fell off the <u>ledge</u> down to the ground.
That old <u>lodge</u> had been great in 1935.
Don't rant and <u>rage</u> at me!
He will climb to the very top of the <u>ridge</u> tomorrow.

Paragraphs with Final /dʒ/

We bought a <u>birdcage</u> on the <u>edge</u> of town. It came from an old broken-down <u>lodge</u>. I like it. I wanted to get an old metal <u>birdcage</u> to grow a plant on my patio. Then it can grow <u>huge</u>.

The <u>gage</u> read, "Empty." We had to drive to the <u>edge</u> of town to buy more fuel for the lawn mower. You can't buy fuel at any <u>age</u>. You have to be 18. Therefore I could not go alone. My dad had to go with me.

He earned a hero <u>badge</u> from our town. Apparently he hung over a <u>ledge</u> to help a family who lived on a <u>ridge</u>. They needed help to get away from a <u>raging</u> river.

Chapter 11 Summary
Onward to the Other Sibilants

- A client who is successful with the Long T Method and the Cornerstone Approach will be able to move from /ts/ and /s/ to the rest of the sibilants – /ʃ/, /tʃ/, /z/, /ʒ/ and /dʒ/.

- The rest of the sibilants are made by altering /s/. The client learns to widen the groove, round the lips and/or add voice.

- Use the Butterfly Position to widen the midline channel for /ʃ/, /ʒ/ and /tʃ/.

- Help the client use his ear to tune his production from /s/ to the other sounds. Auditory discrimination guides him in learning all the sibilants.

- Encourage the client to pause between the sibilant sound and the rest of his syllable or word. This helps him achieve correct oral movement and position while speaking slowly and deliberately.

- The client will need to work slowly in order to maintain control over the sounds. Start slow and work with greater speed over time.

- Rehearse all the sibilants in words, phrases, sentences, paragraphs and conversation.

- Clients who have failed in the Long T Method and/or the Cornerstone Approach will need to move on to the methods described in chapters eight and nine.

Chapter 12

Oral Habits, Oral Structure, Oral Rest and Swallowing

The subjects of oral habits, dentition, occlusion, oral structure, oral rest and swallowing are integral to the remediation of both the frontal and lateral lisp. This is because of the precise and refined movements necessary for correct production of the sibilants. We have discussed these topics in part throughout this text. Let us now summarize basic thoughts on each. The reader will note that the relationship between speech, feeding, dentition and oral habits continues to be an area of great controversy within the field of speech-language pathology. Formal research is needed in each of these areas to back up the claims summarized here. These claims have arisen from the author's direct clinical experience and from those gained through continuing professional education.

Oral Habits

In the best of circumstances, oral habits (like thumb and pacifier sucking or nail biting) are eliminated before or during speech therapy for the frontal or lateral lisp. This is because of the negative effect these habits can have on muscle tone, oral movement, oral position and oral structure. Most speech-language pathologists who work in the public schools are forbidden to address oral habits directly. As a result, this work usually takes place in the private sector. Professionals who help children and adults eliminate oral habits include speech-language pathologists, oral hygienists, dental assistants, councilors, psychologists and others. Some recommend that articulation therapy be postponed for 12-18 months following the elimination of an oral habit. This is because of the powerful and obvious changes to dental structure and oral movement that can occur as a result of habit elimination.

The elimination of oral habits requires special training by professionals who bring this work into their practice. The therapy entails using education as well as environmental and behavioral management strategies to alter the family dynamics around the child's habit. Some speech-language pathologists receive dual certification in speech-language pathology and orofacial myology, and they center their private practice on these types of clients. The best referral source for training in this area is the International Association of Orofacial Myology.

Some orthodontists and dentists place orthodontic contraptions behind the front teeth to prevent an oral habit like thumb sucking. These so-called cribs, cages or rakes are designed to prevent children from resting the thumb or finger in the mouth for sucking. They can break the habit completely in some cases, but fail in others. Failure can occur if the child simply finds another way to suck while the piece is in place, or if he reinstates the habit once the appliance is removed. It is the author's opinion that when failure occurs it is because the contraption was relied upon to be the only source of remediation. Procedures to modify behavior and to educate must also be included.

Dentition and Occlusion

Problems in tooth position and alignment that are related to the frontal and lateral lisps were discussed in chapters three and four. In the ideal situation, dental and orthodontic problems are eliminated before initiating actual speech therapy for a lisp. This is because missing teeth and those that are improperly positioned can impede the development of acoustically correct stridency. For example, it is useless to work on a frontal lisp when a child has no front teeth. It is better to wait until his anterior permanent teeth are almost fully developed so that he can utilize his anterior dental barrier to create appropriate stridency. Once the teeth have emerged, re-evaluation of speech helps us determine if therapy is needed at that time.

Many clients have frontal lisp patterns directly related to dental and occlusion problems. A plan of action for speech must be integrally related to the actions planned by dental specialists. This requires that we develop a close association with our clients' dentists, orthodontists and oral surgeons. For example, consider the child with a frontal lisp and a large anterior open bite. The gap between the upper and lower central incisors prevents true stridency from being established because the anterior dental barrier cannot be formed. Trying to correct a frontal lisp with a child who has a huge anterior open bite is futile. Treatment of the lisp will follow correction of the bite.

In cases where it is not possible to correct dental problems associated with lisps, we must teach our clients to compensate for their structural differences. Our goal in each of these cases is to help the client achieve the best-sounding and best-looking set of sibilants possible given the status of his dental structure. For example:

- Clients with permanently missing anterior teeth can be taught to produce their sibilants by elevating the tongue tip up toward and behind the alveolar ridge. A strident-like sound is created between the tongue tip and alveolar ridge.
- Clients with missing anterior teeth on one side must be taught to direct their air stream toward the teeth remaining on the other side.
- Clients with anterior teeth that are twisted in position (causing gaps between the anterior teeth) also can be taught to use the alveolar ridge to create a strident-like element. Or they can be taught to produce a quieter sound so as to reduce the distortion.
- Clients who are concerned about public speaking situations and who have mild to moderate unfixed gaps between the teeth can be taught to stuff clear dental wax between the gaps for occasions when they must engage in public speaking. This is a quick fix that can be used in some cases, usually with older adolescents and adults. Some of these clients are fitted with an orthodontic appliance that can be inserted into the gaps at special times. Capping the teeth also is an option.

Often the speech and language professional is the first to suspect dental and occlusion problems. A referral is made to the dentist/orthodontist for thorough evaluation. A plan of action for speech is formed *after* the dental specialist determines a course of action for the teeth and dental arches. Sometimes our plan is to wait. For example, we may wait 12-18 months following the closing of an anterior open bite to initiate articulation therapy. This is to prevent wasting time teaching speech patterns that will change once tooth position changes. Appendices nine and ten present sample letters for such referrals.

Oral Structure

Problems in oral structure can reach far beyond simple dental problems. Patients can have significant structural alterations in the lips, cheeks, jaw, tongue or palate due to oral injury, disease, syndrome or surgery. Management of these cases has to be done on a case-by-case basis related to the location and extent of the problem. Speech correction will be toward training compensatory actions when surgical treatments are not possible. Examples are offered below.

Adult: Injured tongue-tip

This adult with lifelong normal speech and language received an injury to her tongue that left the left side of the tongue tip missing. She reported reduced sensitivity in the remaining tip tissue, stating that it tingled all the time. She found that she had begun to lisp during conversational speech. Surgery to fix the problem in the tip was not possible according to her doctors. Speech therapy was recommended.

The client was seen for three sessions during which she was taught: (1) the basics of sibilant production, (2) how to slow down and monitor her speech, (3) how to direct the tip to the right side of her front teeth in order to attain better sound, and (4) how to use cold stimuli and direct pressure on the tip to see if, over time, she could reduce the tingling. A follow-up visit approximately one year later revealed that the tingling had remained but that she was used to it and could tune it out. She reported that she still had to think about her speech production a little bit at times, and that she had to slow down to make sure that she was speaking correctly during important speaking tasks.

Adult: Significant reduction of tongue tissue

This case was reported to me by another speech-language pathologist. The client had lost much of her tongue due to surgery for oral cancer. She had great difficulty speaking and eating because the tongue tissue remaining was very small and could not reach the teeth. The primary concern was eating because she could not use her tongue to manipulate food toward the teeth for chewing, she could not clear the teeth of food for swallowing and she was in danger of aspiration. The brilliant solution was to fit her with a set of dentures that she wore inside her permanent teeth during eating. This gave her two sets of teeth. The inner teeth were closer to her remaining tongue tissue and they allowed her to eat well. Unexpectedly, the dentures also allowed her to speak more clearly.

Child: Cleft lip and palate

This child had a right unilateral cleft lip and alveolus that had left the anterior teeth in odd positions with wide gaps. She was producing a very distorted right unilateral lisp. At five years of age, her surgical and orthodontic management was incomplete, and her deciduous teeth were beginning to shed. I taught this client to use a unilateral lisp to the left instead of the right because she could achieve better sound there. Our plan was to help her use this right unilateral lisp until long term surgery and orthodontia revealed the permanent tooth position. She is still on my caseload today. This client will be monitored through the years to keep track of this process. At each step, she will be taught to use sibilants the best way she can. Hopefully there will be a point where sibilant production reaches a fairly normal state.

Swallowing and Oral Rest Position

In the ideal situation, correct swallowing and oral rest position are established before or during speech therapy for the frontal and lateral lisp. This is because of the integral relationship between speech, muscular development and swallowing. When incorrect swallowing movements and oral rest position are ignored, remediation of the motor-based lisps can be met with limited success because the motor patterns underlying them are being ignored. Many of these clients can achieve a certain amount of success on their sibilants at most levels of speech therapy. However carryover to conversation can be limited.

This is not to say that swallowing problems cause speech problems or vice versa. Instead, both swallowing and speech problems are the result of underlying problems in oral-motor function. If the oral mechanism is delayed or disordered in its movements, both speech and swallowing can be affected.

Most speech-language pathologists in the public schools are forbidden to address the issue of swallowing and oral rest position directly. The work is left to the speech-language pathologist in private practice. This therapy entails facilitating correct swallow and oral rest with appropriate jaw, lip and tongue position and movement. Again, some speech-language pathologists in private practice specialize in these areas as they relate to articulation errors. Readers interested in learning how to do this therapy are referred to the International Association of Orofacial Myology and to other published materials.

The Five-Part Problem

Some clients with a frontal lisp demonstrate a five-part problem. They have:

1. Frontal lisp
2. Anterior open bite
3. Reverse or infantile swallow pattern
4. Incorrect oral rest position
5. Oral habit

Articulation therapy for the frontal lisp is only one part of such a client's remediation process. Treatment for this client can be sequenced as follows:

1. Refer to dentist/orthodontist for evaluation
2. Eliminate the oral habit as soon as possible
3. Establish correct oral rest position

4. Establish correct swallow movements
5. Initiate articulation therapy for the frontal lisp

The time to initiate articulation therapy for the frontal lisp (#5 above) is determined on a case-by-case basis with many factors taken into consideration. One of the following four options can be chosen. We can begin articulation therapy:

1. Simultaneously with #1-4 above
2. Toward the final stages of #1-4 above
3. Immediately after completion of #1-4 above
4. 12-18 months after completion of #1-4 above

The following two cases illustrate this work in progress over time. These children, Casey and Brian, reveal how these principles can be enacted. They represent two ends of the spectrum of treatment. Casey is young and her situation is relatively simple. Brian is older and his problems are complex and long term. Upon intake both children displayed the five-fold problem summarized above.

Casey

Casey represents the easiest of cases. Casey was a three-year-old female of normal development. She had a very strong thumb sucking habit during the day and at night. She was referred to me because the mother was concerned that her upper teeth were beginning to bow outward, and she wondered how this would affect her speech. The family dentist was unconcerned about the habit because these were baby teeth, but the mother wanted to do something about it now. She could see problems coming in the future. Casey had all five problems including a thumb sucking habit, interdental tongue placement during oral rest, an immature swallow, early problems with occlusion and a frontal lisp. The frontal lisp could have been viewed as developmental in nature, but the presence of the other factors strongly suggested a need for action. That action could be taken now or later. My preference was to initiate the process now.

Because of her young age, it was determined that elimination of the oral habit would be our principle means of tackling the problems. The mother read my little book on thumb sucking and then we met twice (without the child) to talk about the ways she could implement these ideas at home. The mother decided on three courses of action:

1. The family had a new baby in the home, and the mother decided to begin talking about the difference between "big girls" and "babies" to her daughter. Part of this included attending more directly to the child's fingernails. She began to file them instead of clipping them, and she began to apply a coat of polish. The child was, of course, fascinated by all of this. The nail activity allowed the mother time to draw the child's attention to her hands and fingers. Grandma also got in the act and had an idea to apply lotion to Casey's hands at night before bed. In any case, Casey was discovering that she was big enough to do things that babies could not do.

2. Casey was rewarded with hugs, kisses and praise for keeping her hands away from her mouth during certain activities like riding in the car and watching TV. The family also made a big deal about telling daddy about specific times during the day when she remembered to keep her hands down.
3. Casey was allowed one "Sucking Time" per day. Specifically, she was allowed her to suck her thumb in order to fall asleep at night. (She didn't seem to mind the taste of the lotion.) But then the parents were going to make sure that the thumb was out of the mouth once the child was sound asleep. I didn't really like this idea because I thought it would only perpetuate the habit. But Casey's mother was a little nervous about giving up the going-to-bed sucking routine. With a new baby in the home, this mom needed a way to get the three-year-old to sleep easily, so I didn't balk at it.

This plan proved quite successful for this family. Casey eliminated her thumb-sucking pattern within one week! Casey was a mature little girl who, despite her age, seemed to understand that this would be good for her. She did not fuss or complain and took it all as a natural step in her development. Within three months her oral rest, swallow and teeth position improved. I then saw the child for one thirty-minute session and taught her the correct way to say /s/. One year later she demonstrated none of the five problems initially observed. A full program of articulation therapy to correct the frontal lisp became unnecessary, as did future orthodontic procedures.

Brian
Brian was an eleven-year-old boy who was referred to me by his school speech-language pathologist. His case was more complex. Brian had been in articulation therapy since kindergarten. He had multiple misarticulations and had worked on a wide variety of phonemes and phonological patterns. He was left with a distorted /l/ and /r/ and a frontal lisp. Brian had all five oral problems, however none of them had been addressed except speech. The parents were unaware that his nighttime thumb sucking habit (a great secret) and his occlusion problems might be related to his long-term speech problems.

I encouraged the parents to schedule an orthodontic evaluation immediately so that we could understand the full nature of his problems with occlusion. And I explained that we needed a thumb-sucking elimination program to be enacted immediately. Brian was both shy and ashamed about this problem because of his age. He wanted to do something about it because he wanted to be able to have overnights with his buddies, and he wouldn't let himself do so until the habit was gone. But Brian did not know what to do. I talked with him about ways he could eliminate the habit at night. He liked the idea of putting a thumb guard on at night. He liked working with bandages and white tape and wanted to put the contraption on every night by himself. He was sure that this would help. We also talked about wearing gloves at night, or just bandage tape alone. Brian began this process that night. He seemed eager to get it done.

The orthodontist recommended that Brian begin the process of wearing braces on both the upper and lower teeth. He had an anterior open bite as well as a narrow and high palatal arch. The braces were put in about two months following our initial evaluation. They were full upper and lower braces with a palatal expander bar on the upper teeth. This bar was like most and stretched across the palate from the molars on one side to the molars on the other side. It had the expected effect on Brian's speech. It made his speech, especially the sibilants, somewhat distorted. It was determined that articulation work would have to wait until the expander was removed. Unfortunately, the expander would stay in place for the entire time that Brian wore the braces. That, of course, would be 18 months or longer.

Articulation therapy was postponed. However, we did begin a process of training Brian to use appropriate oral rest position and correct swallow while his braces were on. This meant that he was enrolled in weekly therapy for about three months, beginning three months after the braces were in place. During this time we worked on strengthening the lip muscles, establishing closed-lip rest posture, increasing jaw strength and stability, and establishing a tip-on-the-alveolus resting posture. Swallowing exercises were developed in a hierarchy of skills and were adapted to the palatal expander. He learned to swallow fairly well even with the bar present.

Training for oral rest and swallowing took three months. Then Brian was scheduled for check-ups every six weeks during the rest of the time his braces were in place. During that time, all areas except speech began to resolve. The teeth moved into correct position and were being held in place by the braces, the thumb sucking habit was eliminated, oral rest was almost completely corrected, and the swallow was good.

Brian's speech did not change, however, so I enrolled him in weekly therapy. We began to develop skills for /l/, /r/ and the sibilants. This treatment combined traditional articulation and oral-motor therapy. We worked the basics including auditory discrimination, jaw stability and tongue mobility. This process of treatment took 14 months during which time the braces were removed.

At the end, Brian's articulation was excellent although he continued to have some problems with /l/ and /r/ in blends, and he still had to think about /l/ and /r/ in rapid conversation. He was able to control these sounds by over-stressing syllables and thinking his way through their production. We quit weekly therapy because Brian had had it. He wanted to finish the rest on his own, and I felt he could. The entire course of treatment with me was nearly three years. But he did not come to my office every week during that entire time. His sessions wove in and out of my office depending upon where he was in the sequence of remediation.

Chapter 12 Summary
Oral Habits, Oral Structure, Swallowing and Oral Rest

- The subjects of oral habits, oral structure, swallowing and oral rest are integral to the remediation of both the frontal and lateral lisp.

- In the best of circumstances, oral habits are eliminated before or during speech therapy for the frontal or lateral lisp.

- The elimination of oral habits requires special training and entails using education as well as environmental and behavioral management strategies to alter the family dynamics around the child's habit.

- Some speech-language pathologists recommend that articulation therapy be postponed for 12-18 months following the elimination of an oral habit.

- In the ideal situation, dental problems are eliminated before initiating actual speech therapy for a lisp. A plan of action for speech must be integrally related to the actions planned by dental specialists.

- Problems in oral structure can include significant structural alterations in the lips, cheeks, jaw, tongue or palate due to oral injury, disease or surgery. Management of these cases has to be done on a case-by-case basis with correction geared toward compensatory actions.

- In the ideal situation, correct swallowing and oral rest position are established before or during speech therapy for the frontal and lateral lisp. This therapy entails facilitating correct swallow and oral rest with appropriate jaw, lip and tongue position and movement.

- Some clients with a frontal lisp demonstrate a five-part problem: frontal lisp, open bite, reverse swallow, incorrect oral rest, and persistent oral habit. Articulation therapy for the frontal lisp is only one part of such a client's remediation process.

Chapter 13

Achieving Carryover

Treatment of the frontal and lateral lisps entails much more than teaching clients to reposition the oral mechanism and listen to the result. It also includes methods of engaging clients so that the things they learn in therapy will be carried over to their conversation in the real world. This means designing therapy in ways that draw the client into and commit him to the process. We are talking about more than games and activities. We are talking about the way we interact with and motivate our clients. This may seem trivial, but when it comes to the frontal and lateral lisps it is not. That is because the work of changing sibilant production is subtle, and, for many clients, unimportant.

A child with an isolated frontal or lateral lisp usually is quite intelligible. He can be understood. Therefore, the client may see no reason to change. Why should he care if he says his sibilants slightly differently than everyone else? I find this attitude especially prevalent among young male clients. They often report that their buddies don't notice or say anything about their error. Thus the client wants to know what the big deal is. He wants to know why his mom or dad is making him come to speech. Designing therapy to draw this client into the process goes to the very heart of treatment. He has to gain a modicum of commitment for treatment to work.

I have no magic to offer you in this regard. There are as many ways to interact with clients as there are therapists engaged in this work. What I can offer is the ideas that guide my treatment as it has evolved over thirty years. These are the underlying aspects of treatment that have helped me be successful with difficult or stubborn clients who have frontal or lateral lisps. These ideas are offered here to help new therapists get started. They also should help the seasoned professional get through that difficult carryover phase.

The Biggest Misconception

The greatest misconception of the carryover phase is that it is something that occurs at the end of an articulation program. For years I thought that working on transferring skills learned in the therapy room to other environments was something that we tagged on the end of the "real" program. Time in treatment taught me otherwise. Carryover must be built into the fabric of our work from the onset of treatment. Each new skill learned must be carried out into the real world for this process to work. The "carryover phase" as a concept still can be used to represent the end of treatment when carryover work is just about all that is being done. But the techniques should not be withheld until then. Carryover techniques should be incorporated into treatment right from the beginning. We shall see how to do that throughout this chapter.

Auditory Acceptance

My first concern in adjusting therapy to meet the carryover requirement is a process I call *auditory acceptance*. Auditory acceptance is the process clients go through to accept the acoustic quality (the sound) of a new way to produce their problematic phonemes. Many clients with frontal or lateral lisps do not like the way they sound when they make the sibilants a new way. Like getting used to the way one's own voice sounds on a tape recorder, it takes a while for clients to acclimate to their new way of producing sibilants. Everything in them cries out to keep things just the way they have been. Their incorrect productions sound better to them because that it what they are used to.

Each of us has an internal auditory image of our own speech. This image is integral to our self-perception, and is intimately connected to our personality and ego. To change the way one produces specific speech sounds is not just a mechanical event. It is a highly personal event that challenges one's very self-concept. And it is resistance to this new perception of oneself that can block carryover for many clients. They just don't think the new sounds reflect who they are.

Therapists can facilitate a client's awareness and acceptance of this new persona by opening up this topic from the very first time a client produces a phoneme within the acceptable range. We can say, "That was it. Perfect. Did it sound right to you?" Most clients are a little shaky in their answer to this question, so we must give them a wide berth of acceptance no matter what they say. The following sample dialogues offer suggestions for responding to client uncertainty.

Sample Dialogue

THERAPIST: Did that sound right to you?

CLIENT: I don't know.

THERAPIST: That's okay. It was correct. Pretty soon you will be able to hear that for yourself. It was very good. Just right.

Sample Dialogue

THERAPIST: Did that sound right to you?

CLIENT: Maybe.

THERAPIST: Yes! It was perfect. It seems weird though, doesn't it?

Sample Dialogue

THERAPIST: Did that sound right to you?

CLIENT: Yes???

THERAPIST: Yes! You are right. That was correct. It sounds like that was not what you expected.

Sample Dialogue

    THERAPIST: Did that sound right to you?

    CLIENT: I'm not sure.

    THERAPIST: I understand. It doesn't seem right at first, does it? It sounds wrong. But that was correct. It was very good. Now, let's do it again. Listen very carefully. Even though it seems wrong, it is the way I want you to do it for now. Don't worry about how it sounds. Just do it exactly the same way you just did it.

The idea here is to teach the client how to talk about and begin to accept this strange new sound. Get him to open up and respond to both the sound and the process. Opening this door early in therapy gives a closer intimacy to everything we do. It keeps the therapist and the client in synch about this new way of speaking. It is a way to initiate carryover practice right from the onset of treatment because it opens up feelings.

Determination

Have you ever tried to change a personal habit? Perhaps you tried to stop cracking your knuckles, biting your nails, licking your lips or twirling your hair. Changing a personal habit is hard. It takes determination. Clients with lisps who need to change the way they speak and who have the cognitive skills to do so also must have the determination to do so. Lack of determination may be the only reason that your client is failing his lisp program. He may want to change. His parents may want him to change. He may even have the skill to change. But he simply may lack the determination to do so.

An inability to change a habit through self-determination can have many causes. The child may be immature or preoccupied with other scheduled events. His parents may make disparaging remarks about his speech that he cannot get past. He may have failed in prior therapy. There are countless reasons for lack of determination to change. It is a hopeless feeling.

Although we are not psychotherapists, we must explore the reasons why each individual client has a lack of determination to change his lisp, and treatment plans must be adjusted accordingly. A change in therapy could mean any one of many little things depending upon the client and his situation. Here are a few ideas to begin your thinking:

- Enlist MORE help from the parents; teach them how to respond appropriately and to be encouraging; show them ways to give the client positive feedback; teach the family to cheer for him
- Enlist LESS help from parents if they are especially bad in interacting with or are unavailable for their child; structure your treatment so that it is you and the child against the whole world working together to conquer this error
- POSTPONE therapy until other lessons or events are concluded, or until the child matures
- CHANGE your schedule with him; enroll the client in individual instead of group therapy, or vice versa, or see him earlier or later in the day

- Challenge the client more; dare him; get him to STEP UP; treat him in a more mature way
- Loosen things up, let things get a little WILD; be funnier; begin a much more liberal reward system; bring cupcakes to therapy; shake loose his hopelessness
- Tighten things up; drill more; get more serious; work at a faster or more determined pace; make him get to work; make a speech CONTRACT; ask the client if he really wants to make this change; tell him you don't want him there unless he gets serious
- Allow more time for the client to TALK about how he feels about all this; take more time to get to know him; talk about how hard this work can be; tell him about the struggles other kids have had with this; empathize with him

Fear

Some clients with a frontal or lateral lisp can perform brilliantly in the therapy room but are very afraid to change their speech in front of others out in the real world. This stops carryover dead in its tracks. The client may act as if he doesn't care about changing his speech, but underlying his bravado is fear. Often this fear stems from not wanting to do anything to stand out. This is especially true of preadolescents. These children usually want to blend in to the crowd as much as possible. It is a funny period of life. They want to blend in yet they want to be noticed and accepted at the same time. But they want to be noticed for the right reasons – like for wearing the right clothes or having the right hairdo. Being noticed because you have changed your speech is not the right reason for many of them.

We can help kids get past this fear by talking very specifically about safe people. Safe people are those with whom the client feels comfortable trying out this new way of speaking. Our first task is to figure out who the first safe person may be. Begin by having the client help you make a list of people with whom he might use his new speech. This list will contain safe and unsafe people, including family members, friends, teachers, scout leaders, bus drivers, and so forth.

From this master list, begin to talk about which one person he can try this skill, and circle that name. Ask, "Who do you think you could try your new speech with?" The best first person probably is his mother or father, or whoever brings him to speech. This is the best first person because they are invested in the process. They also are a good choice because you can guide them in their response. They can be prepared ahead of time to react in a very positive way. But the first best person should be anyone with whom the client feels the safest. I have seen children who pick their grandmother, best friend, scout leader, Sunday school teacher, bus driver, school chef, school custodian, cousin, brother and babysitter. One child even selected his dog. Remember, the client's perception of safety is the key factor.

Once the communication partner is selected, the next task is to figure out when and where to try this, and what to say. Kids need us to help them be very specific about this. Make a plan that they can understand and carry out successfully. The following examples illustrate:

Sample 1

    WHO: mom

    WHEN: on the way home from speech

    WHERE: in the car

    WHAT: *Soup.* Tell mom that I want *soup* for dinner

    HOW: with a correct S on *soup*

Sample 2

    WHO: cafeteria lady

    WHEN: tomorrow

    WHERE: at the cash register

    WHAT: *Thanks.* Say *thanks* after she hands me my change

    HOW: with a correct S on *thanks*

Sample 3

    WHO: brother

    WHEN: tonight

    WHERE: at home

    WHAT: *Stephen.* Ask Stephen for a pencil and use his name.

    HOW: with a correct S on *Stephen* and *pencil*

Make sure to follow up the next week by asking the client if he remembered to try his new speech with the person he selected. Hear him out, and then help him select another person. Help the client gradually expand his list of communication partners over time, and help him be brave in selecting new people. Once having tried this method with a few people, I find that most kids begin to branch out to new people all on their own. They proudly report the results to me. "Guess what?" they ask. "Guess who I said my new S with?" Each little attempt they make in this regard begins to build their confidence in the process. This creates an environment in which carryover is assured. Building a network of safe communication partners should be developed gradually from the onset of treatment.

One Word Assignments

Another method of encouraging carryover is to require the client to say one key word correctly all week long. Chose a common word and make a rule that the client has to say that particular word correctly every time he uses it that week. A common word like *please* or *thanks* will work well. Practice that word in therapy so he's prepared. Add a second word the following week, and so forth. After a few weeks the client will begin to add new words that are important to him and that arise out of his everyday conversations. For example, his class may be doing a project on dinosaurs and he may want you to help him practice that word and the names of several specific dinosaurs.

Along with single words, make sure to include specific common phrases on his list. Have the client help you generate this list. For example, if /s/ is the target, include phrases like:

- Let's pretend…
- Who's turn is it?
- Where's it go?
- What's that?
- I said, 'Don't.'
- Nice shot!
- It's my turn
- This one?
- Score!

Rate

Fast rate of speech often is problematic in clients who have lisps and other mild articulation errors. But even if rate is not a problem, per se, our clients must slow down to practice and they must slow down in order to include their new way of pronouncing these phonemes into connected speech. Slowing down rate of spontaneous speech can be the key to carryover.

I find it does not help simply to ask clients to "slow down." Most of them do not know how to organize that idea into their spontaneous speech. They do it correctly for a moment, and then quickly slip back into their fast conversational mode. You can tell them to slow down all day long and they won't. They just can't.

A different method works better. Structure your entire lesson around slow speech you model yourself by ov-er-ar-ti-cu-la-ting-each-in-di-vi-du-al-sy-lla-ble-with-in-the-words-of-con-ver-sa-tion. Did you get that? I am not just talking about the way the client talks. I am talking about the way YOU talk. Talk with exaggerated syllables the entire time you are working with the client. This will slow the entire rate of conversation. Punching out syllables causes rate to slow naturally. This gives the client enough time to incorporate his new way of producing these sounds into his speech. Teach him to speak with distinction and clarity by focusing on the pronunciation of each individual syllable. This will sound unnatural and stilted. But it will give him tremendous success in his attempts to incorporate his new sounds into conversation. It will teach him how to control his speech. Speed things up over time and challenge him to maintain control as he does.

Frank Discussions

Carryover is enhanced when we have very frank discussions about the child's lisp right from the onset of treatment. During the evaluation, ask, "Why did you come here today?" If the client mumbles something about his speech, try to focus his attention by asking, "What is the problem with your speech?" A direct question like that forces a client to identify his problem. Then, in every treatment session, ask him, "Why do you come here?" This forces him to state the problem again and again. It becomes a way for him to accept the problem. Ask this question until he laughs or complains that you ask him that same question every week. Then you know he's got it.

Clients with lisps need to know the specific reasons they are in speech. We can make blatant statements like, "You stick your tongue out too far during speech" or "You are making the air come out the side of your mouth. That is incorrect." These statements help to draw the client into awareness and acceptance of the problem. Make sure to do this if the client is balking about therapy.

Someone once said that only an enemy that can be named can be defeated. So I pick a name to call the problem we are addressing. I teach my clients words like "lisp," "lateral lisp" and "frontal lisp" if that is appropriate. With younger clients, I might call it, "our S sound" or "the snake sound." One client had such a hard time with his S, and had had so much failure in prior therapy, that he already had begun calling it "the evil sound." So that's what we called it for a while. He was serious about the evil nature of "S." But I began to speak the phrase with a teasingly eerie quality that eventually helped the client to laugh about it. This took the client's hard fearful edge off the phrase. I used his name for the target and helped him change his attitude toward it.

A Reason to Change

Practicing words, phrases and paragraphs will only take certain clients so far in articulation therapy because that work is not functional. Practicing words just for the sake of practicing words has no purpose other than to please the therapist. Practicing words is not pragmatic and may not facilitate carryover into conversation.

On the other hand, functional articulation practice is work that takes our clients to the real reason they should make a change. And the only real reason to change the way one speaks is so that the spoken message can get across. If a client can be understood by speaking the way he always has, then he may have no real reason to change. But if listeners respond to the client as if they don't understand him or are confused about his message, then the client is jolted with a reason to change.

For example, let's say that you have been working on /s/ for some time and the client can say it correctly in words, phrases and sentences in the therapy room. One day, you see the client standing outside waiting for his bus after school. You ask him, 'What'cha doing?" to which he responds, "Waiting for the buth." That is the moment to stimulate for carryover. The way we respond to the child's incorrect production is the key factor in the carryover process, and several options are available. Some responses help the carryover process while others hinder it and enable the client to continue his error. Table 1 (on next page) summarizes several types of responses and their effect on the client.

It should be obvious to the reader that this type of work is not used until the client has full capacity to speak his targets correctly in the therapy room. This is not a how-to-say-the-sound-correctly approach. It is a carryover method. We are talking about techniques to push a client over the conversational edge when it is appropriate to do so. To use this with a client who is unprepared to handle it would be cruel.

What about the client who shuts down after his therapist indicates that she cannot understand him? What if he doesn't care if he gets his message across and says nothing for his next turn in the dialogue? Then the technique is being introduced too early. Probably there is not enough rapport between therapist and client. He does not care if you understand him because he does not care about you and his relationship with you. Drop this technique for a while and build trust in other ways.

Speech-language pathologists typically are friendly, good-hearted people who can build rapport with almost any client. But there always are a few students we cannot reach. Some clients with isolated frontal or lateral lisps fit this category. Usually these are not typical

Table 1

Client Remark	Therapist Input	Client Response	Client Perception	Client Modification
"Waiting for the buth."	"Waiting for the bu<u>s</u>?" (model)	"Yea."	I spoke correctly	None
"Waiting for the buth."	"Say, 'bu<u>s</u>.'" (correction)	"Bus."	SLP will correct me if necessary	None
"Waiting for the buth."	"Can you say that better?" (cue)	"Bus."	SLP will cue me to speak better if necessary	None
"Waiting for the buth."	"Huh?" (communication breakdown)	"Waiting for the bu<u>sss</u>."	She can't understand me if I speak incorrectly	Has to change the way he speaks to get his message across

students. These are students with subtle yet bigger cognitive or emotional issues that interfere with relationship building. The question is how long to keep these clients in therapy before we give up. Therapy intervals (see below) can help but this brings up a broader issue. Articulation therapy programs fail all the time because a client does not have the cognitive, attention, linguistic, motor or auditory skills to back it up. This can be a real problem in the public schools when a parent is demanding articulation services for which the child does not have the underlying skills. For example, what will you do with a six-year-old child with Down Syndrome who has a frontal lisp and a receptive language level of 24 months? You may have to address this issue district-wide if guidelines are not already in place. Develop rules and regulations for articulation therapy qualifications and dismissal criteria for a wide range of clients with lisps.

Therapy Intervals

Once enrolled, some clients can feel like their work on the frontal or lateral lisp will never end. These clients don't push themselves forward to the end because there is no end in sight. With no end in sight, there is no reason to concentrate on carryover skill.

To ease this feeling, we can work in time intervals. In private practice we can schedule clients for three months of therapy subject to review at the end. This way we have the option to dismiss them or schedule for another three-month interval depending upon how things are going. This imposed time limit on therapy works well for clients, therapists and parents. It allows us to think about the process with finality. The child, parent or therapist can call it quits at the end of any three-month period. Time limits make it feel like this sometimes never-ending process is manageable.

A time limitation also can be used in the public school therapy program. Instead of thinking about a full school year, think in two-month intervals for kids with lisps: October-November, January-February, March-April and May-June. That leaves September for testing, scheduling and IEP meetings. And it leaves May and June as a block for make-up sessions, more testing, year-end IEP meetings, report writing, etc. Scheduling this way allows kids to be dropped after two months if necessary. And it helps kids understand what it is they are to accomplish during each individual block. A two-month block or something akin to it may ease an overburdened schedule and help certain clients in the carryover phase. Again, policies may need to be set.

Clear Reinforcement

Kids will do almost anything for the praise of an adult, but our reinforcement should keep carryover in mind from the onset of treatment. Nothing drags out an articulation program for a lisp more than wishy-washy feedback from the SLP. Make sure to give clear signals all through the process so the client knows exactly what to do by the time real carryover work comes along. Use clear words of praise:

- Great!
- Nice!
- I loved it!
- I heard it!
- Outstanding!
- Perfect!
- Good!
- You did it!
- Well done!
- Excellent!
- Yes!
- You got it!
- That is right!

Also use clear words of rejection when the client makes an error:

- No.
- Incorrect.
- I don't think so.
- Not good enough.
- I need to hear a better one than that.
- That was horrible.
- Terrible.
- What!?
- Oh no!
- No way.
- You forgot what you were supposed to do!
- You blew that one, absolutely blew it.
- You have got to be kidding.

Also use clear body language to indicate performance success or failure. When the client's utterance is in error, act like you are choking or ready to pass out, make an obnoxious buzzer sound or close your eyes and grasp your ears as if you head something horrible. On the other hand, raise your arms in victory, smile broadly, sit up straighter or dance a jig for a correct utterance.

Parents

There are parents and there are parents. We never see certain parents while others are there all the time. Some parents never stop talking to us while we are trying to work with their child. Others talk on their cell phones in the lobby while they are "waiting for the kid to get done with speech." And in the public school, a parent can be simply a figment of our imagination. An approach for handling the parents of the client with a lisp must be implemented so carryover will be successful.

I set boundaries with parents that work with me in private practice. I tell them that the child is there to work with me alone, and that each session will include some demonstration for them to see how well he is doing. This means that for every 30 minutes of scheduled private practice therapy time, I get at least 20 minutes of direct one-on-one interaction and treatment with the client, and I get a few minutes with the adult. I bring the parent in a little bit earlier each week until I can work with the client while the parent sits through the entire session. After a few weeks of sitting through entire sessions, most parents ask if they can wait in the lobby.

In the schools, we naturally have less opportunity to interact with parents. We can use one of our scheduled times with the child to call the parents, or we can set aside a block in our schedule for phone calls or visits. Some calls can take the place of scheduled therapy time with the child because communication with the parent is just as important as the direct treatment time.

I find that most parents whose child has an isolated frontal or lateral lisp just want me to be the expert and fix their child's problem. They just want to know that everything is going well. They tolerate information given to them, but, like going to the dentist, they just want me to take care of it. I actually prefer this to the parent who wants me to explain every little thing and who wants to turn into little versions of me. That is hard. Most parents have almost no background to understand what it is we do. I prefer the distance afforded to me as the professional. It allows me to get much more done in a shorter period of time.

Keep parents informed by sending home hand-written notes periodically. Make them personal. "Johnny is doing great in speech. He can read all the paragraphs on page 47 of his speech binder with perfect S sounds. Have him read paragraph four aloud to you tonight. Remind him to do it just like he does it with me in speech." Little positive notes like this keep channels open. This helps all levels of therapy especially the carryover process.

Individual vs. Group Therapy

Individual therapy is an excellent way to do all kinds of therapy, and this includes that for the frontal and lateral lisps. Individual therapy allows you to go to the heart of the problem each and every session. Individual therapy makes for good rapport building, helps children open up, and allows you to be direct about difficulties in the process. All this helps the long-term carryover process.

Small group therapy probably is the norm in public school therapy. I knew one therapist years ago who worked in the public schools and who was an advocate of large group therapy. In fact, she wanted to have full-size classes, one each for "S", "R", "L", "F" and "Th." Can you imagine a full-size class to teach "S" to all your kids with frontal and lateral lisps?

It sounded very interesting to me, but I never had the opportunity to try it. This might be a very nice way to handle large caseloads of older kids in regular education.

Building Rapport Over Time

Old time speech-language pathologists always taught that the first step in therapy is to establish rapport. This is true in essence, but I have found that rapport cannot always be established first. Sometimes you simply have to get to work, and from the work emerges rapport.

Take Mandy, for example. Mandy was a "borderline normal" student of 17 years of age when she began her work with me. She had the lifestyle of an emancipated teenager but the cognitive skills of about a 12-year-old. Mandy did not trust me for several months of therapy. She came every week because she knew better than to skip an element of her schedule, but she clearly did not want to come at first. She had limited awareness of her lisp pattern, and she had great difficulty remembering to do the home practice work. Mandy seemed to forget what we were doing from one session to the next.

Mandy's consistent attendance, however, impacted her in a profound way. Her progress was very slow, and I was unsure of her feelings about therapy. But over time I began to realize that she loved coming to therapy. She had come from a neglectful home environment, and I think I was the first adult who was available simply to listen to her. I listened to her a lot as I tried to figure out how I was going to get certain concepts into her mind. She was drinking up this attention. Wow. Mandy bonded to me and I wasn't even trying. Her speech came along very nicely as a result of her attachment to me. She wanted to work hard to please the lady who was nice to her.

Rapport can make or break any speech and language therapy program. It can be especially important to consider in working with the frontal and lateral lisp because the clients tend to be in late elementary school, junior high or high school. Trust is a critical part of the learning process in this age group. But trust does not always come right away. Often it is built over time as you prove to the client that you know what you are talking about. Nothing builds trust in adolescent children more than proving that you can actually help them. This means structuring your therapy in such a way that each and every session is founded on success. Get to work and help the client see his own success.

Baby Steps

Building a session around success means taking baby steps so that the client can perform brilliantly each time. Baby steps performed very well build the self-confidence a client needs to take him through the carryover phase. When a client says, "This is easy!" you know you are working at the right level for building that confidence.

Building success this way sometimes means cutting the work short. For example, some clients can sustain a new behavior only for a few trials before they begin to fail again. Slowly build your session toward the client's apex of performance, and then let it go. Make a big deal of his performance and then broaden your praise of him. Talk about how much he is growing, what a great kid he is and so forth. Then ask him something to completely remove his mind from the work he just did. Ask, for example, "What were you saying earlier about that baseball game? Did you guys win?" Then encourage a general discussion for a few minutes. In that way, we lead the client to success and quit while we are ahead. Use the rest of the session to continue building rapport. If there is time, return to the work a few minutes later to see if you can build toward peak performance again.

I think all seasoned therapists allow their clients to speak freely on other topics in therapy. I remember watching my first external practicum therapist do this in the public school in which I was placed. Being young and inexperienced, I thought she was wasting time just talking with the kids. But over the years I began to realize that she only had 30-minutes per week to get to know each student, and most of that was in groups. She was using every moment she had with each client to get to know them, and they she. She was allowing them time just to be themselves so she could plan for them in the best ways possible. She was building rapport and stretching things out so the kids could take baby steps.

Don't Be Fooled

Don't be fooled into believing that a sound is correct when it is not. And don't deny that your client cannot produce his sibilants correctly. A program for a frontal or lateral lisp can fail because the therapist works on words when the client cannot even produce a single sibilant sound correctly. Clients, especially those with lateral lisps, can produce sibilants in such a way that they almost sound correct but they are not. They learn to release just enough air that the sloppy lateral sound is diminished, but the air stream channel still is not directed in the right way. Use a straw or other means described earlier to determine exactly what the client is doing to produce his sound, and do not let him fool you. He's not really trying to get away with anything. He is simply trying to comply by making his sound the way he thinks you want it to sound.

If we accept sibilants that truly are not correct because we chose to ignore the oral movement and position problem, we create a situation in which the client is rehearsing sounds time and again that are not correct. The client will never finish the program because when it comes to rapid conversational speech, his sounds will fall apart again. He has not learned anything new. STOP. Return to the sound in isolation. Figure out how to help him say it correctly with a thorough oral-motor analysis. And begin your training again from the start using correct movement and position.

Home Practice

Home practice can ensure carryover. But home practice will only work if the client is practicing things correctly at home. Therefore, home practice is encouraged only under very strict conditions. Use the following guideline: *Assign home practice that incorporates ONLY those aspects of therapy that the client has complete control over in therapy.*

In other words, ask your client to practice only those things that he can do with about 99% accuracy. Why? You do not want your client practicing incorrect oral movement patterns all week long between therapy sessions. This will only reinforce his errors. You want him to gain small well-controlled skills over a period of time. If he practices new correct skills at home, he will be ready for the next new step the following week. Unfortunately, if he practices incorrectly at home, he will have gained nothing during the week and may, in fact, be a little worse off than he was the week before.

Design home practice to be short and sweet. Consider home practice that takes less than five minutes. I prefer practice that takes one minute or less to be done in the bathroom at the mirror after he brushes his teeth. The regular tooth-brushing routine sets the pace for and is a reminder to practice the speech work. It is usually something that parents encourage every day anyway.

The Speech Binder

An old-fashioned three-ring binder can be an extremely beneficial tool in articulation therapy for a frontal or lateral lisp. The individual client binder is a way to store all practice sheets, whether commercial reproductions or hand-made. It helps us build and record the process from conception to maturity, from the cornerstone sound to conversation.

Equipment: Have the following on hand when working with a three-ring binder: plain 8.5"x11" paper, colorful markers, pens, a three-hole punch, stickers.

Include and create pages that reflect the work on which you are focused for the day. For example, when discussing the difference between a midline air stream and the lateral one your client uses, draw a schematic like that in Figure 74. Draw it as the client watches, and describe each part as you do. Say, "Let's pretend this is the your mouth… Here are the flat teeth in the front, … here are the round canines, … here are the molars, … and here is your tongue. Now use your finger to show me where the air should come out." Draw an arrow to indicate the direction of wanted airflow. Then ask, "Now show me where your air comes out." And draw an appropriate arrow.

Visual teaching methods like this are an ideal way to make concrete the abstract oral position work of sibilant production. Visual pages also help present, organize and store phoneme and words lists rehearsed in therapy sessions. With the learning and practice pages bound together and easily accessible, you have made a permanent record of the treatment

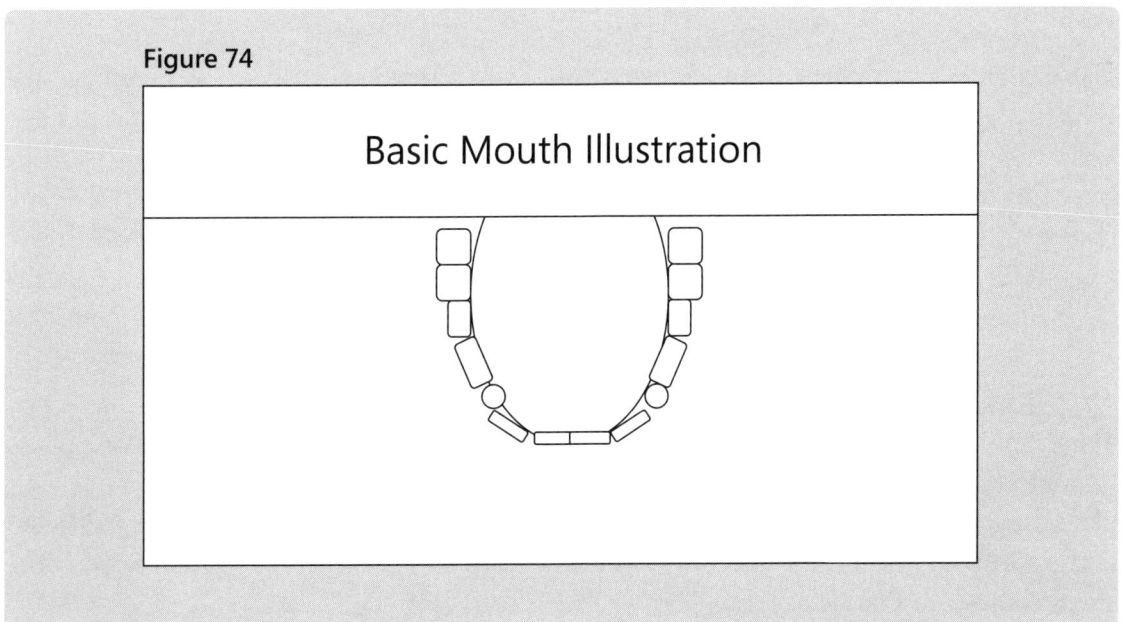

Figure 74

Basic Mouth Illustration

procedures. Have the client date and number each page so that you also have a permanent record of the plan in sequence. Binders make explaining the process of therapy easier for parent conferences. And they are a snazzy way to let other team members know exactly what's going on in speech.

Adopt a special way to indicate which pages are for homework practice. Draw a red star at the top of homework pages, or place a sticker on them. Or make a separate page that lists the pages to be rehearsed at home.

Creating binders like this at school is possible, but it makes for more junk for the kids to cart home and back every school day. Consider making pages that can become part of a speech section in the client's regular classroom binder. Or make single pages to send home. Keep copies in your office if possible. Or create a binder for in-therapy use only and send home a page periodically for the parents. That way you maintain control of the binder, you have a record right there for every session so that you know what you are doing, and the parents are kept abreast of the process.

When possible I prefer to use hand-made pages for the binder for the simple reason that the program can be designed specifically for the client's immediate work. Commercially prepared workbook pages tend to include material for which the client is unprepared. If you use preprinted material, cross off the work for which the client is not ready.

Negative Practice

A fantastic way to solidify a clients ability to carryover his new work into conversation is to practice the old lisping pattern on purpose. This is introduced after the client has learned to produce the phonemes correctly, of course. Use the same word lists you have been using. You can:

- Practice all the words with a lisp
- Practice each word twice: with a lisp and then correctly
- Practice one word with a lisp and the next word correctly

Some clients hate therapy until we reach this point. Then suddenly, when they have the ability to go back and forth between correct and incorrect productions, they find it fun and interesting. Modeling the client's lisp pattern can be a high point of therapy. This can be great fun for the client if he has learned to produce his sounds correctly and is in the later stages of the program. Over time the client will not want to make his error anymore. It will feel wrong to him. It will bother him. This reveals that the client is near completion. A client even can forget how to do it the old way. This is a client who is done.

Content and Carryover

There are several reasons related to the content of the actual program that can cause a client to fail to reach the carryover stage. The first of these is RIGIDITY of approach. For example, a program can easily fail if a speech-language pathologist rigidly approaches treatment with an initial-medial-final mindset. Be flexible in your approach, always open to what the client shows you that he can do.

Second, a program can fail to move into carryover if therapy focuses too much time and attention on SINGLE WORDS. Make sure to work all language levels. Build phrases, sentences, reading and conversation into your program.

Third, the program can fail or stall when we ignore the role of consonant CLUSTERS in word productions. Do not pick random assortments of words to practice. Instead, design your program around very specific oral movement patterns. You are training new oral movements, not new phonemes. Therefore, make your work center around movement patterns. The words *spoon, star, skate, smoke, snake, slide* and *sweater* each require a subtle yet significant change in oral movement and position on each /s/. Rehearse words with similar patterns so that the client learns to habituate the movement patterns.

Fun

Finally, lack of carryover to conversation, and lack of enthusiasm about speech therapy in general, simply can be due to the fact the client is not having fun. Everything about speech-language therapy is serious business – testing, scheduling, writing IEP's, parent approval, staff meetings. This is real serious professional work. But in the midst of it is a kid who wants to enjoy himself. Therapists who are fun are welcoming. If you have a client who is failing to carry over to conversation, ask yourself how much fun he is having with you. Does he like this?

I am not advocating that speech therapy become a laughing matter. In the final analysis, however, therapy should be amusing and interesting to the client. It should pique his interest and his natural curiosity. It should be something that is fun to think about. Not the games; the information should be fun. The knowledge he is gaining should draw him into the process. That is what will ensure carryover.

I have observed that therapy that is not fun usually is void of personality. Either the client or the therapist is holding back and not letting their true personality come through. Make sure you are being genuine with your clients. Model someone your client wants to be with and look up to.

Done

How do you know when an articulation program for a frontal or lateral lisp is complete? There may be one sparkling moment when a child will carry over all he has learned into all speaking situations. But that is not what we usually see. Usually therapy rather peters out as the client gradually gains the skills he needs. In the old days, professors used to teach that articulation therapy is complete once the client reaches 75% correct productions in spontaneous speech. My experience has taught me that this is a very reasonable expectation. Once that 75% is reached, I dismiss kids from regular weekly therapy and put them on a follow-up program. We have one more therapy session at two, six and twelve months. That's the plan, however most kids even don't need that final session.

In order to be able to monitor a child's conversational speech we must structure our therapy in ways that clients feel comfortable speaking up during their sessions. Build that feeling from the onset of treatment by establishing rapport in such a way that you and the client become intimate conversational partners. If you stay away from simply rehearsing words on a list every week, and if your work allows your clients the freedom to speak openly and honestly with you, you will create this atmosphere of dialogue. This will allow you the opportunity you need to monitor carryover skills right from the start. Open communication by your client will help you recognize when your guidance is no longer needed. Then you can celebrate.

Chapter 13 Summary
Achieving Carryover

- Carryover must be built into the fabric of our work from the onset of treatment. It is not something to stick on the end of a program.

- Auditory acceptance is the process clients go through to accept the way their phonemes sound when they are changed.

- Changing a lisp means changing habits. Determination is needed.

- Clients can be afraid to change their speech in front of others. Talk about safe people and the way to speak to them.

- Encourage carryover by practicing one key word or phrase correctly all week long.

- Slow down for practice by emphasizing individual syllables in dialogue.

- Ensure carryover by having very frank discussions about the child's lisp right from the onset of treatment.

- Functional articulation practice is work that takes our clients to the real reason they should make a change.

- Work in specific time intervals to ease the sense that therapy is a never-ending process.

- Give clear feedback signals so the client knows exactly what to do all throughout therapy.

- Set boundaries with parents. Incorporate them as able. Send home encouraging notes.

- Rapport is critical. Get to work and allow rapport to emerge from it. Success is the groundwork for rapport amongst adolescents.

- Building a session around success means taking baby steps so that the client can perform brilliantly each time.

- Don't be fooled into believing that a sound is correct when it is not.

- Home practice will only work if the client is practicing things correctly at home. Limit the home practice to very short activities that rehearse very specific things. Design this work around the client's daily tooth brushing routine.

- A speech binder can be an extremely beneficial tool in articulation therapy. It makes the work visual and keeps it organized.

- Solidify carryover skills by practicing the old lisping pattern on purpose. Kids usually love this.

- Rigidity of approach and lack of fun can limit carryover.

- Professors have taught that therapy is complete once the client reaches 75% correct productions in spontaneous speech.

- Stay away from simply rehearsing words on a list every week. Create an atmosphere of dialogue so you can monitor carryover skills right from the onset of treatment.

Chapter 14

Real Clients in Real Therapy

Our discussion of the evaluation and treatment of the frontal and lateral lisps is complete. This final chapter demonstrates that treatment of the frontal and lateral lisps can be quite varied in terms of content and time involved. It presents summaries of real clients enrolled in real therapy. These examples are meant to help the reader understand the divergent nature of these therapies. Each case presents basic information about the client, his speech problem, the treatment process, results and lessons learned in the process.

David: The Easiest Therapy Imaginable for a Bilateral Lisp

David was a fourth grade student enrolled in public school during the 1970's. David was new to the school district after having moved to the United States from England the prior summer. His teacher had referred him for speech screening during the fall semester. She wanted to know if his problem was one of error or accent. David had received no prior therapy and demonstrated no other developmental or learning problems.

- *Screening:* Initial screening revealed that in addition to speaking a dialect of British English, David used a bilateral lisp on all the sibilant phonemes. Oral-motor skills appeared well developed and the lisp seemed to be the result of simple habit. Articulation on all other phonemes was excellent.

- *Treatment:* During the initial screening session, I described the problem of the sibilants to the student. David seemed to understand the problem and was willing to be enrolled in therapy. David was scheduled to begin weekly therapy the following week.

- *Results:* David returned the following week for his first session and his bilateral lisp had completely disappeared! Stunned, I looked back at my original notes to make sure I was not remembering his problem incorrectly. After assuring myself that I was not imagining things, I asked him what he did to make this rapid and dramatic change. David replied that no one had ever explained to him that he was making these sounds incorrectly. He said that the things I had explained to him the prior week had made sense. During the week between his screening appointment and his first therapy session, David had figured out which phonemes were affected. Then he had figured out how to say them correctly from the description

I had offered during the screening. He explained that he simply made himself say the phonemes correctly from then on.

- *Lessons:* This amazing story of David seems to prove without doubt that the lateral lisp can be the result of simple habit and lack of information. It demonstrates the power of information in the treatment process. It also shows us that a bright client's self determination can result in near immediate change.

Tanika: The Narrow Palate and the Frontal Lisp

Tanika was a twelve-year-old ninth grade student who was referred for a frontal lisp. She displayed no other developmental or learning problems, and she had never received speech therapy.

- *Evaluation:* Tanika had a frontal lisp on all the sibilants and a very high narrow palate. Eating and swallowing skills were age-appropriate. The mother explained that Tanika was scheduled to begin orthodontic treatment in three months. The first plan was to have a palatal spreader placed on the upper dental arch. The mother wondered if we could take care of the lisp before orthodontia began. I explained that most students take longer than three months to correct a frontal lisp. I also explained that once the palatal spreader was placed, Tanika's speech would become distorted due to the bar that would be placed across the palate. Work on the sibilants would have to wait while the spreader was in place.

- *Treatment:* We decided: (1) to engage in two months of treatment to initiate tongue retraining, (2) to abandon therapy while the spreader was in place, and (3) to re-assess speech, oral rest position and swallowing once the spreader was removed. Tanika began weekly half-hour therapy sessions. I taught her to anchor the back lateral margins of the tongue against the upper molars in order to create a central channel. With her tongue in this position, Tanika could produce a decent /ʃ/ phoneme in isolation. From there we worked on /ʃ/ in the initial position of words. By the time we dismissed for orthodontia, Tanika had good control over /ʃ/ in words, phrases and sentences, but we had worked on no other phonemes.

- *Results:* Tanika's wore her palatal spreader for about six months, and then she received a retainer that she was to wear 24 hours per day for at least one year. The wider palate allowed a much better midline sibilant sound. I saw her once during that time and she had maintained her skill in producing /ʃ/, but she was not practicing much and had not generalized the skill to other phonemes.

  Tanika began a second round of weekly half-hour sessions. She was able to produce /ts/ right away, and from there we addressed all the other sibilant phonemes at the same time. Once she could produce all phonemes with her tongue back while reading aloud and while engaging in conversation with me in the therapy room, we dropped to bi-weekly treatment, then to bi-monthly. This process took about nine months during which time I made sure that she was retaining her skill. One year later I had a follow-up session with her and she had retained excellent speech. She reported that she had forgotten how to say the sound incorrectly. When I showed her how she used to do it, she was embarrassed and said it was "really weird."

- *Lessons:* The process of training for a lisp must work around orthodontic appliances. Sometimes treatment is postponed until certain stages in orthodontic treatment are complete. The entire process can take two years or more even when the client is doing very well because orthodontic appliances are in place for a long time.

Will: The Lateral Lisp and Severe Cognitive Impairment

Will was a fifteen-year-old boy enrolled in special education. He was unable to read and he could not count. Skills he learned were gained through rote training.

- *Evaluation:* Will was able to sort, match and name. He spoke in about 50 highly unintelligible yet functional single words, but he tended to be very quiet. Will could follow simple one-part directions. He was severely dysarthric due to neurological and developmental issues. Will had a bilateral lisp on a gross sibilant sound that he used on a few words.

- *Treatment:* Speech and language therapy focused on following directions, speaking louder with better overall enunciation, answering simple questions, and engaging in simple dialogue scripts appropriate to school and home routines. Will had no concept of letter or phoneme, per se, and was unable to follow any directions related to oral placement and sound production.

- *Results:* Will made progress in all targeted areas that school year. However, any work that could have been geared toward the lateral lisp was abandoned due to cognitive interference.

- *Lessons:* Depressed levels of cognition are the greatest impediment to articulation learning, especially when the subject is the refined oral control needed for sibilant production. In cases such as Will's, articulation therapy usually is directed toward general pronunciation to ensure that the words these children can speak are intelligible to their communication partners. Treatment also is directed toward these other people to make sure they are attending and responding appropriately to the few things the client can say. A lateral lisp in a client with severe cognitive dysfunction and related severe receptive and expressive speech and language delay/disorder usually is left untreated.

Arnie: Emerging Lateral Lisp, Cerebral Palsy and Dysarthria

Arnie was a twelve-year-old boy with cerebral palsyy and moderate cognitive impairment. He demonstrated moderate-to-severe expressive language delay and severe dysarthria. Arnie was very talkative in the right situations.

- *Evaluation:* I had worked with Arnie for about three years at the time his sibilants began to emerge, and they were emerging bilaterally. Arnie's most stubborn phonological patterns were initial and final consonant deletion and fronting. The stridents as well as /k/ and /g/ were proving to be the most difficult for him. Arnie had a significant feeding and drooling problem, and he was on medication to keep saliva production at a minimum. Arnie also had very bad occlusion with a very high and narrow palate, very large and protruding anterior teeth, and what looked like a mandible that was too small relative to his maxilla. The teeth and jaw problem caused all his bi-labials to be produced with labio-dental contact, and they contributed to the feeding problem (weak bite and chew, poor bolus formation, incomplete evacuation on the swallow, very messy eater, excessive stuffing.) Arnie was hyposensitive in the oral area and had generalized low muscular tone.

- *Treatment:* As one might imagine, Arnie and I worked on "everything": vocabulary, concepts, auditory attention and discrimination, syntax, semantics, dialogue, question comprehension, direction following, topic maintenance, and so forth. Expressive speech centered on vocal projection, intonation, marking syllables, voicing and devoicing, bi-labial position, back sounds /k/ and /g/, vowel differentiation, diphthongs, and initial and final consonants.

    I held back my work on the stridents because as soon as the first one appeared, it sounded bi-lateral. Closer inspection revealed that these sounds were not in fact bi-lateral. But they sounded that way due to the very high palate and poor occlusion of all the teeth, especially the anterior teeth. A poorly shaped central groove was forming but the shape of the mouth was allowing too much air to escape. I decided to leave the sibilant alone until after he had an orthodontic evaluation. But Arnie was also in school therapy, and his SLP there was working on sibilants. Arnie did not use these phonemes in spontaneous speech, but was beginning to use bi-lateral sounding stridents on word imitation tasks.

- *Results:* Arnie is still on my caseload today and, as of this writing, I am becoming increasingly concerned about his school therapist's push to establish these distorted sibilants. In my opinion, Arnie should be taught to substitute logically chosen phonemes as replacements for his sibilants. For example, he should be taught to use /t/ for /s/, /ʃ/ and /tʃ/. That way we will train him to use his tongue correctly as phonemes /t/ and /d/ serve as placeholders for the sibilants. Then, after he consistently uses these more normal substitutions, we can add the stridency to them. This will serve as a very long-term plan. In the meantime, Arnie needs to visit an orthodontist for evaluation and treatment planning (if any) for his occlusion problem.

- *Lessons Learned:* Writing this story of Arnie is reminding me of the importance of working in teams. I must contact his school SLP today to set up a meeting. She and I have not met or talked on the phone about Arnie for quite a while. I don't know if she will accept my idea of teaching phoneme placeholders, but we have worked well together before and I am hopeful she will see this the way I do. If not, I probably will work to establish correct oral position for the sibilants, and she will continue to work toward establishing them as initial consonants. Arnie is scheduled for an orthodontic evaluation next week. The plan of action to be taken on the teeth and bite will further determine our procedures. My plan is to establish the right conditions for the midline sibilants to emerge over the next several years.

Trevor: Frontal Lisp, Fronting, Attention Problems and General Motor Delay

Trevor was a six-year-old boy in first grade enrolled in a private school. General gross and fine motor skills as well as attention skills were immature, although he received no other therapies.

- *Evaluation:* Trevor had a frontal lisp on /s/ and /z/ which were the only sibilants he used. He also fronted, using t/k, d/g, n/ŋ, w/l, w/y and w/r. And he substituted t/θ and d/ð. Intelligibility was about 60% with an unknown topic. Trevor used tongue protrusion during the oral preparatory stage of swallowing, and he used a reverse swallow pattern on the swallow itself. He had a week bite and chew, a munch chewing pattern, and limited tongue lateralization. Incomplete evacuation of food particles was noted after the swallow. Trevor responded in a hypersensitive manner to oral-tactile stimulation. Receptive and expressive language skills were appropriate for age and hearing was normal. I suspected sensorimotor integrative dysfunction, although the parents refused additional testing in that area.

- *Treatment:* Early therapy focused on three aspects: (1) normalizing oral-tactile sensitivity, (2) stimulating mature feeding skill, and (3) facilitating back sounds /k/ and /g/. As these phonemes began to emerge, we began to work collectively on all four glides through auditory awareness and contrastive auditory discrimination training. We also contrasted place of articulation for the voiced and voiceless stops. This work helped Trevor begin to understand his oral mechanism much better in terms of place. Work on /ts/ helped solidify tongue position for /s/.

- *Results:* The above aspects of treatment took place over one year of time (during first grade and the summer following) after which Trevor was dismissed for a full school year (second grade). The parents wanted to give him a break from weekly therapy and to devote more time to reading and math skills. They also wanted to have his occulomotor skills evaluated by a vision specialist.

    Trevor was re-evaluated during the summer following second grade. He had retained all the new speech skills learned the prior year. And all the strident phonemes now were emerging. The frontal lisp was gone and intelligibility was very high.

Trevor had matured during this year and was doing first grade reading and math. He had been seen by a vision specialist during that year and had received weekly vision training to facilitate improved occulomotor tracking skills for reading and general environmental scanning. Trevor's attention skills had improved but still were not commensurate with grade level expectations. Feeding now was characterized by a strong mature chewing pattern and a normal swallow. The tongue was lateralizing from side-to-side.

Since it was clear that expressive speech skill was improving without direct treatment, Trevor was placed on a three-month periodic follow-up program to monitor his skills over the next year. Trevor is still on that program and continues to demonstrate improvement at each visit. As of his last visit, the sibilant phonemes were completely emerged and produced correctly. Occasional fronting of /k/ and /g/ are still noted, and /r/ has emerged only in the final position. Lingua-alveolar /l/ is used as a singleton and is noted only occasionally in blends.

- *Lessons:* The frontal lisp sometimes is one part of a more complex articulation delay related to poor oral-motor development, auditory attention and discrimination problems and general problems with movement, focus and attention. Therapy must be eclectic, focusing on auditory attention and discrimination as well as phonological, articulation, feeding and oral-motor skills. A longer period of treatment should be expected and normal developmental milestones should be monitored. The frontal lisp is eliminated as oral feeding and speech skills mature beyond infantile patterns, especially when the jaw is stabilized and the tongue can lateralize.

Martin: Fluency and the Bi-lateral Lisp

Martin was three years and two months of age upon entry into my speech room. He had been receiving services from occupational therapy and speech-language therapy since two years of age because of delay in the development of gross and fine motor skills and expressive speech and language.

- *Evaluation:* Upon intake, receptive speech and language skills were roughly age appropriate, and phonological errors rendered him about 85% intelligible in connected speech. Martin had a bi-lateral lisp on all sibilant phonemes and interdental tongue placement on /t/, /d/ and /n/. Glide /l/ had not emerged. Martin also demonstrated fluency problems in the form of whole word repetitions. It was hoped that these were typical preschool dysfluencies. However the recent birth of twins with health and feeding problems was causing much stress in the home. The mother felt that the parents had little time for Martin anymore and she was worried that the fluency problems were getting worse. Martin had had several ear infections.

- *Treatment:* The mother and I agreed to a short period of therapy to facilitate phonological skill, to monitor fluency and to see if he could handle a little work on tongue placement for the sibilant and other phonemic errors. Martin was enrolled in weekly one-hour individual therapy sessions. Therapy was designed to be play oriented with much opportunity for Martin to express himself freely in dialogue with me.

- *Results:* Martin enjoyed therapy, however, the sibling's situation was not improving and Martin's dysfluecies clearly were worsening at home. Although Martin could produce /d/ and /t/ easily with correct tongue placement, and he could produce midline stridency on /ts/ I stopped all our work on these phonemes and devoted a few weeks of simple play with Martin while I monitored his fluency in therapy and his mother and I discussed a new strategy by telephone. I felt that Martin's fluency was the most important problem area and that he needed to be referred to a specialist in that area because it seemed to be getting worse. I explained that work on the lateral lisp would have to wait and that the therapist in charge of his fluency program would incorporate work on it as well as his phonological errors as she deemed appropriate.

- *Lessons:* The lateral lisp can be addressed in young children by working on a /ts/ combination in a playful milieu. The lateral lisp must take a back seat to fluency therapy.

Laura: The Isolated Unilateral Lisp

Laura was a fifteen-year-old sophomore in a home-school high school program.

- *Evaluation:* Laura demonstrated a right unilateral lisp on all the sibilants. No other phonemes were in error. Laura was highly intelligible and highly motivated to change her speech. Oral-motor and feeding skills were excellent and she had no other developmental, learning or dental problems. Her unilateral lisp looked like simple habit.

- *Treatment:* Laura was enrolled in weekly 30-minute sessions during which she was trained with the Long T Method and Cornerstone Approach.

- *Results:* The above treatment regime took about four months after which Laura was dismissed from weekly therapy. She was placed on a three-month follow-up program to monitor her progress. Laura was to read aloud for ten minutes every day using /ts/ as a substitution for all /s/ phonemes. And she was to count aloud from 70-to-80 ("tseventy, tseventy-one, tseventy-two,"…) every day with this substitution in order to train her tongue to produce midline stridency on all /s/ phonemes in rapid conversational style.

    Then Laura was seen three times in nine months during which time it became clear that she had completely mastered midline air stream for her production of all sibilant phonemes in conversation. I called the family one final time about one year later and Laura needed no follow up. In fact, she had almost forgotten all about our work together and could not remember how she used to produce her unilateral lisp.

- *Lessons:* A lateral lisp that is the result of simple habit is quick and easy to correct when the client is motivated to do so and has the oral motor, auditory discrimination and intellectual skills to back up the work. The entire process can take about one year, however, in order to stabilize the skill and to monitor transfer of skill to all speaking situations.

Chapter 14 Summary
Real Clients In Real Therapy

- Treatment of the lisps can be quite varied in terms of content and time involved.

- A lisp can be the result of simple habit and lack of information. A bright client's self determination can result in near immediate change.

- The process of training for a lisp must work around orthodontic appliances. The entire process can take two years or more.

- Depressed levels of cognition are the greatest impediment to articulation learning. A lisp in a client with severe cognitive dysfunction usually is left untreated.

- Communication between therapists working at school and privately can be a critical component of training for a lisp in selected cases.

- A lisp can be part of a more complex articulation delay related to poor oral-motor development, auditory attention and discrimination problems, and general problems with movement, focus and attention. Therapy must be eclectic and a longer period of treatment should be expected.

- A lisp can be addressed in young children by working on a /ts/ combination in a playful milieu.

- Treatment for a lisp must take a back seat to fluency therapy.

- A lisp that is the result of simple habit is easy to correct. The entire process can take about one year in order to stabilize the skill in all speaking situations.

Appendix 1

The Traditional Consonant Chart					
	Stops	**Nasals**	**Glides**	**Fricatives**	**Affricates**
Bi-Labial	[p] [b]	[m]	[w]		
Labio-Dental				[f] [v]	
Lingua-Dental				[θ] [ð]	
Lingua-Alveolar	[t] [d]	[n]	[l]	[s] [z]	
Lingua-Palatal			[y]	[ʃ] [ʒ]	[tʃ] [dʒ]
Velar	[k] [g]	[ŋ]	[r]		
Glottal				[h]	

Appendix 2

The Palatograms

Inferior view of the palate. Gray sections represent areas where the tongue makes contact with the palate. White areas represent areas where the tongue does not make contact with the palate. Adapted from Zemlin, 1968.

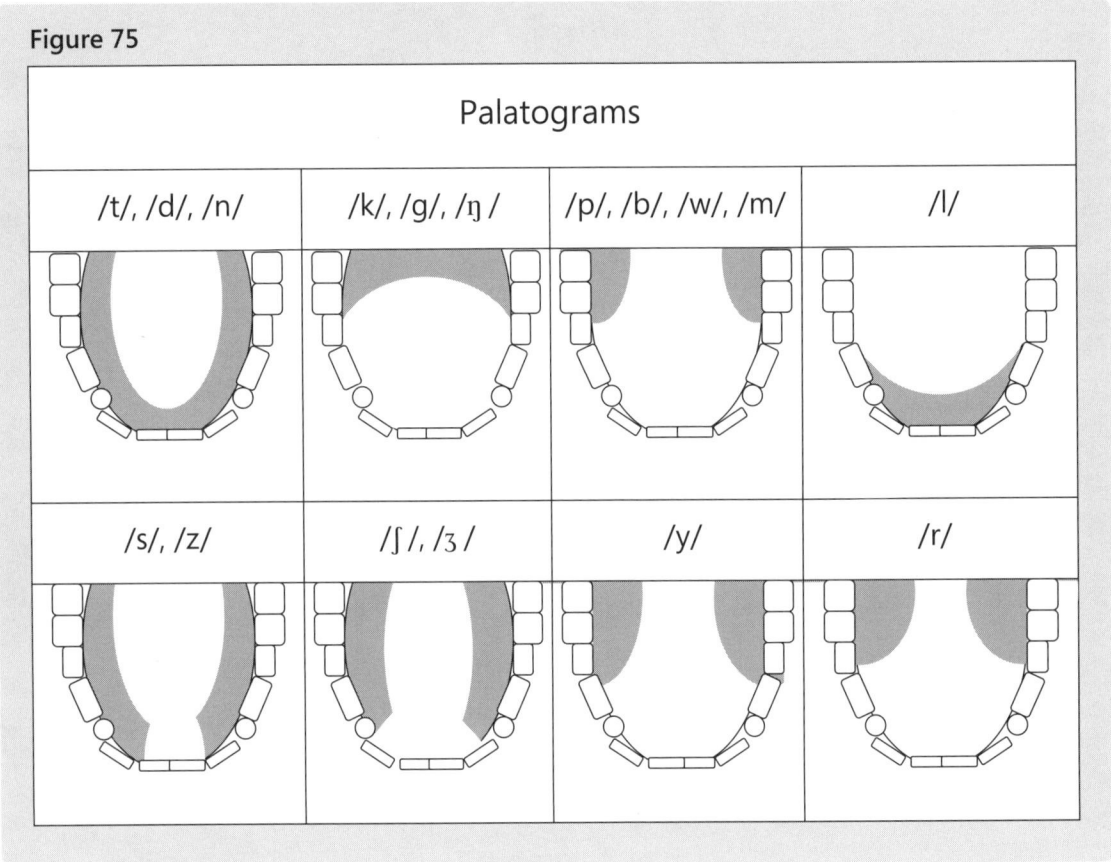

Figure 75

Appendix 3

Zones of the Tongue

Although the tongue is considered one single body part the palatograms reveal that the tongue has the ability to elevate parts differentially. By superimposing the palatograms one atop another, I have arrived at the conclusion that there are distinct "functional zones" of the tongue (adapted from Marshalla, 2002).

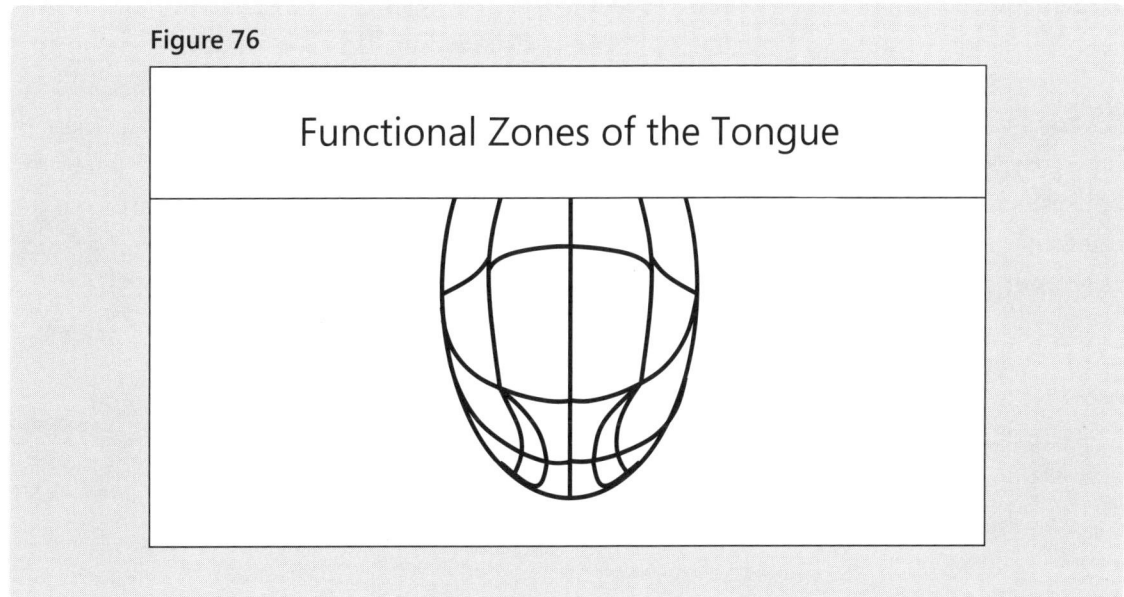

Figure 76

Functional Zones of the Tongue

Appendix 4

The Mature Swallow Pattern

The early dysphagia literature outlined four basic phases in the swallow of an adult who demonstrated no swallowing difficulty. They are summarized as follows and illustrated in figures 77 and 78. Adapted from Logemann, 1983.

Stage 1. Oral Preparatory Phase
Logemann has noted that the oral mechanism prepares food for swallowing and begins early digestion in the oral preparatory stage of swallowing. This is a voluntary stage. This includes biting, chewing, mashing, transferring food to the molars on both sides, mixing the food with saliva and forming the food mass into a bolus. The bolus is a unified mass of food that is mixed with saliva and is the consistency of mashed potatoes. Once prepared the bolus sits in the tongue's center depression (figure 77). The lips are sealed. Formation of the bolus marks the end of stage one. Marshalla has noted that the center depression is formed as a result of the tongue shaping itself as follows:

1. General flattening of the tongue
2. General flaring of the tongue from the middle outward toward its perimeter
3. Slight elevation of the tip
4. Slight elevation of the tongue's lateral margins
5. Slight depression of the middle.

Stage 2. Oral Phase
Logemann has noted that the oral mechanism pushes the bolus from the oral cavity toward the pharynx in the second stage (figure 78). Specific voluntary actions of the tongue accomplish this movement as follows:

1. The tip and lateral margins of the tongue remain elevated and in contact with the palate in a horseshoe shape. This prevents food from moving forward or sideways and out the mouth.
2. The middle of the tongue elevates in a front-to-back stripping action (sequential peristaltic action). This pushes the bolus toward the pharynx.
3. The second stage ends as the bolus passes the faucial pillars and moves into the oropharynx.

Stage 3. Pharyngeal Phase
Logemann has noted that the pharyngeal phase begins when the swallow reflex is triggered at the faucial pillars. The swallow reflex is an involuntary action that can be triggered by voluntary movement. The stage is defined as the posterior movement of the bolus from the faucial pillars to the esophagus. Stripping action through the pharynx accomplishes this bolus movement. The lips remain sealed and the velum elevates. The stage ends once the bolus reaches and passes the cricopharyngeal sphincter at the top of the esophagus.

Stage 4. Esophageal Phase
Logemann has noted that the final phase of the swallow is marked by continual stripping action that propels the bolus down through the esophagus and toward the stomach. The stage ends as the food passes the gastro-esophageal juncture and moves into the stomach.

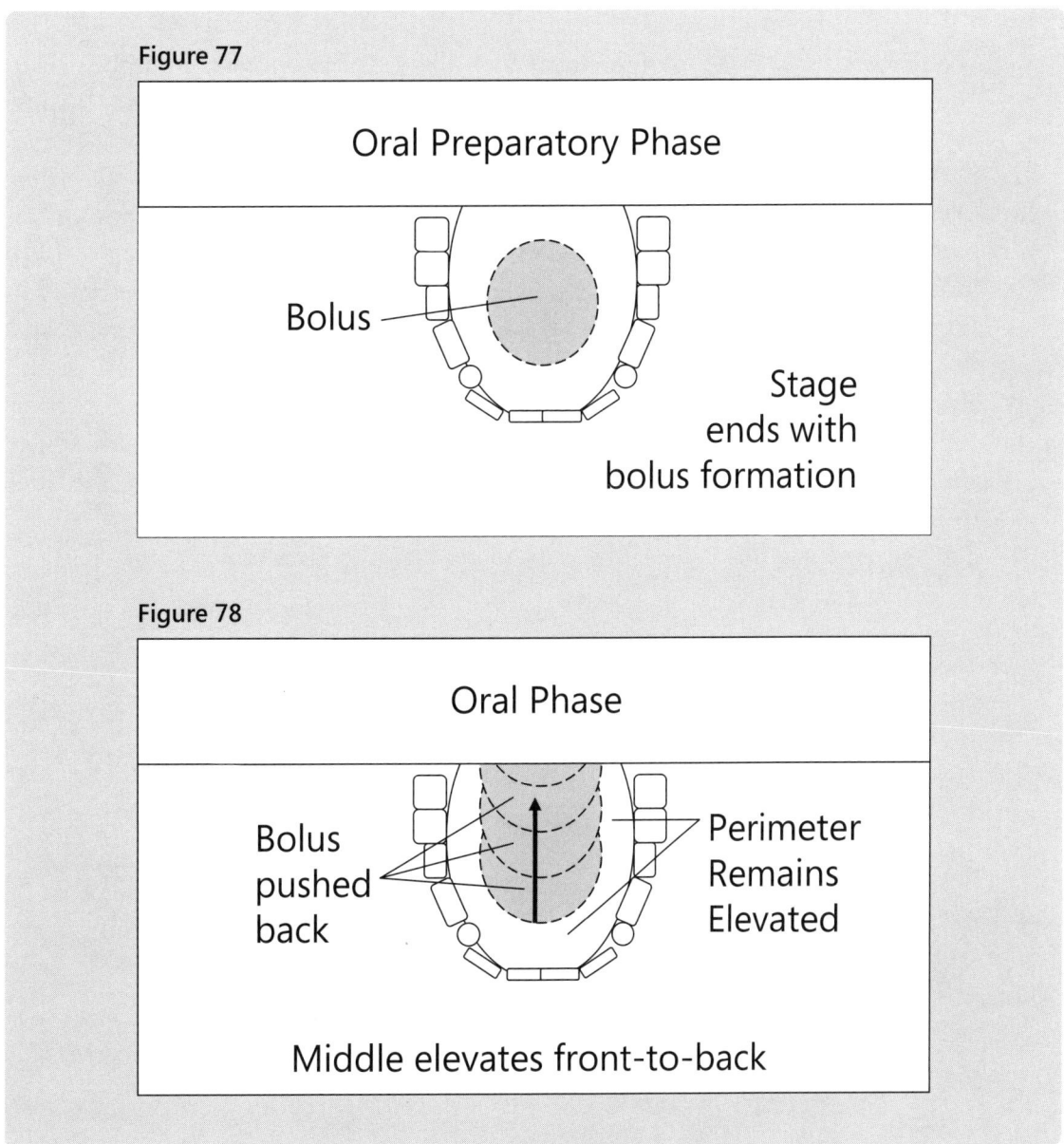

Appendix 5

The Infantile Swallow Pattern

The infantile swallow pattern also has been called the *reverse swallow*, the *tongue thrust swallow* and the *suckle-swallow*. The infantile swallow pattern is characterized by specific oral movements:

1. The tip and lateral margins of the tongue are allowed to lower away from the palate. The middle of the tongue pushes up toward the palate instead. This causes food to move forward and to squeeze laterally.
2. Lack of lateral elevation and midline depressions prevents formation of a solid bolus.
3. The front-to-back stripping action that should occur in the middle section of the tongue does not take place down the midline. Thus, the bolus (which is poorly formed) does not move toward the pharynx along the midline. Instead, food is smashed and pumped back to the oropharynx along the sides of the tongue. And food is pushed back along the tongue as the tongue scrapes forward against the alveolar ridge or teeth.
4. Infants leave the lips parted and much food escapes the front of the mouth. Older children who retain this pattern press the lips together tightly to prevent the food from escaping the mouth.
5. The jaw usually is unstabile, and pumps in big up-and-down movements.

Appendix 6

Simple Screening Test for the Infantile Swallow

A simple test can reveal the presence of an infantile/reverse/suckle swallow pattern. Use one or two crackers (or crunchy cookies), a small glass of water (or apple juice) and a paper towel. Use the following procedures:

1. *Ask the client to eat a cracker.* Watch the jaw, lip and tongue movements throughout. The suckle swallow will be characterized by forward-and-back motion of the tongue. The tongue tip will protrude from between the teeth and lips during mastication, during food gathering, during swallowing or after the swallow. The jaw will lower enough to allow forward slippage of the tongue.
2. *Ask the client to take one sip of water.* Watch the jaw, lips and tongue throughout. The tongue tip may protrude between the lips and teeth during or after the swallow. However, often children press their lips firmly together to prevent liquid from being pushed forward and out the mouth. In these cases, the tip may not protrude. Excess tightening of the lips looks like tight pursing.
3. *Ask the client to take another sip of water.* This time ask him to hold the water briefly in the mouth, to bite, to smile ("Show me all your teeth"), and then to swallow without closing the lips. This will reveal more about tongue movements because it will prevent the client from pressing the lips together. The client with a normal swallow will be able to swallow like this without losing liquid out the mouth. The client with a reverse swallow will not. He will need to close lips so that the liquid does not get pushed forward and out the mouth with the tongue moving forward. He may act afraid to swallow without closing the lips because he knows what will happen. Many clients with a reverse swallow cannot swallow without closing the lips, so let your client do so after trying not to. In some cases, I place a lip retractor on the lips to prevent the lips from closing during the swallow. This assures that the reverse swallow will be seen. Hold the paper towel under his chin to catch the escaping liquid.

Appendix 7

Letter Regarding Tongue Reduction Surgery

The following letter can be used to inform a client's primary physician about a tongue that may be too large.

Dear Dr. Paige:

I am writing about Billie Barton. I would like Billie's tongue to be evaluated for size. As you probably know, Billie speaks with his tongue protruding from his mouth. He also holds his tongue out when the mouth is at rest and while eating and swallowing. Most children who keep the tongue out do so out of habit or due to neuromuscular problems, especially hypo tonicity in the oral area. Billie's oral tone is slightly low, and this could be the main reason that the tongue protrudes. However I am concerned that the actual size of his tongue may be too large. I want to rule out any possible size problems so that speech therapy can progress appropriately.

I have asked his parents to schedule Billie for an appointment at the Craniofacial Clinic at Children's Hospital for this assessment. They will be calling you for the appropriate referral.

Sincerely,
Susie Speech, M.A., CCC-SLP
Speech-Language Pathologist

Appendix 8

Letter Regarding Referral for Tonsil and Adenoid Examination

The following letter can be used to refer a client with a frontal or lateral lisp to the physician for evaluation of the tonsils and adenoids.

Dear Dr. Washington:

I am writing about Jessica Jones and the relationship between her tonsils, adenoids and speech. I would like Jessica to be considered for tonsillectomy and adenoidectomy in order to improve her breathing for speech.

Jessica has a *frontal lisp*. This means that she lowers the jaw and thrusts the tongue forward too much while speaking. It appears that Jessica's speech problem is directly related to her inability to breathe through the nose. I believe she is lowering the jaw and carrying the tongue forward so that she can create a bigger air space in the oropharynx.

Creating a bigger air space in the oropharynx through surgical management of the tonsils and adenoids would allow her to carry the tongue inside the mouth where it belongs. This should contribute to a better oral rest posture and better speech sound production.

I would like you to evaluate the status of her tonsils and adenoids, and to determine if she is a candidate for tonsillectomy and/or adenoidectomy. I am pleased to report that Jessica has none of the nasality problems in speech that would caution us against this surgery.

Sincerely,
Stephen Speech, M.A., CCC-SLP
Speech-Language Pathologist

Appendix 9

Letter Regarding Tooth Position and Speech

The following letter can be used to inform a client's dentist or orthodontist about tooth position and its relation to speech.

> Dear Dr. Arlon:
>
> I am writing about Patty Paige. I would like Patty's teeth to be evaluated for occlusion. In specific, Patty has difficulty positioning her tongue correctly for certain speech sounds. I am wondering if her occlusion supports proper tongue movements at this time. I am also wondering if she will be a candidate for orthodontic treatment. Information about Patty's possible course of orthodontic treatment will help me plan her speech therapy program.
>
> I have asked her parents to schedule Patty for an appointment to assess occlusion. They will be calling you for an appointment. I look forward to your assessment.
>
> Sincerely,
> Sam Speech, M.A., CCC-SLP
> Speech-Language Pathologist

Appendix 10

Letter Regarding Supernumery Teeth and Speech

Dear Dr. Hennesy:

I am writing about David Hollas. I would like David's teeth to be evaluated. In specific, David has difficulty positioning his tongue correctly for certain speech sounds that require delicate tongue-to-palate articulation. My visual inspection suggests that he may have extra teeth emerging through the palate.

I have a few questions I would like to see answered so that I can plan appropriately for David's speech therapy program. Specifically, does he have extra teeth, will they be removed and, if so, when?

The parents will be calling to set up an evaluation with you. Thank you ahead of time for providing me with this information. It will help me tailor David's articulation program.

Sincerely,
Sandy Speech, M.A., CCC-SLP
Speech-Language Pathologist

Appendix 11

Following Sanitary Procedures

Speech-language pathologists are required to follow sanitary procedures at all times when touching a client's oral mechanism for diagnosis or therapy. The following procedures are recommended in Marshalla, 2001:

1. Wash the hands with a sanitizing cleanser
2. Dry with a paper towel and dispose of it – or dry with a cloth towel and place it in the laundry
3. Slip hands into latex or vinyl gloves (beware latex allergies)
4. Work with one client
5. Dispose of gloves after working with one client
6. Wash hands with sanitizing cleanser and dry appropriately

Toys and tools used in and around the mouth also need to be used in a sanitary way. The following procedures are recommended.

1. Wood objects must be used only once and then discarded. (e.g., tongue depressors, craft sticks)
2. Paper and cardboard objects must be used only once and then discarded. (e.g., paper towel tubes, toothette handles)
3. Sponge objects must be used only once and then discarded. (e.g., toothettes, oral swabs)
4. Cotton objects must be used only once and then discarded. (e.g., glycerine swabs, cotton balls)
5. Rubber and plastic toys must be used once and then sanitized. (e.g., baby chew toys, Nuk brushes) Use a commercially available sanitizing product, or soak for ten minutes in 1-part bleach and 10-parts water.

Appendix 12

The Emergence of [s], [ʃ] and [tʃ] from [t]

The Long T Methods is based around the idea that children can learn to produce the sibilants correctly by using [t] as a springboard. This idea was born in me after reading Smith *The Acquisition of Phonology*. The following notes are abstracted from that source. Smith divided his son's phonological acquisition patterns into stages. As he explains, stages 19 through 24 demonstrate the emergence of [s] from [t] through [tˢ].

Stags 1–16
No stridency in sample.

Stage 17-19
[tˢ] and [dᶻ] make rudimentary appearances

Stage 20
"…stage 20 again showed a number of changes. Most important is the appearance of alveolar affricates [tˢ] and [dᶻ] in contrast with their plosive congeners…" p122

"It should be mentioned that, phonetically, there were one or two occurrences of [tʃ] and [dʒ] for [tˢ] and [dᶻ], and also one or two occurrences of pure continuants–[s]." p123

Stage 21
"Stage 21 is virtually identical to stage 20, except that… the affricates [tˢ] and [dᶻ] have now been normally replaced by [s] and [z]." p124

Smith presents word samples that illustrate the evolution of [s], [ʃ] and [tʃ] from [t] through [tˢ] These are located in appendix C of his text. Samples of specific word changes are offered below. Each sample word is followed by pronunciations at sequential stages. Notice how each word changes over time as stridency is infused into the child's phonological system. Notice how [tˢ] is used as a transition from [t] to [s]. Also notice how [h] is used to help the child gain [tˢ]. Note too that the child uses the [ts] process even when he is substituting [s] for [ʃ], [tʃ] or [θ] Readers are referred to appendix C in Smith for examples of the same process as it occurs in the child's acquisition of [z] from [d] through [dᶻ].

Word	Pronunciation	Stage
Sandwich	/daemdit/	10
	/tambid/	19
	/tˢaembit/	20
	/saembiz/	24
Say	/de:/	6
	/tˢei/	20
	/sei/	21
Scissors	/didə/	1
	/tidə/	13
	/tʰidə/	14
	/tˢidədᶻ/	20
	/sizəz/	22
See	/di:/	2
	/li:/	5
	/tʰi:/	13
	/tˢi:/	13
	/si:/	21
Shake	/geik/	12
	/tʰeik/	19
	/tˢeik/	20
	/seik/	23
Sharpener	/da:pənə/	10
	/tʰa:pənə/	14
	/tˢa:pənə/	21
	/sa:pənə/	24
Inside	/in'daid/	2
	/intaid/	14
	/intˢaid/	20
	/insaid/	23
Lucinda	/'du:dənində/	4
	/lu:'tində/	13
	/lu:'tˢində/	17
	/lu:sində/	21

Word	Pronunciation	Stage
Mouse	/maut/	7
	/maut^s/	20
	/maus/	22
Much	/mut/	4
	/muts/	21
	/mus/	24
	/mutʃ/	29
Nice	/nait/	1
	/nait^s/	21
	/nais/	22
Outside	/autdait/	1
	/autdaid/	7
	autt^{h}aid/	13
	/autt^{s}aid/	21
	/autsaid/	22
Shoe	/duː/	1
	/tuː/	13
	/t^{s}uː/	21
	/suː/	21
	/sjuː/	29
Shut	/dʌt/	2
	/lʌt/	6
	/dʌt/	12
	/tʌt/	16
	/t^{s}ʌt/	20
	/sʌt/	22
Sick	/t^{h}ɪk/	14
	/t^{s}ɪk/	20
	/sɪk/	23
Sing	/gɪŋ/	12
	/tɪŋ/	16
	/t^{s}ɪŋ/	20
	/sɪŋ/	20

Word	Pronunciation	Stage
Sock	/gɔk/	1
	/kʰɔk/	13
	/tʰɔk/	14
	/tˢɔk/	20
	/s̠ɔk/	22
Stay	/de:/	2
	/tʰei/	13
	/tˢei/	21
	/sei/	22
	/stei/	26
Stop	/bɔp/	1
	/dɔp/	1
	/tʰɔp/	13
	/tˢɔp/	20
	/sɔp/	20
	/stɔp/	26
This	/dit/	11
	/ditˢ/	20
	/dis/	21
Thumb	/wʌm/	4
	/dʌm/	10
	/tʰʌm/	13
	/tˢʌm/	21
	/sʌm/	24
Yes	/dɛt/	1
	/rɛtˢ/	20
	/rɛs/	22
	/jɛs/	22

Appendix 13

Sample Dialogue

Learn to do articulation work at a conversational level by studying this dialogue. The therapist combines articulation work with a subject of the child's interest. She balances work on phoneme with topic elaboration to help the client learn to think about his speech work at the same time he is thinking about other things. Notice that the therapist uses every opportunity to bring up target words, but she allows the conversation to sound as natural as possible. Also notice that she ignores sound and words for which the client is not ready.

THERAPIST: Do you like <u>rats</u>?

CLIENT: I have a rat in my classroom.

THERAPIST: Many <u>rats</u>, or only one rat?

CLIENT: Only one rat.

THERAPIST: Do you like rats?

CLIENT: <u>Rats</u> are okay.

THERAPIST: Hey. You remembered to use the Long T. Very nice.

CLIENT: My teacher's rat is fat.

THERAPIST: A fat rat! Fat <u>rats</u> are funny.

CLIENT: Yea.

THERAPIST: Say, "Fat <u>rats</u> are funny."

CLIENT: Fat <u>rats</u> are funny.

THERAPIST: Oh, you forgot to use the "Long T" we practiced.

CLIENT: Oh yea.

THERAPIST: Sat it again, but use the correct "Long T." Say, "Fat <u>rats</u> are funny."

CLIENT: Fat <u>rats</u> are funny.

THERAPIST: That was good. Why is that rat so fat?

CLIENT: I guess he <u>eats</u> too much.

THERAPIST: (Smiles.) Yea. He probably eats too much. Now there's another word with a Long T. <u>Eats</u>.

CLIENT: <u>Eats</u>.

THERAPIST: That was perfect. You said "<u>eats</u>" with the Long T.

CLIENT: (silent)

THERAPIST: What color is that rat?

CLIENT: Brown. And a little white.

THERAPIST: White?

CLIENT: Yea, he has white on his feet.

THERAPIST: What if we said, "He has white on his feets."

CLIENT: (laughs)

THERAPIST: Say, "<u>feets</u>."

CLIENT: Feets.

THERAPIST: You used the Long T. Let's do a few more Long T words. Say, "<u>rats</u>."

CLIENT: <u>Rats</u>.

THERAPIST: Perfect. Sat, "<u>bats</u>."

CLIENT: "<u>Bats</u>."

THERAPIST: Correct. Say, "<u>cats</u>."

CLIENT: "<u>Cats</u>.'

THERAPIST: Very good. Do you have a cat at your house?

CLIENT: Yea. Two.

THERAPIST: Two <u>cats</u>?

CLIENT: Yea.

THERAPIST: Say, "Two <u>cats</u>."

CLIENT: Two <u>cats</u>.

THERAPIST: Did you use the Long T on that one?

CLIENT: Huh?

THERAPIST: Did you use the Long T when you said, <u>cats</u>.?

CLIENT: I don't know.

THERAPIST: Try it again, <u>cats</u>.

CLIENT: <u>Cats</u>.

THERAPIST: How was that one?

CLIENT: I think… okay, I guess.

THERAPIST: Yes! It was perfect! <u>Cats</u>. You said it correctly. You put the Long T on it. Say it again.

CLIENT: <u>Cats</u>.

THERAPIST: Perfect. Now, tell me about your <u>cats</u>. What are their names?

CLIENT: Well, one's "Bootsy." He's black. And one's orange with these… well, like these stripes all over him.

THERAPIST: What's his name?

CLIENT: Sissy Cat.

THERAPIST: Sissy Cat? Why do you call him Sissy Cat?

CLIENT: Because he always runs around like he scared of everything. Like, if he hears a sound, then he stops dead in his tracks and he, like, stares around for, like, five minutes.

THERAPIST: He sounds like a funny cat.

CLIENT: Yea. He always stops dead in his tracks.

THERAPIST: His name is hard. It has so many "S's."

CLIENT: Yea.

THERAPIST: But, you know what? The other <u>cat's</u> name is one we could add to your speech book.

CLIENT: The other cat?

THERAPIST: Yea, <u>Bootsy.</u> Watch as I write it down. B-O-O-T-S-Y. Do you see the T and the S. We should say, <u>Boo-tsy.</u>

CLIENT: Oh yea.

THERAPIST: Say, <u>Boo-tsy</u>, and put your Long T right in the middle.

CLIENT: <u>Boo-tsy</u>.

THERAPIST: Perfect! What does <u>Bootsy</u> do? …

Glossary of Terms

acceptable range of production. The limits within which phonemes vary.

affricate. An affricate phoneme is one that begins as a stop and ends as a fricative. This set in English includes /tʃ/ and /dʒ/.

allophone. Slight variations of phonemes that are accepted together as representing one.

auditory acceptance. The process clients go through to accept the acoustic quality of a new way to produce their problematic phonemes.

back lateral margins. The sides of the tongue in the back.

bi-labial. Pertaining to relationship between both upper and lower lip. The bi-labial consonants of English are /p/, /b/, /m/ and /w/.

butterfly position. A tongue position achieved by pushing the tongue's lateral margins upward against the lower surfaces of the molars while keeping the midline low.

carryover. The act of using newly learned speech skills in spontaneous conversation outside of the speech and language therapy room and away from the therapist supervising the work.

consonant. Speech sounds made with or without voice by constricting somewhere in the oral cavity. The consonants of Standard North American English are:

- *Stops* /p/, /b/, /t/, /d/, /k/, /g/
- *Nasals* /m/, /n/, /ŋ/
- *Glides* /w/, /l/, /y/, /r/
- *Fricatives* /θ/, /ð/, /f/, /v/, /s/, /z/, /ʃ/, /ʒ/, /h/
- *Affricates* /tʃ/, /dʒ/

developmental error. A speech sound error expected in the speech of young children. Phoneme production errors made naturally before full maturation of expressive speech has been realized.

discrimination training. Therapy techniques and procedures that facilitate perception of differences in phonemes, syllables, words and the like.

distal. A point relatively further away from the spine on the body map. The opposite of proximal.

distortion. In speech, the description of speech or speech sounds that are recognizable but not accurate due to alteration or bending of the sound.

facilitation. The act of bringing forth. In motor or oral-motor therapies, the act of bringing forth, stimulating or increasing the influence of a movement.

fricative. A fricative phoneme is one that is formed "by directing the breath stream with adequate pressure against one or more surfaces, principally the hard palate, alveolar ridge behind the upper teeth, and lips." (Nicolosi, Harrymann and Kresheck, 1983) This set includes /f/, /v/, /s/, /z/, /ʃ/, /ʒ/, /θ/ and /ð/.

glottal. Pertaining to the glottis (vocal apparatus of the larynx)

infantile swallow. The suckle swallow pattern characterized by strong up-and-down movements of the jaw and forward-and-back movements of the tongue.

inhibition. The act of holding back. In motor or oral-motor therapies, the act of holding back, preventing or reducing the influence of a movement.

interdental. Pertaining to the space between the upper and lower teeth.

interlabial. Pertaining to the space between the upper and lower lip.

labio-dental. Pertaining to the relationship between the tongue and teeth. The lingua-dental phonemes of English are /θ/ and /ð/.

lateral margins. The sides of the tongue.

lingual. Pertaining to the tongue.

lingua-alveolar. Pertaining to relationship between the tongue and alveolus. The lingual-alveolar phonemes of English include /t/, /d/, /n/, /l/, /s/ and /z/.

lingua-labial. Pertaining to relationship between the tongue and lips. There are no standard English phonemes made with lingua-labial contact. Children produce raspberries and other non-standard sounds with lingua-labial articulation.

midline. A center line.

midline of the tongue. A conceptual line drawn down through the center of the tongue from tip to back.

mobility. The act of moving or being moved.

nasal. Pertaining to the nose.

nasal phonemes. Phonemes made through the nose. The nasal phonemes of English are /m/, /n/ and /ŋ/.

ombissure. Shape the mouth assumes while playing a wind instrument. We are expanding this term to refer to the shape the mouth assumes while producing speech sounds.

off-glide. The final or concluding movements of phoneme production made away from the apex of phoneme production.

on-glide. The first or initiating movements of phoneme production made toward the apex of phoneme production.

oral. Pertaining to the mouth.

proximal. A point relatively nearer to the spine on the body map. The opposite of distal.

resonance. An increase or prolongation of a sound or tone caused by secondary vibrations. In speech, primary resonance occurs in the oral and nasal cavities. Resonance of sound also is made in the head, neck, chest and upper body.

reverse swallow. The persistence of an immature or infantile swallow pattern characterized by coordinated up-and-down movements of the jaw and forward-and-back movements of the tongue.

safe people. Those with whom a client feels comfortable trying out his new way of speaking.

shoulders of the tongue. The tongue's back lateral margins that serve as the tongue primary points of stability.

sibilant. A sibilant phoneme is one whose production is accompanied by a hissing or turbulent noise. This set includes /s/, /z/, /ʃ/, /ʒ/, /tʃ/ and /dʒ/. The term comes from the phonetics literature.

stability. Resistance to sudden change or fluctuation in movement or position. In motor or oral-motor therapy, stability is a relative term used to describe the ability of body parts to resist movement. Accurate and advanced movements are dependant upon stability of body parts.

strident. A strident phoneme is one that is characterized by noisiness resulting from a fast rate of airflow directed against the hard surfaces of the teeth. This set includes /f/, /v/, /s/, /z/, /ʃ/, /ʒ/, /tʃ/ and /dʒ/. The term comes from the phonology literature.

suckle-swallow. An infantile swallow pattern that is characterized by coordinated up-and-down movements of the jaw and forward-and-back movements of the tongue.

target. As a noun, the *target* in articulation therapy is the phoneme being taught or stimulated. As a verb, *to target* a phoneme means to work toward its correction.

tone. A muscle's strength and speed of reactivity.

tongue stability. Anchoring of the back lateral margins of the tongue accomplished with flexible fixing of position against or near the molars.

tongue thrust. A strong downward thrusting of the tongue. The term also has been used analogously with the infantile, suckle-swallow or reverse swallow pattern characterized by up-and-down movements of the jaw and forward-and-back movements of the tongue.

tongue tip. The anterior portion of the tongue.

velar. Pertaining to the area of the velum.

velum. The soft palate.

vowel. A voiced speech sound made with unrestricted passage of the air stream through the oral cavity. The vowels of Standard North American English are:

- *Front* /i/, /ɪ/, /e/, /ɛ/, /ae/
- *Back* /u/, /ʊ/, /o/, /ɔ/, /ɑ/
- *Middle* /ʌ/
- *Diphthong* /ɑi/, /ɑu/, /iu/, /ɔi/, /ei/

zones of the tongue. Areas of the tongue differentiated by their movement function. (Marshalla, 2001)

References

Carrell, James and William Tiffany (1960). *Phonetics: Theory and Application to Speech Improvement*. McGraw-Hill Book Company: New York, NY.

Hanson, Marvin (1983). *Articulation*. W.B. Saunders Company: Philadelphia, PA.

Hodson, Barbara Williams and Elain Pagel Paden. (1983) *Targeting Intelligible Speech*. College-Hill Press: San Diego, CA.

International Association of Orofacial Myology. Please see: www.iaom.com.

Logemann, Jerilyn. (1983) *Evaluation and Treatment of Swallowing Disorders*. Pro-Ed, Inc.: San Disgo, CA.

Marshalla, Pam (2001). *How to Stop Drooling*. Marshalla Speech and Language: Mill Creek, WA.

Marshalla, Pam (2001). *How to Stop Thumb Sucking*. Marshalla Speech and Language: Mill Creek, WA.

Marshalla, Pam (2001). *Oral-Motor Techniques in Articulation and Phonological Therapy*. Marshalla Speech and Language: Mill Creek, WA.

Marshalla, Pam (2001). *Successful R Therapy*. Marshalla Speech and Language: Mill Creek, WA.

Morris, Suzanne and Marsha Dunn Klein (1987). *Pre-Feeding Skills*. Communication Skill Builders: Tucson, AZ.

Nicolosi, Lucille, Elizabeth Harryman and Janet Kresheck (1983). *Terminology of Communication Disorders*. Williams and Wilkins: Baltimore, MD.

Oller, David K. (1978) "Infant Vocalization and the Development of Speech" in *Allied Health and Behavioral Sciences Vol. 1, No. 4*. Milwaukee School of Allied Health Profession, Milwaukee, WI.

Smith, Neilson (1973) *The Acquisition of Phonology*, Cambridge University Press, London.

"Tongue Reduction Surgery, Efficacy and Relevance to the Profession" (1990) ASHA

Travis, Lee Edward (1971) *Handbook of Speech Pathology and Audiology*, Prentice-Hall: Englewood Cliffs, NJ.

Van Riper, C. (1939). *Speech Correction, Principles and Methods*. Prentice-Hall, Inc.: Englewood Cliffs, NJ.

Zemlin, Willard (1968). *Speech and Hearing Science*. Prentice-Hall, Inc.: Englewood Cliffs, NJ.

More Books by Pam Marshalla

How to Stop Thumbsucking
80 pages $14.95

How to Stop Drooling
64 pages $14.95

Pam Marshalla's How-to Series gives you easy-to-understand resources that help to reduce or eliminate your child's thumbsucking and excessive drooling. Includes practical guidelines, solutions, and activities for home or therapy.

Becoming Verbal with Childhood Apraxia
New Insights on Piaget for Today's Therapy —112 pages $19.95

Particularly relevant for minimally verbal children who have been diagnosed with apraxia or dyspraxia of speech. Includes the organization and facilitation of early sound and word emergence.

Oral Motor Techniques in Articulation and Phonological Therapy
128 pages $49.95

Includes all the basics of oral-motor therapy for improving jaw, lip, and tongue control, and for normalizing oral-tactile sensitivity. Written for both the professional and student speech-language pathologist, the text guides the reader through fundamental techniques used in treatment. An excellent supplemental text for courses on motor speech disorders, articulation, phonology, feeding, and dysphagia.

Questions? Call **(425) 379-6443** or visit **www.pammarshalla.com**

Successful R Therapy

Fixing the Hardest Sound in the World — 240 pages..$49.95

Learn how to train the most difficult R clients. From the cornerstone R to conversational speech, this takes you through every stage of articulation therapy for the misarticulated R. Includes deep insights into the relationships between oral-motor skills, auditory processing, and articulation control.

Breastfeeding Blues

Advice from a Dairy Queen — 160 pages..$12.95

Breastfeeding Blues reveals those hidden experiences our mothers forgot to mention to us on the way to the delivery room. Laugh along with these new mothers as they discover that God must have designed breast-feeding as a way to keep us all smiling.

Audio Seminar

Apraxia Uncovered

The Seven Stages of Phoneme Development

Full Seminar — 3 audio CDs & 164-page book..$89.95

Book Only..$19.95

A revolutionary audio seminar on articulation, phonological, and oral-motor therapy.

Discover the seven stages of sound acquisition and apply it immediately to your therapy. This innovative program integrates proven essentials from articulation, phonology, oral-motor, and infant vocal development into a comprehensive program of treatment for all consonants and vowels.

- Three audio CDs of practical instruction and exercises
- Handy reference book of easy-to-use methodology
- Nearly 30 years of research
- Pam's famous practical style!

Order Today

	Title	Price	Quantity	Total
1. Select titles	How to Stop Thumbsucking	$14.95		$
	How to Stop Drooling	$14.95		$
	Becoming Verbal with Childhood Apraxia	$19.95		$
	Oral-Motor Techniques	$49.95		$
	Successful R Therapy	$49.95		$
	Breastfeeding Blues	$12.95		$
	Apraxia Uncovered — Full Seminar	$89.95		$
	Apraxia Uncovered — Book only	$19.95		$

2. Calculate total	Wholesale prices available on request
	SHIPPING AND HANDLING (1–4 books = $5.00; 5–10 books = $10.00)
	WA residents add 8.9% sales tax
	TOTAL

3. Mail order

Name: _____

Street: _____

City _____

State: _____ Zip: _____

Phone: (___) _____

E-mail: _____

4. Send check or money order to:

MSL Marshalla Speech and Language
914 - 164th Street SE #128, Mill Creek, WA 98012-6339

For Credit Card orders, order online at: www.pammarshalla.com

Questions? Call (425) 379-6443 or visit www.pammarshalla.com